DATE DUE			
Aug 9 '77			

PRODUCERS ON PRODUCING

Stephen Langley, editor

Stephen Benedict	Herman Krawitz
Sir Rudolf Bing	Paul Libin
Warren Caro	Harvey Lichtenstein
Alexander Cohen	G.A. McLellan
Akila Couloumbis	Theodore Mann
Zelda Fichandler	James Nederlander
Morton Gottlieb	Anthony Reid
Adrian Hall	Alvin H. Reiss
Norris Houghton	Norman Singer
John Houseman	Ellen Stewart
Robert Kalfin	Vantile Whitfield
Marketa Kimbrell	Peter Zeisler

Drama Book Specialists (Publishers)

New York

Library of Congress Cataloging in Publication Data

Producers on producing.
  A series of interviews with theatrical producers.
    1. Theatrical producers and directors—United States—Interviews.
I. Langley, Stephen.   PN2285.P7   792'.0232'0922   75-26817
ISBN 0-910482-68-3

Printed in the United States of America

Interior book design by Melanie Jeanne Ray

Photo credits:
p. 3 Alan Ginsberg; p. 9 Alan Ginsberg; p. 17 Alan Ginsberg; p. 39 Alan Ginsberg; p. 43 Alan
Ginsberg; p. 49 Alan Ginsberg; p. 71 Alan Ginsberg; p. 80 Trinity Square Repertory
Company; p. 86 Alan Ginsberg; p. 113 Alan Ginsberg; p. 119 Alan Ginsberg; p. 134
International Theatre Institute; p. 153 Fritz Menle; p. 180 Martha Swope; p. 206 The
Shubert Organization; p. 227 Alan Ginsberg; p. 233 Metropolitan Opera Association, Inc.;
p. 239 Alan Tannenbaum; p. 265 *Arts Management;* p. 272 Alan Ginsberg; p. 279 Alan
Ginsberg; p. 299 Blackstone-Shelburne; p. 309 Alan Tepper; p. 324 Alan Ginsberg.

Contents

Preface by *Stephen Langley, editor*

Associate Professor of Theatre,
Brooklyn College of the City
University of New York;
Managing Director, Falmouth
Playhouse, Cape Cod,
Massachusetts; author, *Theatre
Management in America.*

First, how did this book come about?

For a number of years I have invited leading theatre people to appear as guest lecturers for my performing arts management classes at Brooklyn College in order to gain a proper "mix" of professionals and professors; and for an even greater number of years I've been fortunate enough to meet and to learn from some of the finest people in the business. Theatre talk, it seems, has a richness and a fascination that is quite unique. Invariably, if you are talking amongst professionals, it is charged with tremendous energy, commitment and humor—three qualities absolutely necessary for success in theatre as they are, I suspect, in most endeavors. Happily, the busiest and most successful people are often the most eager and generous in sharing their experience and knowledge with beginners. Listening to the advice and the insights of theatre managers and producers over the years, I have always thought how wonderful it would be to collect and publish such comments so they could be shared by a wider audience. I was delighted, then, when just such an opportunity presented itself in the Spring of 1973.

Ethyle Wolfe, the Dean of Humanities at Brooklyn College of the City University of New York, through the Chairman of Theatre, Howard Becknell, informed me that there was a little money available to sponsor a special seminar in my field of specialization. Naturally, I jumped at this chance and set to work organizing eight three-hour sessions, each one devoted to a different branch of the theatre with the emphasis in all sessions placed on management and producing. The most difficult task was not in convincing leading producers and administrators to participate but, rather, in deciding *which* people might provide the most valid and representative picture of the field. A few, of course, could not attend because of other commitments. A few others (namely: Morton Gottlieb, Warren Caro, Ellen Stewart, James M. Nederlander and Robert Kalfin) could not attend the original sessions in 1973, but did address students of mine during the following year. To serve as moderator for the original sessions, I asked Tom DeGaetani, whose far-ranging experience at Juilliard, Lincoln Center, the U.S. Institute for Theatre Technology and as a performing arts consultant, quickly made him a central force in the whole concept of the series. Without his contribution I cannot imagine how this book could have been possible. Another friend, Robert Feinstein, undertook the arduous task of supervising the tape recording and transcribing of the sessions and helped in many ways to see the project through to its conclusion. Our official photographer was Alan Ginsberg; and I must thank Mrs. Sally Schwimmer for her loyal and efficient secretarial assistance, as well as Dr. Charles Whipple for providing the gracious seminar rooms in the Brooklyn College Student Center. Too, the class of thirty eager students from the Colleges who attended the sessions contributed much through their attentiveness and their questions to the guest speakers. I trust that those students are all now producing plays somewhere!

The reader of these pages, of course, must bear in mind that, with the exceptions that I have mentioned, all of the comments were delivered in the Spring of '73, and there are a number of references to events that were happening at that time. I do not feel, however, that this diminishes the importance or even the immediacy of the book. The core of the statements, value judgements and advice is every bit as pertinent now as it was then. Also, I wanted the book to retain, as much as possible, the atmosphere of candid informality which characterized the sessions themselves. The speakers were not asked to deliver formal papers or prepared remarks but, rather, to speak off-the-cuff for a short while and then answer questions from the students.

At the beginning of each meeting, I requested that each speaker spend a little time discussing the following four questions:

> (1) How did you become involved in the theatre?
> (2) How did you become involved in your present position?
> (3) What do you see as the differences between a producer and a manager?
> (4) What advice do you have for aspiring arts managers and producers?

While you will read the answers for yourself, it is rather fascinating to compare the similarities as well as the differences amongst the various responses. Obviously, for example, there is no single formula for launching a career in the theatre, even less so a career in theatrical producing. The arts leaders herein represented began, variously, in such fields as zoology, social psychology, law and medicine, and found their way into theatre from such startlingly diverse places as a European camp for displaced persons, a Viennese bookstore, the Argentine pampas, the Territory of Alaska, Texas, the White House, the Geneva Peace Conferences and, inevitably, from the Borough of Brooklyn! From such beginnings each has found a highly satisfying life in the performing arts and each has made a significant contribution to the arts field.

The purpose of bringing together in one volume several dozen of the theatre's most productive leaders is to seek an experiential definition of theatrical producing and arts management, although with cognizance that definitive answers concerning the contemporary, *living* theatre are impossible to acquire. Most writing in the field of theatre—both journalistic and scholastic—continues to emphasize the work of the performer, the director, the playwright and

the designer. The role of the producer is less apparent.
Many people, for example, believe that the producer in the
commercial theatre is almost exclusively concerned with
raising the production money. In non-profit theatre organizations, where he is usually called "artistic director," there
appears even more confusion about the producer's role,
perhaps because that situation is burdened by boards of directors, financial subsidy and other factors which tend to
disguise the importance of a single, artistic head. Yet, such
a person is always essential to the success of a theatrical
production or organization. Almost always, it is the producer who originates the idea and provides the impetus for any
theatrical product or group. He must then gather around
him others who subscribe to his idea and are capable of ex-
pressing it in terms of their respective crafts and talents.
Specifically, the producer (or the artistic director,) is a person who must have ready answers to the "five W's"—Why?
What? Who? Where? When? The arts *manager,* on the other
hand, is primarily concerned with "How?"

Producers on Producing is, I think, a logical progres-
sion from and companion to my recently published book,
Theatre Management in America. The latter attempts a sys-
tematic description of theories and practices in performing
arts management today, while this book offers a first-hand
accounting by leading practitioners and, even more important, provides some rather inspiring evidence that—armed
with commitment, passion, discipline and humor—one can
carve out a deeply fulfilling and meaningful life in the arts.
And I think that is a key phrase—"carve out"—because that
is what a producer must do and what each participant in
this seminar has indeed done. The business of creating
one's own special niche in the long history of theatre-
making is exactly what producing and creative managing is
all about. It requires a kind of drive and leadership ability
every bit as rare as are the talents of a gifted artist (try
counting the producers who *have* made an impact on our
culture and you'll see what I mean!). A blazing commitment to one's own individual standards, dreams and goals,
and the passionate desire to express these through the medi-

um of the living arts are the qualities most likely to produce a producer.

In the few short years since the 1965 publication of the Rockefeller Panel Report, *The Performing Arts: Problems and Prospects*—which best marks the beginning of a new era of development for the performing arts in this country— there has been a huge amount of promising activity in this field. The variety, the substance and the vigor of much of that activity is reflected by the participants in this seminar. In short, if anyone doubts the continuing survival of theatre in America, this book should be good tonic. There is enough energy, experience, creativity and humanity represented in the following pages, I think, not only to insure the theatre's survival, but also to help provide through the arts the kind of medicine that is more and more needed to insure the survival of our society as a whole.

To the tremendously distinguished participants in this series, then, I express humble gratitude for the opportunity of sharing their knowledge, experience and warmth with my students and now with you, the reader.

New York City, 1975

Grassroots Theatre

Akila Couloumbis
Marketa Kimbrell
Vantile Whitfield

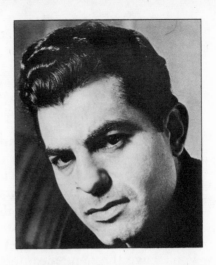

Commentary by *Akila Couloumbis*

Co-director, Theatre for the
Forgotten, New York City

My own beginning came about six years ago when I was a sometimes employable actor in quest of an audience for which to perform. I decided to go into prisons and my co-artistic director, Ms. Beverly Rich, and I got together and formed Theatre for the Forgotten, and in the last six years we've been enjoying a rather long run. Statistically speaking, we've done fifty-seven plays. We just finished one on Friday and we are in rehearsal with two others now. But those are only numbers.

We found a ready-made audience for theatre and theatrical culture in the prisons. We found, also, that the fellows who are doing time are very much interested in becoming involved in all aspects of theatre. Bear in mind that most of them have never seen a play, which at the beginning rather shocked me—that in Twentieth Century America, in New York, there should be that many people who have never seen a play in their lives. I think that the first audience that we had was about five hundred, and only one fellow had ever been to a theatre. But what was even more shocking was that of all the officers I talked to, perhaps thirty or forty, none had ever seen a theatre or been inside one. They wanted to know when the movie was going on! "Well, fellow, that's not a movie, it's a play."

"What's that?"

And those were the reasons, I suppose, that we became

so immersed in it, because it did not exist either in prison or in their lives outside. It seems as though an awful lot of theatre is only done for certain groups of people, or was at that time, some six or seven years ago. There are so many other groups now, thank God for that.

In that space of seven years I have gone from just being an actor to what could be called a "schlepper," and that is what the theatre is all about. If you are going to do one thing and not the other, forget it. You won't get it done or it won't have the same meaning to you. You won't love it as deeply as you will if you really get into it on all levels, or on as many as you can possibly handle. I don't know what the hell anybody means by "administrate something!" All I know is that one must be able to treat the theatre as if it is a venture. You can say it is a business venture. Yet, it deals in art, it deals in culture, and it's anathema to put business next to that: but you won't succeed unless you know what it is you are selling, or you are doing, and for whom you are doing it, and whether or not it's going to work and be accepted.

The differentiation, perhaps, between a producer and a manager, to me, is semantics. How can you do one without the other, or how can you get to be one without having been the other? Managing what? Managing people? Managing a product, which is the ultimate play? Managing the theatre, the props, or whatever—they're all interrelated. They have a very direct relationship to the actors. They also have a very direct relationship to the audience.

What we have also done in prisons, aside from just going in and doing fifty-five some-odd plays, is drama workshops—in all the facilities in the city, some in New Jersey, some upstate, I think thirteen altogether. Marketa [Kimbrell] is teaching two of them for us. Her accomplishments and the reactions of the inmates to Marketa and the workshop are overwhelming, really overwhelming. It makes me ashamed for supposedly having come from the right side of the tracks not really to have known where it's at, until I mingled with inmates and saw the great need, the great desire, the great amount of imagination that exists. You will read books on theatre and you will read books on what this thing called "theatre magic" is, but it never really hits you until you see somebody who has never been in a play, never been onstage, doesn't know his left from his right insofar as stage lingo; and they come up and they create little things, props for example, that are really overwhelming.

I remember one incident in '67 when we were doing the trial of Sacco and Vanzetti and I'm playing Sacco and I'm putting on a prison uniform and the guys who are in prison are putting on civilian clothing. There was one fellow who was over in the corner cutting up little strips of black cloth and I said, "Willie, you're on in thirty seconds, man, you're on."

He says, "I know, but it's going to have to wait."

"Willie, it can't wait!"

"It *can* wait, man, I'll be ready.""

So what he did was to tell me that he was playing the part of a courtroom attendant, "I've been in this racket for ten years doing the courtroom attendant and, man, I gotta be a sergeant," and he immediately put three stripes on his sleeve.

I mean, there you go! You can read about Ethel Barrymore and theatre magic, but this kid did it and he didn't know what he was doing. Really, they have no knowledge of how creative, how immense they are at talent, because no one has taken the time to say, "Hey, that's pretty good, man." All that is said is, "You've got the wrong name, the wrong skin, and you come from the wrong neighborhood; therefore, you cannot amount to anything!"

Well, I've had my head played with, turned around in many, many ways and I am pleased that I have a chance to say all this. I don't think I am worthy of your attention, but I certainly have had the greatest seven years of my life doing something that I jumped into out of enthusiasm, and it's led to wherever we are right now, with a budget of perhaps $180,000. I don't even keep figures any more—running something that is almost a self-destruct program, and I hope it is *that.* Perhaps with your help it might be, because can you imagine where I would be without prisons? Unemployed! I am looking forward to that day.

But to get back to the original question: Why a "theatre for the forgotten?" What are its objectives? What does it do?

All I am is an entertainer. Now, an awful lot of things can be tacked onto that. We have been able to find that, given an opportunity, people will rally to something—something which is positive. Going into prison and taking twenty individuals, not asking them anything except, "Do you want to be in a play?" and "When is your release date?" That's all. These are the only stipulations I have: Do you want to be in a play, and, am I going to lose you three weeks after rehearsals? Do you have enough time to spend with us?

You can turn anybody into an actor. Nobody comes on and waves a magic wand at anybody. It's work. There are times when I wish that I *could* wave a magic wand and turn them into carpenters, because they're sure as hell going to make a lot more bread making cabinets than being actors. But what we have seen is that people *do* change. They change even for the amount of time that they're involved in the seven-week rehearsal period and performance schedule. Bear in mind that we do six or seven productions a year. We entertain close to fifty thousand offenders a year. Now, what happens to an individual who, for the first time in his life, doesn't have to prove anything? He is accepted by the mere virtue that a judge said, "You are doing a year and a half at Rikers Island." There are guys who have come up and said to us, "This is the best thing that has ever happened to me. I am glad I got busted." Sad, isn't it, for somebody thirty years old to say that the first thing that ever happened in his life that's worth anything is that he got busted, to be in a play! Perhaps that is the strength of the theatre. It can do that to people, however temporarily.

We've got people running workshops in prisons all over the city and what happens is that the fellows who graduate from the workshop (graduation means "release date") come to the studio and we either employ them in some capacity or refer them to other agencies. I don't have enough work to involve the two hundred and eighty-five people who have been in the workshops since September, or the five hundred who may be involved by the end of this year. God knows, there are not that many jobs in the theatre, let alone in my own organization. What we do is try to channel them into other areas: schools, drug rehabilitation programs, jobs. We have been able to retain four or five people. My whole staff, practically, is made up of exconvicts: the secretary, the road manager. The counselor is an ex-junkie. So, we try to create positions for them. But, again, to stress the importance of the theatre—the importance of a guy coming up and saying, "Listen, I don't want to act, I am not an actor, but I do want to stage manage, I do want to learn how to work the lights" —theatre has those other possibilities for them to learn the crafts, all the crafts that are necessary in a production. Therapeutically speaking, it also has virtue. People from the outside who do not know the situation in prison come up and say, "These are trained actors."

I say, "No. They're inmates. Some of them cannot read."

There was an incident a few years ago when I had to read the script to somebody so he could memorize the lines. And when you see this kind of thirst in a human being, where he now does something that he can be proud of— wow! When a guy is stopped in the hallways and told, "Hey, man, you were *good*!" He thinks, "The guys are talking about *me*!" It is the first high that he has ever had without anything that is illegal or alcoholic. So from that point of view it's got something going for it.

We once did a study. We asked the warden to give us the infraction record of the ten guys who were picked for the play and he found out of the ten, seven had no infractions. Of the other three, one had five in the period of six months. During the production we had one infraction and nothing after that, which implies to me that there was only one infraction out of ten people who cumulatively had fifteen infractions before we got in there. Any time that there would be any hassle between an inmate from the play and a guard, the whole group would more or less surround this individual and tell him to cool it, because it wasn't worth it. So we see a whole kind of communal spirit. Marketa can attest to this because we had a problem with a workshop and somebody tried to point a dirty finger at one of our guys and in the space of five minutes Marketa came up with twenty-six letters and ninety-seven signatures, and that was only for five minutes! I am sure that by now she's got everybody in the institution underscoring the program and verifying its virtue. There is nothing that they can feel proud of that they've done before, but for the first time in their lives, they're doing something that has a communal spirit where a guy says, "Hey, man, listen! It might be me up there! I can get up there and do that, because this is a guy I sleep with and I know he's not talented, but all of a sudden he's got something that I never knew existed in him."

You see, if there is anything we're doing in the Theatre for the Forgotten, it is to let people know that they have a hell of a lot more than they give themselves credit for.

Commentary by *Marketa Kimbrell*

President and
Artistic Director,
New York Street
Theatre Caravan

The first grassroots theatre I ever created was in a displaced persons camp in Europe after the Second World War. I was held prisoner because, as a refugee, I lacked the proper identification to prove that I belonged somewhere. Several of us in the camp persuaded the proper people on top to permit us to prepare a program for the entire camp population. We found an amazing group of motley artists of every conceivable nationality and talent—dancers, singers, serious musicians, just about every category of entertainment was represented. We started with simple pieces and soon were permitted to tour different camp units with our theatre. It was there that I learned to tap resources in search of costumes, props and instruments—you can't imagine it! The payment for our efforts was an extra sandwich or doughnut, which enormously supplemented our diet, or a loaf of bread and a can of Spam for a week. The camp was American. After my release, in fact, I met an American and we got married.

After coming to America a few years later, I had a burning ambition to make good as an artist here. We first lived in Fort Hood, Texas. My expectations were great, but Fort Hood was very small and not much larger than nearby Kileen, Texas. I ended up studying in the Theatre Department of the University of Texas in Austin. I think my total English vocabulary then amounted to about three dozen words—most of them learned from singing English songs in a nightclub in France! So I noted down all the words phonetically, as I heard them, and later looked up their meaning in the dictionary at home. A fantastic way to learn English, by the way.

Eventually, I came to Hollywood. An old Viennese actor became my coach. One day he called me, all excited: a touring company from Stratford, Ontario, was coming into town. They were doing Shaw's *Saint Joan* and had lost their leading actress.

"I think you can play Joan," he said.

I got an audition with them. I would have made a pact with the devil to play that part! I burned my heart out at the audition and they said, "Yes!"

I played Joan for months to come. I started eating salted bread and wine for breakfast, I saw Joan in every sunset, in every moment of my life. I played Joan for over one hundred and twenty performances and—I am a little embarrassed to admit this—I never really stopped playing her! When you're an actor, a little bit of each part you play remains with you.

Before Joan, I had permitted myself (or, rather, the *image* of myself) to be affected by the artifice of Hollywood. The women here know what I mean—a little bleach and makeup, clothes to make the rounds in, and whatever other tricks I could think of. But under the grip of Joan, I cut my hair, wiped off my lipstick and started on a road searching to save—not only Orleans—but the whole world! Someone from CBS saw me play Joan and I was cast to play a lead on Playhouse 90. After that, I started doing lots of TV and a movie, *The Pawnbroker*. I had come to New York, leaving Hollywood with the urgency of a refugee. New York was such a challenge in the beginning. My first Broadway show was playing George C. Scott's wife and had me kind of breathless throughout the entire run. George is great to work with. I can't even *begin* to tell you what happened to me, playing Camille in *Camino Real* at the Circle in the Square Off-Broadway—the opposite of Joan! I set myself up as a "Magic Mountain" character in Thomas Mann fashion. I even smoked hash, once, to get her entrance right (in the play she comes in "high and feverish!").

By the time I had finished a season with the Lincoln Center Repertory Company I was thirty-eight years old and in urgent need of a reassessment of my life and my future. Christ, was I shaky, just walking into the Center—shaky in any space except on stage. I felt that the theatre as it is set up commercially made me a lesser person. So much energy seemed to be spent on thinking up ways to stay up— thoughts about promotion, manipulation, competition, calculation, became the inner dialogue of my life and I felt my tormented head growing increasingly neurotic. But to confront the hyprocrisy and vanity I had developed in competing in the commercial world of theatre also meant to give up my weapons. I needed to continue in theatre, I really loved theatre and could not imagine any kind of life for me without it. But at that time, all attempts outside of commercial theatre were, to me, just poor and unprofessional and amateur.

My first step of rebellion against the continuation of my symptoms came at the gala opening of *The Pawnbroker,* in which I played Tessie. Instead of expensive dresses, a hired limousine and a publicity agent, my kids and I just snuck unnoticed into the balcony to watch the movie. Getting out of the elevator after the showing, I was suddenly pushed out of the way while cameras were flashing, taking pictures of the departing "stars"!

I am sure we all pass through yearnings and needs for more love and recognition than normal life has to offer us. Some people sublimate that unfulfilled desire and need into creative, hard work. Let's face it, the reasons why people enter the performing arts are not always noble. Very few young actors seek out the theatre to illuminate the human condition. Most actors are on stage to fulfill a personal need, to fill a void in their emotional lives or in their sense of self. How many bruised hearts and egos—including my own—hope to be healed by the realization of that dream of "Making It"?

There is a beautiful passage in Ansky's *Dybbuk.* It

speaks of seeing the world through a glass. Now, a little silver in back of the glass blocks the view of what's behind the glass, and one can only see oneself. Clean the silver off and, suddenly, there is a whole world discovered behind the glass with people in it, and each face carved to behold another world within. Something like that happened to me about this time. Out of the protected world of dressing rooms in plush theatres and television studios I suddenly began to discover and, eventually, to touch the lives of people across this country I lived in—people in ghettos, poor neighborhoods, people in prisons, trapped and disinherited—wasted, human lives and hunger of all kinds, mixed with anger, viciousness, despair, but also beauty. There were millions of people across America (and I came to learn this slowly) struggling for livelihoods, people with simple needs and very little investment in the wealth of the land. I remember once, when performing on a Hopi Indian reservation, how silent and embittered they felt, collecting welfare checks they were rendered useless, as are the migrant workers, living in shacks in controlled areas that look like the DP camps I did time in after the War.

Soon my entire world changed. Slowly, but radically. The '60's were a time of search, I feel, a search into individual and collective consciousness. I am glad to have been part of it all. But the great question remained: how to create or build a theatre that could contain all this search and anguish and discovery of an emerging world of the disinherited? A theatre that has in it all the wealth of experience from the past, added to the urgency and immediacy of the present and arriving from this to a vision of the world to come?

My second season at Lincoln Center was to start with my playing Federico Garcia Lorca's *Yerma*. In my first meeting with the director of the play I laid out my ideas of the part and the play: "See, Lorca was murdered by Franco's troops. He had a passionate love for Spain, as a poet would for his motherland. Yerma to him was Spain. It's so simple. Yerma is the earth of Spain, forced to remain barren because her life is ruled by an impotent dictator, right? Her husband, Juan, is Franco in reality. Sanctimoniously, he uses the rules of the church to hide behind, he counts his money all night instead of making love to his wife. And Yerma, driven to love, to bear fruit like nature and earth itself, strangles her oppressor for the sake of life."

I'll never forget the face of the director when I had finished with my interpretation of the play. His whole body was tense with indignation. He ran into Jules Irving's office and shouted, "It's me or her—I refuse to work with her!"

After that year of clashes, politics, firings and chaos at the Center, I was ready to start out on my own. My first production was to be *The Life of Federico Garcia Lorca, The Man and Poet*. With the help of a colleague, Richard Levy, and a group of wonderful people from the lower East Side, whom I recruited into a workshop I taught for them (a shoe salesman, a waiter in a deli, a cab driver—just ordinary working people), we began to build this play. A carpenter wrote out some of the scenario with me and he built the set. We worked on the production for seven months. It was a work of love and had much beauty in it. When it was all ready, we said, "Here it is, our theatre for the people, by the people. Come, beloved audiences, people in the streets, come. It's for you, and we work for free!"

And we waited, but no one came. Actually that's not true. People *did* come, especially after we received a wonderful review in the *Voice*, which said we brought to Lorca a reality and the truth of *The Grapes of Wrath*. But the people who came were not the ones for whom we had prepared the play. The audiences were sophisticated theatregoers who were interested in our experiment. No one came from the streets and neighborhoods of the poor or from the working class. So, we decided to go to the audiences. We moved to Coney Island, sharing the Old Boston Theatre with Peter Shumann's Bread and Puppet Theatre. Our next production was a Brecht piece. By then we had brought many people from the ghettos into the company as actors, making a very motley group. We made wonderful-looking programs and ran thirty blocks up and down the Coney Island neighborhood, delivering personally all the invitations, talking to our audiences, performing small skits for them, beating a big drum and playing instruments. We knocked on door after door, smiling and telling them, "It's free and it's close. Please come."

Then we would run back to the theatre, put on our costumes and makeup and wait. No one, except a trail of little kids, followed us. They sat there waiting, so we performed for them. Day after day, we went back but no one ever came. Later, as the weather got warm, we just opened the door and the people strolling by came in. But never neighborhood people. Coney Island is one of the most hopeless neighborhoods I have seen. It almost looks like some bombed-out European city after the War. Dope and alcohol and a state of demoralization and lethargy keep the poor people there from struggling for anything more. We were heartbroken. What was the next step? It came organically and we took it.

We rented a float the next summer and on those hot nights when everybody was sitting on their stoops because they couldn't stand their rotten apartments, we took our plays right into those desolate streets—not just in Coney Island, but Brownsville, Fort Greene, Bedford Stuyvesant, East New York, Harlem, South Bronx, South Jamaica and Corona. The people sat there dumbfounded, and they loved it. They just sat there piled on their steps or in windows and doorways and they watched and listened and loved it! We became a street theatre, you see, not because we *decided* to become a street theatre, but because we could not get through to the people in any other way. We were in the streets that summer of riots and street fights—in fact, we were often in competition! That summer, foundations gave us our first money and we could pay salaries to actors. They had a lot of guts, because the streets were battlefields at times. There were times when we were scheduled to perform at a place and, between the time of checking out the place and performing there, a couple of days later, the whole block had been burned down! Violence and destruction became like a steam valve that helped release some of the pressure. One *had* to let go, so one could live through tomorrow. That was before the mass recruitment into the Vietnam War took thousands of black and Puerto Rican young men out of the streets and arranged for them to die and to kill more profitably!

The summer after this we decided to take the theatre all across the country. We got a stake truck that carried our stuff and was to be our stage at the same time. The itinerary was to cover Appalachian coal mines, performing for coal miners and their families between work shifts, as well as in their communities. Sometimes we so baffled a local sheriff of a mining community (the sheriff is often also the owner of the only local bank, and the mayor) that we were followed and harassed every step of the way by his local posse.

That summer we went to our first Indian reservation. First the Cheyenne, later the Navajo and Hopi tribes saw from our truck their first live theatre. We returned to them years later and were treated as their guests. Since that first summer, we have played in dozens of migrant camps, prisons, workcamps, fields and factories all across the country. My God, I remember Bufford, Georgia! There were still chain gangs there in the late '60's and young kids used their sledge hammers to smash their leg bones in order to get out of the terrible work and conditions with which they were punished.

And I remember the cold chills we all felt, entering the Cummins Prison Farm in Little Rock, Arkansas. We did three shows for the inmates there. Only a few years ago the *New York Times* printed the horrible findings of medieval torture and killings there. Conditions are much better now.

One thought that occupies me very much: There are a lot of people out there who start in the theatre but who can't make it. And there is a lot of money around and it helps these people, even though they have no tools or knowledge, to start amongst the poor and use them as a stepping stone to the commercial theatre, because that is where they basically want to go. I think that if you learn amongst the poor, which we did, then you learn your craft among people whose everyday life is involved with this moment to moment struggle for sheer survival. And theatre is most alive and vibrant where it plays for people who struggle hardest in the world. But finally, when you get good, God damn it, stay there and show them the proof of what you learned from them! I feel very strongly that one never ought to leave.

Now you have an idea of grassroots theatre. Make it good. Make it professional. Our standards are very high and we work hard to become good, but once we *are* good that is where we are going to be: right in the street, in the ghetto, in the factories, in the mines, in the migrant camps! Give them the best thing you've got, because it is not fair to use them and then step right by them when you make enough money to leave.

I swear to God you can learn more about theatre among these people than any other people in the world. I know. And so that is my story.

Commentary by *Vantile Whitfield*

Program Director, Expansion Arts
Program, National Endowment for
the Arts, Washington, D.C.

After I got out of high school, I wanted to be a set designer
and in my community that was really out of the question. In
fact, most people, including my own mother, didn't know
what I was talking about. To make a long story short, I
thought the way to do it was to go to school. This is after my
transition from the streets and all that. I went to Howard
University and got a pretty good background and I went to
UCLA and decided what I really wanted was films, that I
wanted to be an art director in films. I went through all the
changes that you go through at school, with a little hustling
on the side, and finished at UCLA and started knocking on
doors to get into an art department at one of the studios.

I tried for about a year and a half, but nothing was happening around 1960. So I became a painter for quite a while
and then I was a layout man in a commercial art studio,
where I worked up to assistant art director. And then I got a
job in juvenile detention, working with kids, and I liked
that because I had been in similar situations several times
as a young person in Washington, D.C. So I started trying to
find activities for the kids in Juvenile Hall in Los Angeles.
There are a lot of restrictions. They didn't really let us get
involved in the theatre. But by this time I had done a little
acting professionally, I had not worked anywhere as a set
designer. Nowhere. I had been involved in some small

theatre groups. So I tried working out some ideas with the kids. But the turnover in the detention center was so heavy that you couldn't really establish any kind of continuum.

Anyhow, the period of time from 1960 to 1965 passed and I got my first job in the industry. I was called early one morning when Watts was burning, because they couldn't get any white cameramen to go into Watts. I didn't even know it was a riot, because I was living in Hollywood at the time and Watts is across town. I said, "I'll call you right back," and I called up some friends of mine who were in the camp, as we call it, and found out there was a riot going on. But, since I had never worked in the industry, I didn't know what kind of money you could get for going out there. So I called up some other friends and said, "What kind of money can you get for going out there?"

The cat says, "The sky's the limit, man. You can ask for anything you want."

So I called Metro-Media and told them I'd go. And that was really my first job!

The weird thing that happened was we got some very good footage on a lot of the things that were happening out there. The only other people able to shoot were from KTLA. And they were shooting from a helicopter. The guy who was the producer of the show, the host of the show at that time, Louis Lomac, was so nervous and uptight under these battleground conditions that he gave the cans of film as we were shooting it to this courier who didn't even know where KTLA was. That was a heavy thing. But we did manage to salvage about twelve hundred feet of that situation. Anyway, that was my first job anywhere near the industry that I wanted to get into. So I started pounding the doors again, but nothing happened.

Then I started a project, this was the third project that I started in Los Angeles, called "The Performing Arts Society of L.A." We opened up a theatre but, as in Marketa's case, we couldn't get people to come to it. So we performed, and we took the plate glass out of street corner windows. We created a stage in a street corner area that was a very well populated area because of the liquor store, and the bar-be-que, and stuff like that. And we managed to do pretty well.

Then we got a flat bed truck and set up in the parking lots in shopping centers, which are a real big thing. And we did pretty well in that situation. Finally, we got back into our own theatre and got some luck and a lot of things happened around that time, 1965, '66, right after the riots.

We got a television show called "From Inside Out." We did daily shows, we did variety shows, a little poetry, a lot of talk—some plays. We did that for about two hundred and sixty shows.

Then I started traveling around to other places in California and Chicago as a consultant—making speeches about what was happening on a grassroots level in theatre and in other kinds of arts projects. Meanwhile, my own theatre was coming along pretty well and we were at the point where we were getting people into the house to see theatre. But the problem that always confronted us was that we couldn't get any money. Everybody in the world would get money in '65, '66, '67, '68. But we couldn't get any because we were not defined, we were not a professional theatre and all the sources of money were going to professional theatre or to children's theatre or something like that. I had a lot of problems. I managed to raise maybe about a hundred and fifty thousand dollars over a three year period. That just kept the theatre going. Nobody got paid, that just got us through the productions. Occasionally, we would have to pay somebody, but most of the money that went to individuals was to get people out of jail, people who got busted for tickets and stuff like that. They got busted at 3:00 o'clock, and we needed them for a performance at 8:00 o'clock. So money went for that. But nobody actually got paid any salary.

Constantly I was traveling around, trying to find out how all these other theatres—I'm primarily talking about white theatres—how they got money. A lot of my partners, like Marko with the East-West Players, an Asian group, and people in L.A. and Los Otros, a Chicano group—none of us were getting any money at all. We weren't doing anything that was right. I'm not saying it was anybody's fault, but, on the other hand, you know how it goes. We weren't doing anything right. So I got more and more interested in that whole process of developing better press than Center Theatre in L.A. We were getting press in the trades that said, "This is really not a community theatre, this is as professional a theatre as L.A. has to offer." But we weren't getting any money from anywhere. Center Theatre was raising five hundred and six hundred thousand dollars a year. So I really got angry, because I had all those beautiful people working with me, spending long hours at the theatre, trying to convert this old building into a theatre, walking up and down the streets, passing out handbills. We were doing all the kinds of things that theatre people have to do to survive. And we couldn't get enough money to know that we were going to put on the next production. And this problem wasn't unique with us. It's the top problem right across the country with what people are calling grassroots arts projects, or grassroots theatre, or emerging arts, or developing arts.

People in the community I was in, which was Watts, were happy we were there, once they realized what was happening. So when I had needs for certain things, like we needed some typewriters to type proposals and what not, they miraculously appeared. You understand? We needed a tape recorder to do a track for a production we were going to do. And in a few days a tape recorder appeared. We kind of had a funding system going on! And I didn't complain about it because we really needed these things, and we had no other way to get them. I certainly didn't solicit. I was just mentioning the fact that we needed these things. Anyhow, certain elements in the community were very happy that we were there doing what we were doing. My whole theatre at that time—I had about sixty people in my workshop—were people who had never studied before. They admitted, once they got involved, that they hadn't been to the colleges, and some of them hadn't been to high school. We had a lot of ex-offenders come in. In fact, one of my students is playing in a picture, *The Mack*, and does a very good job in it, and he was an ex-offender. During this period I'm talking about, a lot of people in our workshop started working in TV shows. Several of the people out of this theatre managed to get work in Hollywood and all of these things started adding up: the press that we were getting, the press that individuals were getting, and some of the consultant gigs that I went on.

When the National Endowment decided they would create a program that would deal with community arts, I was one of the people recommended for it. But I didn't want to leave my theatre at the time, although there's a time when leadership in some situations should change or else the people who are being led don't get strong enough. Finally, when I was convinced that I was the only person to do this job in community arts around the country, I felt that my theatre was strong enough to continue without me. It's had its problems, its growing pains, but it's still out there. They have a full season ahead of them and they're in production. I've been at the Endowment now two years this month—traveling around all over the country, looking at things, responding to inquiries and letters, proposals, applications for what people are calling grassroots arts or community arts. I like to refer to them as "community arts," and I named this program in opposition to what people wanted to call it. They wanted to call it "emerging arts," but it's not that at all, because these arts have been existing. They've been existing, but they've been untended. I decided if the government would take the leadership to start trying to give assistance to this level, then it was an expansion on the level of government or bureaucracy. I call the program "Expansion Arts," and that's how the program got the title. It means just that—it's an expansion on the level of thinking in terms of what is art in America.

I manage to fund a lot of innovative projects. A lot of theatre gets funded—small community theatre, usually involved in social purposes like identity—the need to be able to express in a certain community—theatre with what I guess you'd call therapeutic value. I fund both Marketa's and Akila's projects. A lot of interesting things are happening and I manage to find out about them. The grapevine is better than normal sources of information, going into the government and out from the government—people in the field—and I make trips based on that kind of information. Some of the people whom I'm funding, some of the projects that I've funded around the country, are so good, so well-recommended, that I don't even have to see their work. Only a few like that, but I must say that Marketa's project is one of those. The recommendations were high, but at the same time these recommendations were coming from people who could have given money quite frequently themselves, but they didn't. So, here again, it was because what was being done on this community arts, grassroots level was not defined by any of the major or established foundations. They don't have a category for it—they claim. Now that I'm involved, I'm on the same side of the fence. They're still saying the same thing, so I get into a lot of arguments about that. And I think something will happen in terms of a transition that will make major funding sources look seriously on what we're calling "main jobs." In fact, a lot of small foundations are beginning to think only about community arts, because they realize that the big piece of the pie is going for the established things. I've been a consultant with several of the larger foundations, talking about really strengthening programs for community level projects. But I don't know when something is really going to break through with the larger foundations.

Meanwhile, my program is still in good stead as far as the Endowment is concerned. We've doubled the appropriation money every year. If we get the proper appropriation this year, I can start beefing up some of the projects that I've identified. By "beefing up" I mean giving them a larger amount of money. And I don't know how long that will last. We don't know how much money we're going to get this year. The administration has recommended eighty million dollars, fifty of which could be program money, and that would mean twenty-one million more than we had last year. But if we don't get that—and there's a lot of opposition in both houses—then we will do what we've been doing. I'm very concerned about structuring a program at the Endowment so that community arts projects are a more visible part of the American lifestyle, in terms of being recognized by financial sources. I'd like to leave and go back to what I was doing, but I won't do that until I'm sure the program is in good shape. Meanwhile, for therapy, I'm

Robert Hooks' artistic director for the D.C. Black Repertory Company. If you push paper around as much as I've been pushing it around for two years, you need therapy—or somebody is going to be coming to visit you!

In some kind of nutshell, that's what I've been into. That's my involvement in theatre.

Questions to *Akila Couloumbis*
Marketa Kimbrell
Vantile Whitfield

QUESTION   Mr. Whitfield, I wonder if you would comment about the extent to which foundations and corporations refer to the lack of good administration and management as one reason for not funding certain theatre projects?

MR. WHITFIELD   That was constantly, in my own case in L.A., the thing that I got. But then switching over and getting on the other side of the fence, one of the big fears is that the money will be messed up—the fear that they don't know how to keep books or they don't keep the books properly. They get involved in such heavy petty cash expenditures that they can't account for the money; and that's one of the strong, strong fears. The other fear, quite frequently within conservative business organizations and the private sector, is that community groups are involved in controversial, extreme-left issues and things. And they don't want to spoil the image of their foundation or their business by being involved with some of these projects. Yet, the Endowment has been involved in community arts—and that's the *federal government!* The legislation that gives the Endowment the right to operate specifies that the Endowment will not be involved in *what* art is done, but in the *excellence* of the art. So the whole Endowment and all of its programs are able to fund artists who are quite frequently controversial, plus some of the material they are doing. We are able to fund them. And we have funded them, and there have been only one or two incidents that were kind of bad in the eight years since the Endowment has been in existence. So I think that, down in the business sector, where the business sector begins to start thinking about some isolated community arts projects, they don't have to have that fear as much—especially if they are strongly involved in how the money will be handled.

One of the biggest problems that I notice across the country is that we have to develop a curriculum, a method of training community arts administrators, and that is different than arts administrators on an established level. To give one example, I found that none of the merchants, the major merchants like hardware stores, lighting stores, or electronic supply sources, trusted a little theatre for a check. It may be a simple problem (individuals have this problem) so, therefore, if I had to buy a tape recorder—let's use that as an example—that costs four hundred and seventy dollars, I had to write a cash check and get the cash and then go pay for the tape recorder. They would not accept the check. That's one incident. On weekends, if you're operating, the smaller merchants are not going to accept your check. Quite frequently, you have to keep a backlog of cash for the weekend—for any eventuality. Well, according to procedures, loan bookkeeping procedures that the business would have you keep, or the endowment for that matter, this is too much cash for you. So it's a problem. But most of the people in the arts—and I've reviewed and involved myself in minor audits of a lot of my projects—are very honest people, so that in a shoe box or an old brown bag will be the receipts for money spent. An imaginative bookkeeper or an imaginative accountant could show these people just how to keep good books. Regardless, they have to function with their funds the way they have to function. A lot of people are afraid of the smaller arts group for that reason. But I am able to establish credibility at the Endowment for a lot of my arts projects, and we are not finding that any of the people in this field are dishonest and misusing funds or misappropriating funds. They just may not be using established methods. What an arts administration course would have to do for community arts administrators would be to bring in a lot of community arts people to teach such a course—not the professionals in the field who work in major arts institutions—but people who work in community arts, people who can give a real picture of what it's like to administer a community arts project.

Like, how do you get advertising? How do you get visibility? Most of the time we cannot compete with commercial ventures for the space in newspapers. Quite frequently, just by the way you get shoved around, you can't get public service time on radio and television, although you are eligible for it. But if you had a sharp administrator who was hip to the fact that you're going to get pushed around and approached it another way, with some clout, with some methods that would work, it would be a different story. What we need are community arts administrators rather than administrators who come from the establishment and try to fit into that slot. That just doesn't work. At the Endowment we're beginning to identify one or two places, programs where we can begin to train community arts administrators. But it's a real big problem. And when a community arts project begins to get some money, then a lot of problems happen. First, there was a problem of not getting *any* money. Now there are a lot of problems *because* of money. Now you need management. But just about across the boards, I would say that eighty percent of the managers in community arts are artists who have had to learn management also. This is very difficult for an artist—to continue wearing both hats. You can do it for a while, if you believe in your project enough. But it's difficult for an artist to do that—ultimately the art gets affected or the administration gets affected.

QUESTION   Could Mr. Couloumbis further define the difference between a manager and a producer as he sees it, since he introduced the term "semantics" in this area.

MR. COULOUMBIS   What Van says is absolutely true. I have had to become an administrator and a manager. And it is a time-consuming situation. We're getting funds now from the National Endowment for the Arts, as Van pointed out. The New York State Arts Council funded us at the very beginning with the first sizable grant that we received. The last big grant we received was from the Criminal Justice Coordinating Council. When you begin working with federal agencies, you need to give out monthly reports as to how the money is being spent, as to whether you're following every line in that budget that you set down. Triplicate receipts for everything! You run up a hell of a bill on photocopying alone. We don't have a copying machine, therefore I lean on Xerox. I call them up, I say, "This is what I got, give me a machine!" Well, they're kicking that around someplace—to give us a machine. But, in the meantime, I've asked them to let me do *free* copying. So every so many days we trot down to 666 5th Avenue and Xerox is doing all our copying for us, which is great. There are an awful lot of people you can put the bite on, providing you have some kind of clout, as Van pointed out.

Now to get back to the semantic thing—I don't know, I find myself wearing the hat of a producer because, ostensibly, I am producing plays. What does that entail? It entails finding the script, it entails making out the traveling schedule, the touring schedule of the show. We go to thirty-five prisons, we do it in seven weeks. We do seventy performances in those seven weeks. Monday through Friday, that's two performances a day, sometimes three, sometimes one, but they average out at two performances a day. That is a lot of producing and it requires a lot of management. I don't have a big staff and I don't want a big staff at this particular point because it's difficult to give up a child, you know, kind of as if I don't feel that I'm in it, it's not mine anymore. I don't even want to go see a play if I haven't really put some effort into it.

MS. KIMBRELL   I'd say that a manager manages what *is* and a producer is someone who brings or finds things from the outside to bring into a particular venture. The manager organizes what is available.

MR. WHITFIELD   I think there is a third element. Community arts projects have to become non-profit corporations in order to get Internal Revenue to recognize that they have a way to receive money—it's called an IRS Determination. A lot of the theatres that we are talking about are non-profit corporations, and I think what needs to be in all of them (and there are only a few in the country that have good ones) is a *developer.* A developer is a new breed, a new name. I guess it's a cross between the old fund-raiser and the old program-developer. The developer has a strong idea as to what the project should be, and is imaginative about how the project should develop or expand, and has the ability to produce the funds, to *raise* the funds. Now, most projects need a developer. I don't know what makes a developer, except a certain kind of guts, a certain kind of moxie with some knowledge in developing, with imagination and creativity—it's a kind of art in itself. You feel things out, you feel where you can get your money and how to hit for it and who to hit. And then you're backed up, hopefully, with an administrative staff that can bang out proposals for you, that can develop budgets for you, that can break one budget into four or five parts, so you can send four or five different proposals out, because some people will fund you for bricks and mortar, some people won't. Some people will fund you for salary, some people will fund you for travel, some people will fund just one play out of your whole program or one project out of your whole program. A smart developer just *deals*—that's the best word I can use—just *deals* for that organization and gets what that organization needs.

Now, when you get to theatre, if this organization is a theatre, I would define a producer as that person who can develop a whole package concept in terms of a given amount of money with which he can get the best artists and put together a package that can be presented. Once that is together and presented, it is, as Marketa said, the manager who takes over to keep it together. We operate on three levels, now don't forget it's not only the producer-manager or the producer-administrator—it's that developer-producer-administrator. Sometimes you can get—out of necessity or out of the graces of God—one person who can handle it all, if the operation is small enough. Artists, because they believe in what they are doing, have had to learn how to make things happen, how to wear those other hats. But it can break down to four people with a group such as Akila or Marketa has. Four people: a developer for the corporate structure, a producer for the productions, a manager for the productions and/or an artistic director. That's the ideal situation and many of your major organizations form structures like that.

We are coming into a time when the community arts are growing a lot and are able to generate funds other than public money. Public monies are difficult monies, as the accountability is very heavy, as in the audit situation surrounding public monies, because it is taxpayers' money. Public monies bring you special bureaucratic problems. Every time you start picking up public money, you pick up a whole bag of things that really need another body to handle. It is very difficult for an artist to do this well.

QUESTION   How should a theatre group go about applying for a grant from the National Endowment?

MR. WHITFIELD   The easiest way is to write to the National Endowment for the Arts, Washington, D.C. That is the address. You can make your inquiry in your letter. Your letter is one of inquiry. If you describe what your project is, very briefly, you will be sent appropriate guidelines from the program that handles it. That is the simplest way of reaching the Endowment—write, and it will get routed to the proper program, and I might mention that I think most public funding sources are like this. I know that the Endowment is a responsive agency in that we respond to whatever comes in. We don't go out looking for things; although I look for things in my program area a little more than anyone else does, because we're still identifying the community arts process, and my panel and I decided we needed at least two to five years to do this.

Six months after I had the job at the Endowment, I found the one thing that would be a big help to a lot of my people (especially in rural communities) was that they needed help in filling out forms and in getting basic ideas about how to develop a practical proposal. So I was able to get an accountant-type person loaned to the Endowment for one year by IBM. IBM loaned that person to us and paid that person's salary. The Endowment paid for the travel, and I was able to send this young lady out to projects either before I funded them, quite frequently before I funded them, or right after I funded them, to make sure that the whole office situation was set up. We spent two or three days with the people at the project, talked with the board of directors, made sure that the books were set up properly, that the procedures in terms of handling the money were set up properly. Now I've lost that person, but at the same time I've picked up a permanent staff person who is my assistant director. So a lot of that responsibility, in terms of technical work, is performed by my assistant director, although I do a lot of it when I'm on my trips.

QUESTION   I'd like to ask Mr. Couloumbis how he got permission to perform in the prisons.

MR. COULOUMBIS   I didn't know who to deal with. I knew that there was a Commissioner of Correction, both on the city level and the state level, and all we did was just drop off a letter to them and say, "This is our idea and would there be any objection?"

Since we were not going to charge any money, I felt rather confident that we would be invited. In the back of my mind was the thought of political blackmail—because they've no right to keep us out as long as we have a program that is of value to someone. And to my surprise it has been a rather happy marriage. They've never stopped us from giving any plays. As a matter of fact, we get letters and calls from wardens and prisons in which we haven't performed, inviting us to go. So that was the simplest thing in the world. Problems developed afterwards, because of the security situations in different cities. But it was pretty much an easy thing.

QUESTION   Did you have trouble raising money for your program?

MR. COULOUMBIS   Well, for two years we had no funds. We got a lot of actor friends of ours, who were also unemployed, and said, "Listen, we are doing a play and most every actor on earth would love to perform for money—or otherwise." And they all came and we performed for no money. After we had set up some kind of track record, if you will, we invited governmental agencies to fund us, such as the New York State Council on the Arts. They were the first to fund us, and once you get one, you gain some respectability. From there we went to the National Endowment for the Arts, and after that came other agencies. After those, the players got small grants from foundations, banks, Rockefeller, Mellon—all in all we got small grants from maybe fifteen or twenty different groups. And that's how it started with us. We submitted proposals, as Van said. Some of them were rejected because a private foundation would only fund you if you happen to be doing the thing that its director liked. And you have to know: is Ford Foundation doing anything for the prisoners? Are they into that? If they are, they'll fund you, and if they're not, forget it!

MS. KIMBRELL   A small point: we like to operate on a limited budget in my particular group. All our props come out of garbage cans. We collect things on Wednesdays or whenever the city is full of unpicked up things. I find it important to my emotional balance to know that if ever we should *not* get funded, there is still enough substance within the group so that we will work for nothing for that period until we get funded again. In other words, even though sometimes you receive an extra grant or more money, so that you accelerate your operation, the substance of the operation, the purpose you are really working for should remain so contained and independent from expansion that, if you fall back financially, you always have something to continue with. If you don't, you have demoralized the people with whom you have been working. Actually, we never got so much money that we did not have to find materials for props and costumes in the city's garbage cans; but that's part of the theatre's strength, creating something out of nothing.

QUESTION   What type of plays do you present in the prisons?

MR. COULOUMBIS   Well, as I mentioned earlier, we do a number of plays each year. There are different categories of plays. One category is the touring show. That is the one that goes to thirty-five prisons. Because of the financial situation, it is a small cast play. No set. Most of the plays that we do run an hour, an hour and ten. That's one category. That's a traveling show with a minimum of people, no more than four or five in the total cast, a regular play, a one act, or a play that is full length and cut down with no big sets. I am sorry for the scenic designers, but we have a problem. We play on stages that are immense and we play on stages that are very, very small, so we can't have scenery.

The other category is the play that we do in the prison with a crew involving twenty inmates. Ten girls and ten fellows. That's a full length play. That's a big production with a full staff, some of whom are offenders. The stage manager that we have now for the production, *No Place To Be Somebody,* is an offender who wanted to concentrate on stage managing and therefore I didn't hire a professional. He is getting that experience and the production will have all that it needs. We go to a lighting firm that has been kind to us for the last five or six years, giving us all the lights that we need and cables and a dimmer board.

Another category of production is the one that we have in the "work release" program. We have a program that releases to our custody six offenders for a period of twelve weeks. In that space of time they are counseled and they are rehearsed for the first eight weeks. The last four weeks they are on the road touring with the production: six people, plus a stage manager, and small props, props that we can put into the station wagon and travel from Brooklyn to the Bronx, to Queens, to the Tombs, to Rikers Island. And those are the three different plays or categories.

Marketa's workshops, both in the Bronx and in Queens, just recently finished doing productions that they evolved from the workshops. She makes do with the things that are available in the institution. They'll give you chairs, they'll give you tables. Like Van's experience with his theatre group out in California, coming up with tape recorders and things, the first experience that I had in prison was when we wanted a couch. The warden said, "There's no couch in this prison." Well, nobody left the scene, but somehow the word went out and we got a couch. They dragged it out of the doctor's office and brought it in and there was the couch. I swear that nobody left, but the word went out. We got a couch. They are very resourceful in prisons!

MS. KIMBRELL   In the production I had with the inmates in Queens there was one thing very necessary—a gun. So I said to the guy, "Sorry, but we have no gun. Just tuck your hand under your coat and pretend." So opening night— opening morning, as the prison productions are always at 9:00 o'clock in the morning—suddenly, this Walter White comes out as the landlord and had a gun! The most fantastic, really fantastic gun! So the captain jumped, everybody jumped. When we looked, it was a piece of cardboard that he had molded with toothpaste and let dry and then colored the toothpaste so that it looked like a real gun, more than any real gun you will ever see. It was beautiful, you know, we all thought it was great!

QUESTION   Do you ever use professional actors?

MR. COULOUMBIS   Yes, that has happened. It happened more in the past than it does at present. Now I find, because of the great work that is being done in the workshops in prison, more and more guys are coming to us after their release, wanting to become involved. Therefore, the opportunity is given to them. The last play that we did on the road was a play written by an offender at Trenton State Prison. He got royalties for it. I don't pay professional playwrights royalties, but inmates do get paid. And the two fellows who were in the play were ex-offenders and professional actors. So I am more into using offenders.

QUESTION   Do you believe that your program actually helps to rehabilitate the prisoners who get involved with it?

MR. COULOUMBIS   No way that I can answer that. I don't know. I hope and only hope. I hope that, if nothing else, it involves them in a play, gives them for a space of seven weeks a new profession. But beyond that it would be presumptuous for me to say that I have changed their lives. All that I can say is that perhaps we have shown them another way.

I have been able with four or five individuals who have had as many as twenty-nine years in prison, to see their progress. One man is Chuck. He has not gone back to it. As a matter of fact, just recently he beat me out for a commercial. We both went up and we got an appointment from the agency and he got the commerical! It's a Hertz commercial and he is the fellow who says, "We give the guy a nice clean car." That's Chuck. We both went for the same part and he got it, and it delights me because Chuck needed that. He needed that very badly, and now he has done a number of films. But that is only one example. I can also tell you about the guy I bailed out of jail and he turned around and skipped bail and I was stuck with five hundred dollars out of my pocket.

MR. WHITFIELD   I could say something about that, I think. There are about fourteen prison programs across the country; some programs with theatre, some with painting and visual arts, and other performing arts. Now I'm beginning to talk to the Justice Department in Washington and to the National Science Foundation about opening up other funds for prison arts programs. And the reports that they have gotten from prisons where arts programs are involved are good. There is a strong feeling in Washington that there may be a whole area opening up here. So that means that there seems to be some good in them. There must be some. I haven't seen any reports that have not been positive. I think they are making that kind of report because they've been able to watch about fourteen projects around the country and somehow the results are good. That doesn't necessarily mean that the guys rehabilitate overnight. It just means that the consensus of opinion is that prison arts programs are good.

QUESTION   Why do you think it's so difficult to get people in ghetto areas to attend a theatre?

MS. KIMBRELL   I think the first thing that really overpowers them is all kinds of agencies coming in—politically—with a lot of promise and leaving without ever fulfilling the promise. So a lot of people in the ghetto feel cheated when some politician comes in and gives them a lot of hope. They feel cheated when their own personal cycle of accomplishments has been degraded. They no longer have any faith that going out or extending themselves to any activity is going to change their lot. I am speaking now mostly for the societies that are totally demoralized, such as ghettos we have in Chicago, in Cleveland. I think that the reason that in Coney Island people don't even go to the beach is because there seems to be no vibrancy, not enough fight left in the people to make them believe that they can change anything. So they just stay where they are. The other thing is a well-grounded skepticism that they have for anything that is offered to them free—for which the price they pay is the perpetuation of the very thing that they live in.

Also, it seems to me that the traditional theatre in America, or Europe for that matter, is basically concerned with middle-class complexities. I was very much part of that scene at one time. And I found, too, that experimental theatre caters to colleges, caters to the avant garde, to the liberalism of America, but no one within that experimental theatre ever experiments with the communication necessary to reach people who just don't have the time or the inclination to go to a theatre. What kind of communication do they need? Do they need to be seen attending a theatre? Do they need to see people taking their clothes off? Do they need an actor to sit on their laps? They don't. They don't want it. I feel that experimental theatre and theatre as a whole has very little to explain to the people who are hungering for some expression, but who aren't necessarily involved in the middle-class, sexual-erotic aspects of theatre. They aren't hung up on that because they're hung up on life!

Educational Theatre

Anthony Reid
Norris Houghton
John Houseman

Commentary by *Anthony Reid*

Executive Director, American
Theatre Association, Washington,
D. C.

I began as a college teacher and taught for seven years. I was involved in that period with directing and acting, scenic design, some management, some promotion; whatever you do in a small college department and, as one of the staff people, you do a little bit of everything. I went from there into a non-academic theatre situation—a community theatre which, however, had some permutations to make it a little unusual. In that situation I became involved with budgeting and fund-raising, professional box office management, promotion, administration, professional music events, booking and management of films and road show productions. During that time, of course, I was still involved with directing, acting, design—all of the production aspects of the theatre. After thirteen years of that, I went into what, for want of a better term, is called "arts administration." This was as the executive director of the California Arts Commission, and then the Oregon Arts Commission—both of which, may I say, are totally different from the New York Arts Council; for many reasons, but including about fourteen million dollars! With the arts commissions I was involved with the development of community and state-wide programs in all of the arts, not just the performing arts. This gave me an education in the governing structures of organizations and involved me in legislative liason, relations with state and federal agencies, and in the creation, as well as the analysis, of funding proposals. That went on for about seven years and, since then, I've been with the American Theatre Association, which is more of the same, except that it's on a national level and involved with multiple interest groups. That's enough of me; I think you've got a sort of skeletal outline that tells my points of reference.

ATA is a membership association. It is a professional association as well as being a service organization. It is a publisher of journals, books, pamphlets, newsletters, monographs, whatever. In addition to the direct service that our publishing offers to our members, a placement bureau is maintained for people who work in theatre. Our national office maintains liason with and advises federal agencies, legislatures, foundations and other bodies. We also maintain relationships with as many of the other theatre-related organizations as we can, including some international organizations. We're involved in basic research in theatre, we produce the American College Theatre Festival, as well as the Community Theatre Festival. We sponsor an annual convention.

The actual constituents that make up ATA are: the American Community Theatre Association, the Army Theatre Arts Association, the Childrens' Theatre Association, the Secondary School Theatre Association, and the University and College Theatre Association. All of those are associations which have individual members (both professional and student) as well as organizational members. We have two associations which have organizational members only, these are the University Resident Theatre Association and the National Association for Schools of Theatre.

Now to get to the part that's very difficult for me, because I'm asked to define what, in my mind, is the difference between a producer and a manager. In my experience I think one of the primary qualifications for a producer is to be like Roger Stevens and have a lot of money! Then it's very easy for you to produce. So—if you want to be a producer, go into real estate!

It seems to me the differentiation in those functions depends a great deal upon the situation in which you find yourself. In the commercial theatre I think the producer is the person who is responsible for the money aspects of it and, because he is, also makes the decisions on what show is going to be done, who the director is going to be, who the designer is going to be, who the stars are going to be, all the rest of this. He usually is the "front man" for the corporation, or the limited company which is providing the money to produce; he acts as its agent and has charge of the decisions. The manager in this kind of situation, it seems to me, is the person who implements those decisions for the producer, takes care of or has the responsibility (and may delegate it) to make all the arrangements with the various guilds and unions that are involved. The producer, of course, is the person who approves the budget; the manager is the person who puts it together, provides the original skeletons and seeds that can make it work. He has responsibility for the organizational structure that supports the production itself; including, if there is such a thing, a permanent staff, which he heads.

Now, are there any words, gems of advice, to be given in relation to aspiring producers/arts administrators/arts managers? Obviously, my qualifications lie much more in the area of the managerial or administrative end, so I will speak primarily to that and say that, even though you are involved in theatre, if you are going to become an arts manager or administrator, you're going to have to have a pretty basic familiarity with *all* the art forms. I can find no way in my work in the theatre to separate them. Theatre is one place where, it seems to me, they all come together. So you need that basic familiarity, you need to know how the various arts are produced; in other words, what are the mechanics, the similarities, and the peculiarities between art forms; and, particularly, how to work with the people who are involved in these various forms. Believe me, on the average, dancers are different kinds of people than most theatre people, and people who work in the visual and plastic arts are different from theatre and dance people. They have their own kinds of hang-ups and if you're going to be working in arts administration, you're going to have to learn to recognize those and do it very quickly. Then, secondly, as the administrator, you've got to know the kind of nitty-gritty stuff that is not confined to management of the arts, but to management in general: organizational structure and group dynamics, marketing, budgeting systems, personnel management, small office organization, and then the whole gamut of things like state and federal tax regulations, postal regulations—you've got to learn to live with printers and printing. All of these things are involved in any management situation. I think this was something that perhaps Vantile [Whitfield] was talking about when he was saying that too many arts organizations are managed or administered by creative artists, which in my experience is not such a good idea, simply because they have no training and little interest in such things as structure and systems analysis. These do not really interest them very much and they do them badly and they are taking time from their own creative work. I think it's really a waste of their time and, quite frankly, it's usually bloody hard on the arts organization. A lot of organizations disappear because of sheer bad administration.

Commentary·by *Norris Houghton*

Dean of Theatre, Purchase College
of the State University of New
York; Co-founder of the Phoenix
Theatre; Author of *Moscow
Rehearsals, Advance From
Broadway, Great Russian Plays,
Return Engagement* and
*Masterpieces of Continental
Drama*

The last seminar apparently emphasized that, to be a producer, you really should be everything *but* a producer. If
that's the case, I'm eminently qualified. I come to you not as
a producer, but as a college dean!

My own beginnings in the performing arts field were
very far from that of a producer. In high school I thought I
was God's gift as an actor, but in college I found I was not.
Coming out of college I thought I was God's gift as a scene
designer, and I managed sufficiently to persuade myself of
this fact that I could persuade others to give me a certain
number of jobs as a designer. I also worked as a stage manager for some quite prestigious managements—for the
Theatre Guild and Gilbert Miller, and I worked for a number of other producers. From these associations I came to
some ideas of what I would define as the difference between a producer and manager, and what I consider the ex-
cellences that can be found in a good producer. Also, not
being particularly successful in any of these, I went on to
try my hand in other matters, such as book-writing, which

is not necessarily the province of a producer, to even writing some criticism for small and relatively unknown magazines, associate editing one that was quite distinguished, called *Theatre Arts*. My first role as producer happened because I found a play that I wanted to direct. (I forgot to say that by now I was getting to be a director.) And I couldn't find anybody to produce it, so in order to get it on, I became the co-producer; but then immediately I acquired a co-producer who didn't want my name on the program as such and, therefore, *Billy Budd*, if you go back and look at the annals, names me as its director but not as its co-producer. However, if you look at the partnership papers, you will find that I was one of three. Those were my beginnings.

The point to be made in connection with that kind of beginning is that, if you're making it in the New York City theatre, if you're doing it on Broadway, in order to function you have to belong to a union. If you are seeking to function in a number of different ways, you have to belong to a number of different unions, so that I have in my time been a member of Actors' Equity Association, the Society of Stage Directors and Choreographers and of the Brotherhood of Painters, Paperhangers and Decorators of America, of which Local 829 is the United Scenic Artists. And it is through being a union member that one comes to learn how awful the unions are, as well as how useful they can be. Mr. Houseman, who is presently being picketed by I don't know how many of them, can speak of the unions with more immediate concern than can I, since today I belong only to the American Association of University Professors!

A knowledge of the theatrical craft unions and how they affect one's life is very important to anyone who is producing on the Broadway scene and, I suspect, in a number of other areas in other parts of the world. My own role as a producer really began when I revolted against all of this, by which I mean the Broadway scene, and with the help of a friend and colleague, founded the Phoenix Theatre. Phoenix in part was to be a revolt against the commercialism of Broadway. It was also an idealistic undertaking to bring to pass the kind of theatre that T. Edward Hambleton and I dreamed of being able to create, the kind of theatre which would involve us in a continuing operation.

That brings me to a new kind of producer who is becoming a more recognizable, more constant figure on the scene nowadays—the man who runs a non-profit, resident theatre, whether it be a repertory theatre in actuality or repertory theatre in name only. This poses a different set of producer's problems and a different set of management problems, principally resulting from the effort to create a sense of continuity, whether it be a resident company that stays year in and year out, or whether you have people for a season, or whether you have them only for one play. That company or theatre is not going to stand or fall on a single production, but is undertaking to be a continuum. This means a kind of long-range planning that the Broadway manager or the Broadway producer seldom has to deal with. Each play, each production becomes a problem in itself that must be resolved, hopefully happily—usually unhappily—and then the attack begins all over again. So such producers today (people like Zelda Fichandler and Nina Vance and Duncan Ross and Michael Langham) find themselves in an unusual position, because they are both producers and artistic leaders. The relationship of the producer to the artistic leader, I would like to say, is one of identity. They are identical; a producer *should* be the artistic leader. He should be the artistic leader of a production on Broadway, as well as Off-Broadway, as well as in the repertory theatre or the resident company. This is one of the things, I think, that cannot be lacking or overstressed. The Theatre Guild was much more than a producing organization. It had artistic muscle that it exercised vehemently over everything it did. It was a hydra-headed monster. Those of you who are theatrical historians know that it was founded and run by a board of six managers, all of whom together managed somehow to pull off some rather extraordinary enterprises. There are many instances which separate such producer-directors from Roger Stevens and such other producers as, to the best of my knowledge, have never undertaken to direct a play. I'm not saying that it's necessarily a good idea for the producer to be a director, or for the director to become a producer; but I think that it is important that the producer be the artistic leader, as well as the business management leader. And, therefore, there is a similarity between a person like the artistic director—or whatever title he or she is given at the Arena Stage in Washington or at the Guthrie Theatre or at the Phoenix—and the producer himself or herself or itself.

There is a point also that comes into this when we talk about the resident theatre, or the permanent theatre organization, as opposed to the producer's role in the Broadway scene and, indeed, in the academic theatre scene, and that is the presence of what is usually known as the board of trustees or the board of directors. This brings the realm of management into the realm of producing—a new factor. One can't imagine the Brahmses and the Michaelangelos bowing to the will of any kind of board that would tell them what they could do next, what they should do next. By and large the non-profit organizations of the country—whether they be symphony orchestras, opera companies, dance companies or theatres—have a board. And that board exercises some kind of control, or should. I remember, rather ironically, that I wrote a chapter in the *Rockefeller Panel Report on the Performing Arts* on the subject of the board of trustees, because this is an area with which I have had some experience (but not nearly enough, because I don't think we ever quite resolved the relationship of the producer or the managing director or the artistic director or whatever you want to call it, to the trustees). If you allow the trustees to run the situation, then you get something like the fiasco of the Vivian Beaumont [under Jules Irving]. If you allow the director or the producer to run the organization, then the board claims it is nothing but a rubber stamp. Presumably, the board in this kind of theatre has the financial responsibilities of the individual producer. They're supposed to raise the money. But, as we read in the papers, the first board at the Beaumont has somehow not been able to accomplish that. Now we'll see whether Mr. Papp, who does seem to be able to get boards to raise money for him, can accomplish it. Time will tell.

Ten years ago, I resigned my co-managership of the

Phoenix Theatre, saying that I was the only man I had ever heard of that had gone into teaching in order to improve his financial condition. What happened was that it seemed I couldn't afford to go on the way I was from a monetary point of view, so I accepted a professorship and the directorship of the Vassar Experimental Theatre and the chairmanship of the Department of Drama at Vassar. Vassar doesn't pay very well, but it pays better than the art theatres in America and this was a kind of welcome haven. I tried for the first two years to hold both jobs. But, both were full-time jobs and were separated one from the other by about seventy-five miles. So I then went into teaching, and then after five years went to the State University of New York, being an arsonist by nature and being interested in the idea that the State University was lighting a fire in Westchester County, which was to take the form of a four-year college—the unique thrust of which was to be in the performing arts. I was asked to be on the planning staff and to be the dean of a nonexistent school, and I accepted. I've been there now for almost six years, but the first students in the School of the Arts arrived only last September. So my life has been spent for five of those six years in planning what would be the ideal educational theatre experience. The objective of this school is very much the same as Houseman's Juilliard, it being in the private sector and we being in the public sector. I form a good link into what Houseman will probably end up by saying, theorizing a discussion of his present position, because I, too, am hoping to make a very strong professional theatre school. And I, too, am hoping that out of that can come, as has come, brilliantly in the case of the first class of Juilliard, a continuing operation which in his case is an acting company. In my case I hope it may be a total theatre organization with directors and designers and technicians and arts managers, all being part and parcel of what I hope we can do: graduate theatre companies rather than graduate individual artists.

The producer, I have already stressed, is the man who I think *does* need to have the kind of background that Houseman and I, myself, have had, and this is part of the advice I would offer to aspiring people in that area who have immersed themselves in a number of different aspects of theatre. So that if the costume designer comes with a portfolio of sketches for a play that you are producing, and you're the one who is going to have to pay the bill for the costumes, you have some sixth sense about those clothes— you know that they are the right kinds of things. When a dispute emerges between the director and the playwright and the actor, which you're going to have to arbitrate, you should know something about the problems a director faces, something about the problems a writer faces, something about the problems an actor faces, and so on down the line.

I think I'll stop *now*!

Commentary by *John Houseman*

Artistic Director, City Center
Acting Company; Director of
Theatre, The Juilliard School;
author of *Run Through*; Academy
Award winner as Best Supporting
Actor in *The Paper Chase*; Earlier:
Managing producer of the Negro
Theatre and the Classical Theatre
of the (WPA) Federal Theatre
Project; Co-founder of the
Mercury Theatre; Artistic Director
of the American Shakespeare
Festival (Stratford, Conn.); Artistic
Director of the Theatre Group
(UCLA)

My own beginnings in the performing arts are irrelevant and rather squalid. I entered the theatre at the age of thirty, having been in the international grain business, having been a gaucho on the Argentine pampas, and all kinds of things having nothing whatever to do with theatre. I had a secret love for theatre, but it was buried under other activities. Then, just as I was about to become a rich man, the Depression came and I found myself unable to earn a living in any other way except in the theatre. I started adapting, translating, writing and generally messing around with playscripts, on which to my surprise and pleasure I found I was able to sell options. Very rarely and not very successfully, they were even performed. Then, by a stroke of sheer luck (all of which you can read about in my book) I encountered a gentleman named Virgil Thomson, a composer who had just arrived from Paris with the *Four Saints in Three Acts* opera by Gertrude Stein. This very hard-headed, practical little man turned out in this instance, to be a lunatic and invited this person—myself—who knew almost nothing about the theatre, had never directed a thing, and really was a sort of theatrical hanger-on, to direct and produce his opera—*Four Saints in Three Acts*. It turned out very nicely and that was my beginning in the theatre.

From then on most of my operations in theatre were of a vaguely lunatic nature and were the result of incredible luck, skulduggery in obtaining jobs, and a great store of energy. But always my activity in theatre was entirely opposed to what was then the theatrical establishment—the Broadway scene. It took me into the Federal Theatre of the WPA, which was an entirely unique phenomenon without precedent in any theatre in the world. It was an extraordinary enterprise having only partially to do with theatre. It was part of an enormous relief project designed to get people off the bread lines.

In due course my activity has led me to organize and operate no less than seven theatres, all institutional theatres of one sort or another. Some of these were successful and distinguished; all of them lost a great deal of money—as much money as was available at the time to put into them. In those days losing money in the theatre was considered vaguely disgraceful; indeed, financing a theatrical operation was a fairly crooked endeavor in the sense that you went to your angels and backers (from whom you got your money to start these theatres), you offered them something artistically exciting or something that stirred their imagination. Never for a moment did it occur to you that you would ever repay a penny of the money they invested in your theatre—you knew you were running what was inevitably a deficit operation. In those days "deficit" was a dirty word in the theatre. "Subsidy" was an unknown word. Mistakenly, sometimes people talk of the Federal Theatre as the first subsidized theatre in America. That's absolutely erroneous. For all its artistic accomplishments the Federal Theatre was essentially a relief project having nothing to do with artistic subsidy.

Norris Houghton made a good point about the difference between institutional theatre or, rather, continuity in the theatre, as opposed to current Broadway speculative, one-shot production. Here I think it's worth bearing in mind that Belasco, Miller, Frohman and all those great producers of the past did in fact have a very pronounced continuity in their operations. These men produced a number of plays each year over a great many years, and it's interesting to note that Frohman, who was America's leading producer when he died on the *Lusitania,* left five hundred dollars as his entire fortune after years of being the most successful producer in the American theatre. But for better or worse they ran a serious, continuing business. It was only later that the Broadway "plunger" appeared and this development occurred largely for tax reasons. Almost every play produced on Broadway today is produced under a limited partnership and each play is considered a separate entity. So that if by any chance the play is successful and makes money, you can dissolve or sell the company and make capital gains out of it. And if the play is a flop and you lost your whole investment, you can deduct the entire loss from your taxes. And that's perfectly legitimate. But it is also very dangerous and it represents, I think, the fatal flaw in today's Broadway commercial theatre. The great old commercial producers, for all their faults, had a sense of theatrical continuity, had a sense of responsibility toward themselves and toward the people they employed.

The idea that theatre may be a deficit operation is now finally beginning to be accepted in this country as it has previously been accepted in one form or another in every other civilized country in the world. The kind of institutional theatre we are thinking about is not capable of sustaining itself through the box office. But then, neither is anything else nowadays. The people who revolt at the idea of subsidy to an art institution or a theatre are perfectly willing to accept it for public highways, hospitals, railroads, fisheries and what have you. We operate strangely in this country. You still encounter violent opposition to the idea of government or state subsidy, although, in fact, it is now becoming increasingly common. The truth is when a foundation gives you money, it is giving you government money because it's tax-free money! Similarly, everybody screams and objects to socialized medicine while, in fact, we have an elaborate structure of insurance which is already very close to national socialized medicine. So we must face the reality and accept the pragmatic truth that the kind of theatrical continuity, the sort of institutional theatre that Norris and I are talking about *does* have to get it's money from somewhere other than the box office. Either from the state or from the city or from the federal government or through these elaborate devices called "foundations." If any of you are thinking seriously about the theatre, you *are* thinking in terms of institutional and continuous theatre, because that is the only theatre that makes any artistic or material sense for this particular era in which we live. But, having accepted that fact, you should not have any illusions about this being an easy or comfortable life.

Raising money for the theatre is not an easy or agreeable job. You have to prove your worth. But also you have to woo, maneuver and finagle. And you have to make personal conquests and that goes even as far as the government. I worked for many years for two of the toughest and most lucrative corporations in the American entertainment business—the Columbia Broadcasting System and Metro-Goldwyn-Mayer—and I never spent any of my time while I was working for these two organizations thinking about money; I was expected to make a certain product. If the product was unsuccessful, they tended to look past you in the corridors or they cut you in the commissary, and, finally, the chances were that your contract would not be renewed. But in fact, terribly little time was spent worrying about or discussing money. Since I went back into the "culture business," I do nothing else from five in the morning, when I wake up sweating with anxiety, till I go into a troubled sleep, *than* think about money! I think that is true of everybody who runs any kind of artistic enterprise in this country at this time. An organization with which you've heard that I have been involved—the Phoenix Theatre—presents a classic case of worrying about money—over a quarter of a century. But we all do.

At an advanced age, through my present position as Director of the Drama Division of the Juilliard School, I believed I was getting out of this rat race. I was getting out of this theatrical racket that I've described to you and becoming an eminent educator. When I was invited to form the Drama Division, I was very flattered at the idea. I'd done a certain amount of lecturing and vague kinds of practical teaching, including a year at Vassar many, many years ago. I found at Juilliard the opportunity to develop the kind of training which goes beyond what most of the theatre arts departments in universities or existent drama schools were giving their students at that time. There were some excellent schools. Carnegie Tech had been for years a remarkable school; so had the Neighborhood Playhouse. Yale had been a good school, concentrating on scenic work without very much consideration for actor training. The Juilliard School for theatre arts was set up primarily for actors—just as the Juilliard Music School devotes itself primarily to musical performance.

Actually, to my great regret, we never developed the other areas of theatre, although we may one day have a technical department, a scenic department and a writer's department, which should exist in a theatre conservatory. *We* concentrated on actors. I personally would never have taken this job had I not been very sanguine about the development of regional, institutional theatre in this country. To do a four-year course of a rather elaborate, highly integrated nature, training actors in order then to send them out to knock on Broadway producers' doors, or to hope for a job in a television series, or to wait for some scout to come along and think they're good-looking and get them a job in pictures—is no great inducement to somebody who is trying to run a school. On the other hand if you have the conviction, as I did and many of us did at the time, that the institutional theatre movement was spreading throughout the country and that it would increasingly attract and give opportunities to well-trained young actors, then it was certainly worth trying to establish a conservatory in the manner of the Juilliard School. And that is more or less the way it's turned out.

I think it's fair to say that not for many, many years has a talented and well-trained young actor or actress found it as easy to make a living as in the American theatre as it is today. Of course the picture is not all rosy and the truth is that when the actor reaches his late twenties or early thirties he suddenly finds it less easy because he is no longer willing to work for the Equity minimum, he's not willing to travel and it does become more difficult to make an adequate living. But as far as turning out well-trained graduates from a school—I repeat that they do have a pretty good chance today of earning a living.

So—to return to my personal experience. About the time we were ready to graduate our first class something very unexpected and very strange happened at the Juilliard School. It was, as I have said, our intention to train students for the growing body of institutional theatres in this country. We had hoped in the beginning—and my associate in forming the school, Michel St. Denis, had had some experience of this in Europe—he and I always assumed or, rather, hoped that a school like ours would ultimately be attached to a repertory company. Our obvious hope was that the Vivian Beaumont Repertory Company at Lincoln Center would be the company to which the school would be attached, feed into and derive a certain amount of experience from, and would supply a certain amount of new blood to. Unfortunately, it didn't turn out that way for many reasons which I won't go into here. There never was a connection between the Repertory Theatre and the School. In fact, there never was a repertory company at Lincoln Center. So, we were reduced to hoping that, when they finished our four-year course, our students would be well enough trained to give successful auditions and then be hired by various regional theatres all over the country. By a very fortunate and very fortuitous series of developments, our first batch of graduating students turned out (because, I suppose, we chose them with incredible care from all over the country and because we lavished an obscene amount of love upon them and because they happened to be very talented) they turned out, I repeat, at the end of their third year when we first sent them out to perform in schools and in universities, to be so cohesive and to make so much sense as a young ensemble company and to be so awfully good at their jobs that we found ourselves confronted with the wonderful but alarming realization that we had a full-fledged young theatre company on our hands—and that we really hated to let go. The company was so cohesive and so successful in its own modest way that the idea of letting them break up and scatter and go to work at all kinds of different places became absolutely repugnant and horrifying to us. And so through, again, the skulduggery and the knavery that I've mentioned earlier as a prerequisite for any kind of satisfactory operation in the theatre, and because of the real quality of this company, we found ourselves gradually receiving offers of engagements to the point where the company, which is now an Equity company, a fully professional company in every way, finds itself with more than forty weeks a year of guaranteed engagements. They're not all profitable engagements, of course, and for this reason we have to go get help from the National Endowment and the State Arts Councils and foundations and other places.

So there it is. As the result of running a school, we found almost overnight and almost by accident that we were operating a permanent, or rather a continuing institutional company. It's a kind of miracle. We're all amazed by it. We try to run it, we try to manage it as well as we can, but it's not easy. In the first year of a mad venture like that it is difficult to organize any kind of rational or intelligent management—because the situation is changing all the time and doors are suddenly opening and dire catastrophies are threatened and miracles suddenly occur to save you from them. But now, after a year, we have built up an eager and competent organization; we have made an affiliation with a national booking agency and we have every hope that we are going to enter into a period of calm and reasonable operation. We are probably doomed to disappointment, but that *is* our hope.

Questions to *Anthony Reid*
Norris Houghton
John Houseman

QUESTION Could I ask Mr. Reid to comment about theatre education on the secondary school level—how common are theatre departments in high schools and what standards do they maintain?

MR. REID Well, now we come to the gloom-doom chapter! The state of theatre or drama on the secondary school level is absolutely appalling. We completed a survey about two years ago of the status of theatre in the American high school, which is a terribly depressing book to read. All kinds of lip service was paid by high school principals to the idea that theatre and drama are marvelous activities, but only something around five percent of those schools that were surveyed had anyone on the faculty who had any training in theatre at all. A tremendous number of schools where there is some sort of theatre activity use the physics teacher or, usually, the English teacher for this, because some place in his or her career he or she had taken a course in Shakespeare, and therefore knew all there was to know about theatre. Another interesting aspect is that the guy who coaches the golf team has either release time or a little extra money put in the pot for him, while very few of the people who are doing theatre get either release time or extra money. I think, quite frankly, we can lay this right back on our own shoulders, as people who are involved in theatre who, in effect, are professionally in theatre in the sense that we're making a living out of it, whether we're teaching it, or producing, or acting or whatever. I don't think we've ever decided to come out and say whether or not there ought to be any theatre in high school, but I think part of the problem lies in the fact that we all have a little difficulty in recognizing that theatre is not only a product but also is a process. This is one of the things that the Association is getting very involved with at the moment—that is, in treating theatre as a process. What does it do in the educational sense? What is its value?

I personally would have some qualms, for instance, about a strong production program in high schools if some of the things that go on out here in Long Island are typical—teachers beat themselves to death and a whole group of kids, and their parents, and everybody else, to do *Man of La Mancha*. I really have some qualms about the educational value of that, even though it is very popular in the community, just as is the football team, and they get something of the same level of support, too. But I would have some of the same questions that I would ask about high school football. I think part of the problem in the high school situation lies in our colleges and universities, and the kind of training that they provide and the kind of liaison that they have with the schools of education in their respective institutions. I mean, literally "kinds of communication," because there are departments of education in universities around the country that haven't spoken to anybody in the theatre department for years.

This whole thing is so damned interrelated you really can't pick it up at one place, because when you do you're picking up the whole thing.

No matter how talented they are, or even what kind of training they've had, it's extremely rare to find a high school actor who has any level of competence, simply because they're so immature. I think, as a matter of fact, that there are some things that need being looked at very carefully in the two-year college where they have a very strong production emphasis. I'm wondering whether that production emphasis is happening too soon in terms of artists' maturity (of the student actor particularly but, also, I think it has to be true in the area of design). Technically, I've seen some absolutely first-class students come out of high school and be very good in such things as lighting and stagecraft, but I've never seen in my experience a really good actor or actress come directly out of high school.

QUESTION   Mr. Houghton, could you discuss the peculiarities of managing a theatre or theatre department on the college level? What are the politics that are involved and the special problems?

MR. HOUGHTON   Well, to talk about this from experience is silly because we have no theatre at Purchase and we have only an entering class of thirty-five students; therefore when you say that there are politics, I don't think about students, I think about Albany. One has to consider school boards (if you want to talk about secondary school education or administration); if you're going to talk about colleges and universities, then, is the state prepared to give the kind of support that is necessary to make theatre in the public educational sector work?

It must be said that Purchase is a threat to most of the other campuses of the State University of New York, because we have become the most favored, we're the baby and, as often happens in a large family, there's an awful lot of sibling rivalry, and then a baby comes along and is treated as the most fair-haired and the rest of the family is then in a rage.

We have sought to make Albany understand the difference between a performing arts program and a regular liberal arts course, or a liberal arts college in which you can major in drama, or major in music, or major in sculpture, or another individual art. There's quite a difference in a professional program as opposed to a major within a liberal arts context—most of it in the money and in the teaching. For instance, we are trying to persuade Albany that it's impossible to run a school of the arts on the student-faculty ratio of more than ten to one. Ten teachers per every student—I mean, ten students per every teacher! At Purchase, we're trying to have ten students per every teacher, no more. Actually, the ratio so far is 8.3 to 1, but that's because the music division has to operate on the average of about five students to one because, you know, you can't have forty oboes, and there aren't forty people who want to study the oboe. But you've got to have at least two or three people studying the oboe, or you can't have an orchestra. So you have to have somebody to *teach* oboe, and the person who teaches the violin is not likely to be able to teach the oboe. Therefore, you've got to have a very small faculty-student ratio. And in theatre, if you're going to make it a professional training program, the people who teach acting are not likely to be able to teach stagecraft, the people who teach scene design are not likely to be able to teach arts management, are not likely to be able to teach directing. So, as the School grows, it's going to be necessary to have an enormous faculty and we hope to be able to keep a very small student body.

All this and, of course, a large physical plant requires a tremendous amount of money. The state has put up the money, which is to say it has authorized the bond issues. But, think of what it is going to cost to run! I tremble at the fact that I believe it's going to cost the state a million dollars a year to run the arts center. Supposing they say "no"? Then we'll have the same thing that has happened at so many places, where all the moey goes into the buildings and none is left for operating costs. Now this is management, this is politics, this is Albany, this is the problem of learning to establish a performing arts operation within a state university.

QUESTION   With the creation of performing arts schools at City College and at Brooklyn College and given the number of professional training schools that already exist in the New York area plus Purchase College, I wonder if Mr. Houseman would comment about the duplication or proliferation of these schools, especially in light of recent objections raised by the President of Juilliard and other private schools?

MR. HOUSEMAN   The opinion I will give you is not the opinion of the President of the Juilliard School, who feels terribly strongly that it is morally wrong and close to criminal for institutions directly supported by tax money to be competing with private institutions. I don't altogether agree with him because, as I said earlier, there *are* today no really private institutions. Juilliard is supported by endowments, gifts, and foundations, all of which are tax exempt; so there isn't an enormous amount of difference between "public" and "private" institutions. It is, of course, true that as long as the distinction remains, the private institutions *are* being endangered to some degree by the activities of the State institutions. It makes it terribly difficult and tedious to raise the ever-growing sums of money needed to keep these so-called "private" schools going at their present size and standard of quality. I feel that state-supported schools or conservatories should not slavishly imitate or duplicate the already existing institutions. For example, in the case of City College, I was invited to go up there and discuss what they should do with their two-and-a-half million endowment. In listening—they listening to me and I listening to them—I discovered that they had a rather special problem up there. They have an enrollment which I believe is made up of more than sixty percent black, Puerto Rican and all kinds of other minority groups. It seemed to me that, rather than try to set up an art center or conservatory along the same pattern as those that already exist, they had an opportunity to develop an entirely new kind of theatrical training, specializing in the problems of how you deal artistically and theatrically with these not very cohesive minority groups. How you deal with street theatre; how you deal with participation theatre and all kinds of things which are enormously important and which institutions like ours at Juilliard simply cannot even begin to cope with. Well, they disregarded my advice and they are setting up what I believe is a performing arts center not very different from existing institutions.

Next comes the vexed question of staffing these institutions. The great danger I see in proliferation of the performing arts schools or professional schools or conservatories is that available personnel—quality personnel—are so limited that the competition for their services degenerates into a sort of auction. Who's going to pay the most money to the few really qualified people? It may end up in something of a mess. That's my only objection to premature formation of too many performing arts centers. My other concern, sanguine as I am about the future of our theatre, is that we should not be training more young people than there are jobs. Will the graduates of our proliferating institutions be able to find artistically and even professionally valuable employment? I'm not absolutely certain. Yet, on the other hand, you do have to assume that there will be an expanding market. If you *don't* assume that, then we're all in trouble anyhow. But I repeat, the amount of really skilled— what you could conscientiously call *expert* personnel—in this field is limited and if you have more institutions than you can staff properly, then I think the situation is dangerous.

QUESTION   What is the American Theatre Association's "Army Theatre" group?

MR. REID   The Army Theatre Association is composed mostly of civil service personnel who are part of the Department of the Army's program—actually, they call them "entertainment specialists." In effect what they do is to run community theatres on army bases, using both army and civilian personnel. As a matter of fact, as far as groupings are concerned, the Army produces more musicals in a year than any other grouping in the country. It is guided by civilians, but it is supported by the Department of the Army, which finances the program.

QUESTION   Could you clarify your comments about high school theatre programs—are you against teaching theatre on the high school level?

MR. REID   I knew I was going to get a "hoof and mouth" on that one! Let me say this: I see nothing at all wrong with production on a high school level. But now I'm talking about a place where the high school has, in effect, a department. You have ten of them in Brooklyn alone. I want you to know, however, that there are at least thirty states that don't have one high school with a department of speech and theatre. The point I was trying to make clear is that I think that we have to learn to differentiate between theatre and drama as a *process* and as a *product*. The production is the product. The process is what happens to the student in the educational sense while creating a production. What educational values are there for the student, educational values which cut across the whole spectrum? I'm not talking about specific theatre skills, like how to put on a dutchman, I'm talking about what happens to the student. I think you've all probably read about this concept of accountability in education? All right, if we get to the point where we have to justify high school performance in terms of educational accountability, then we'd better be able to do it or maybe there will only be two high schools in Brooklyn with a program, because somebody asks, "Why are we spending this money? What—to have fun?" I don't say that there's anything wrong in their having fun and enjoying themselves, because in my experience when students are having fun they're learning and learning a great many things that don't really have much to do with what they're actually doing. So I'm not saying "cut it out." I would say, however, that it would be dangerous for a high school to emphasize too strongly the production-performance aspect.

MR. HOUGHTON   I think that Houseman and I would agree with you on that score, because to the best of my knowledge, students at Juilliard are not before any public before their third year and my students are not going to be put before a public before their third year. You know, you take music lessons and you don't get hired the next year at Carnegie Hall. You've got to learn the process, you've got to experience the thing before you're prepared to present the finished product. But there is an awful lot of emphasis on result-oriented programs in which students are pressed too hard and too quickly.

MR. HOUSEMAN   I know specific examples in which a very talented and energetic teacher—in order to give a great show and make the parents happy and the kids happy—is likely to force a production crisis in order to get his great opening night. Although he may be an excellent teacher and the kids may have gotten a great deal out of him, that kind of strain, that kind of intensity, may do a certain amount of harm in the development of those kids, if they have serious theatrical inclinations. But that depends very much on the teacher.

MR. REID   Let me go back to the "process" thing. The Theatre Association has been deeply involved with a program, which the federal government has now ceased to fund, called "Impact." And what it boiled down to was a pilot project in five different school districts across the country to use the arts—visual arts, dance, music and theatre—as the central curriculum in varying kinds of situations. One of them was an elementary school in Eugenia, Oregon; one a series of elementary and secondary schools in Glendale, California; an inner city high school situation in Philadelphia; a rural school system in Troy, Alabama, encompassing two counties. This was an experiment and each one of these places went at it in their own way. The amazing thing about it—and the thing that infuriates me as far as the feds are concerned here—is that in each one of these situations there were positive results better than anything else that's been tried in God knows how long. And so the federal government says, well, all right, that's marvelous, now we know, but the hell with it—and wipes it out instead of finding another couple of million dollars and doing it in five different school districts. Interestingly enough, though, in each of these five districts they have found, stolen, or begged the money to continue these programs. Because the administrators of many of them suddenly began to realize that the bloody thing will work—that the stimulation of the arts is in itself an educational process!

MR. HOUSEMAN   I think that theatre in high school is an absolutely marvelous thing.

QUESTION   Mr. Houghton, do you agree with John Houseman's statement regarding the proliferation of performing arts training programs on the college level?

MR. HOUGHTON   Well, of course, the great multi-versity enterprises present quite different problems from the individual conservatory or university. The New York State University system has seventy-two campuses, or seventy-two units. Some years ago—about eight or ten, I think—a university-wide committee of the arts was created to advise the chancellor. It was given a budget, it has some money, and the purpose of that committee is to try to bring some sense of cohesiveness to this sprawling thing with campuses stretching from Buffalo in the west to Plattsburg in the north, to Stony Brook in Long Island, to New York City. It has worked fairly well in terms of linking campuses with what's going on. When it came to defining the missions of the campuses, vis-à-vis the theatre particularly, here's where part of the difficulty arose about Purchase, because the central administration decided that they would create a particular School of the Arts at Purchase, which would be the professional training school. It would probably start with a BFA program and the next step would be an MFA program in theatre. This is one of the very few BFA programs in the State University system. We are not, therefore, supposed to be training people to *teach* in the arts of music, dance, visual arts and theatre. Other campuses in the University have long-established and very fine music schools, but their particular thrust is into music teaching. There are, I think, excellent training programs in theatre at Brockport and Cortland and a number of the colleges, but they're not professionally oriented. There is also at Binghamton and at Albany emphasis on theatre scholarship, which we are not undertaking to do much about. So that if you want to get a Ph.D. within our system, you'd be well advised to go to SUNY at Binghamton. In other words, I don't think that you could ever have one *single* center within these sprawling institutions. But I think you *can* find ways to focus on certain aspects of arts training and say, here we'll teach people to teach, and here we'll teach people to perform publicly, here we'll teach a general appreciation of theatre, and here we'll teach theatre criticism and scholarship. Another campus could become a great center for children's theatre. It would be ridiculous to say that no theatre should be taught anywhere except on one campus, and deprive all these other colleges of anything to put into their theatre building or into their art museum or into their music hall. I think you can differentiate in your objectives.

Where actor training is concerned, John and I are both influenced by Michel St. Denis. Certainly, actors should start at the beginning as soon as possible—that is to say, as soon as they get out of high school.

MR. HOUSEMAN I'm told that the English drama schools, LAMDA and RADA [London Academy of Dramatic Art and Royal Academy of Dramatic Art] are going the other way. They prefer not to take anybody until they have sowed their wild oats and have maybe resolved their doubts about what they want to do in life; they favor taking them at twenty-two, twenty-three. I don't altogether agree. I prefer to take them younger when they are completely malleable and impressionable. However, this is a generalization and it applies only to *actor* training. I don't think it applies to directors, I don't think it applies to playwrights, I'm not sure about designers. I think that if you have an artistic talent in drawing and painting, and a visual eye, and you're madly in love with the theatre, you probably could start at seventeen or eighteen learning how to be a scene designer, and if you are good with a hammer or a paint brush, you could learn how to be a technician at that age. I don't want to start a program in directing or playwriting professionally, because I think that probably really flowers best at the graduate level.

QUESTION What in your opinion is the best background that an aspiring producer or artistic leader could attain?

MR HOUGHTON I suppose that he has to be knowledgeable about at least one aspect of the artistic side of the project. It would probably be as a director, (that's my personal opinion). I have not seen very many successful scene designers or technicians become producers; I haven't seen very many successful actors become producers; I haven't seen very many successful playwrights become successful producers. But there are a number of examples, which we all know, of directors who have become producers or producers who have become directors. There seems to be a closer relationship between the talent the director needs and the talent that the producer needs to have.

QUESTION   What do you think about the establishment of professional companies-in-residence on college campuses?

MR REID   Well, you put your finger on a very sensitive spot, particularly in relation to the undergraduate student who feels that, when there is a professional company on campus, it takes attention away from the undergraduate program. The pros are a bit better than the kids in the undergraduate area and get all of the newspaper attention and lots of money is spent on them. One of the things that the Resident Theatre Association is attempting (and I think they're going to hack it, too) is to establish a case for a resident professional company as being a resouce to the campus in much the same way that the library is; and to prove that it does not infringe upon, or in any way take from, an undergraduate program. It does mean, of course, that in most cases the college or the university has to come up with the extra money—in other words, they are not *substituting* the resident company for their normal theatre program.

MR. HOUSEMAN   Ten years ago we ran into this with the Theatre Group at UCLA. We had formed a professional theatre group performing on the campus of UCLA under the protection of Extension. There is no question that, although our board was made up fifty percent of members of the Theatre Arts Department of UCLA, there was a distinct cleavage—and on the part of a large portion of the faculty, considerable resentment and opposition exactly on the ground you mention. The Professional Theatre Group was getting attention and publicity to the detriment of the Theatre Arts Department. And it was never really resolved because, finally, the Professional Theatre Group moved downtown and became the Center Group [at the Mark Taper Forum of the Music Center of Los Angeles County]. I, myself, think they should have stayed on the campus. We were, in fact, offered a fine piece of land on the campus and the Ford Foundation's half million dollars toward building our own theatre was already in the bank when Mrs. Chandler decided to move the Theatre Group downtown.

But to answer your question, there never really was a *modus vivendi* between the Theatre Arts Department and our professional group. There was a cleavage. Whether that would have straightened itself out in time, whether today—twelve years later—with a great many more such institutions developing, the adjustment would be easier to make, I really can't answer.

MR. HOUGHTON   I would like to answer for Purchase. I said earlier that we were interested in graduating theatre companies, rather than graduating individual artists. And originally, we had hoped to have a resident professional company. But at that time we observed what happened to the APA and the Phoenix and their program at the University of Michigan and we came to the conclusion that we didn't want this problem to arise. And we had just observed how it happened at Yale, when Dean Brustein created the Yale Repertory Theatre alongside the graduate students and their own work. And so we said, at the end of four years of working together with a group of twenty or so actors, and some directors and designers of scenery, costumes, and lights, and some technicians, and some management people—in the *fifth* year let us send them out into the state university system, which has, as I have said, seventy-two campuses. But if fifty of them said "No!" we could still get out of the twenty that are left ten or twelve weeks of performance per season in the fall, then come back to the campus for a refresher period after Christmas vacation, and then perform a ten or twelve week tour in the spring. Even if we couldn't get a full ten weeks out of SUNY, we could augment it in other ways.

In the sixth year, they would come back and be the resident professional company at Purchase. They could or not, as they pleased, be working on a Master's Degree. When I say "professional," I mean that at that point they would be paid. In the seventh year we would undertake to send them out on their own, but that sixth year would mean that the resident professional company was, in fact, part of the educational process. If the third year students or the fourth year students fussed, because they were not playing in a repertory situation on the Purchase campus, we'd say, "of course not, but two years hence it will be you." And so you then integrate the professional program with the educational process.

QUESTION   Mr. Houseman, how do you select the students for your school; what criteria do you use?

MR. HOUSEMAN   There is no definite formula. Some young people come in with one set of qualities and change drastically somewhere along the line, and vice versa. We do think about maintaining some proper kind of balance between male and female, but not much beyond that. We found in selecting that you simply take the best you can find and hope for the best. After about two years, you've lost a number of them. Those that remain begin to take on the qualities that are the result of our teaching. Each year varies and you just keep working at it.

Resident Theatre

Zelda Fichandler
Adrian Hall
Peter Zeisler

Commentary by *Zelda Fichandler*

Artistic Director,
Arena Stage, Washington, D. C.

Our theatre started in 1950 along with what has been called the "resident theatre movement." I call these theatres the "what-do-you-call-them-theatres"! Nobody has found a name for them because they're really just theatres. Any other country that has a theatre tradition would call them "theatres," because they are collectives that unify the disciplines and talents required to produce that form of behavior and entertainment and contribution to culture which is known as theatre. We've had trouble in this country giving them a name because we *haven't* had them. We were first, I think, given a name around 1957 when the Ford Foundation came into the picture, and Mr. McNeil Lowery—who is the pioneer in giving to the arts—called us "residential theatre," I think because we have residents or because we were squatted in one place or because we were quasi-permanent. But that didn't suit us, and then we were called "resident theatre" and sometimes we were called "tributory theatres," because we flowed into (or away from) New York. But really I think we are "spokes people;" spokes people for theatre companies or for the idea of theatre companies. Ours [The Arena Stage] was one of the first. It was not *the* first.

This new wave probably seems very old but is, culturally speaking, very new. Anything that is twenty-five years old is very new in the history of the ages. The impetus for this new wave came from Margo Jones, who in 1948 set up a small theatre in arena form in Dallas, Texas, in a two hundred seat reconverted building. She called it "Theatre '48," and then she called it "Theatre '49," and then she called it "Theatre '50," and so on. There had been efforts before then: there was the Barter Theatre, there was the Cleveland Playhouse, which I think is now celebrating its fiftieth anniversary. But this whole new impetus started with Margo and it was Margo to whom I was sent when I called up ANTA [The American National Theatre and Academy], which was then a service organization, and said, "We are starting a theatre and whom do I go to?" I had a meeting with Margo Jones in New York—she died shortly thereafter at a very young age, about forty. But people tend to forget, because human memories are very short, that this quite extraordinary lady came to Dallas and set up the first professional company. It had eight members and they did classics and new scripts and that was her bible—classics and new scripts. She had a great definition for classics, and that was anything that was over fifty years old. She had no problems with "what's a classic"; it had to be fifty years old, and she also did a lot of new material.

The only importance that autobiographical information can be to any group of learners (among which I consider myself) is to prove that one can come from any background or any composite of fields, and still get to theatre. I think theatre is so close to life you can use anything that happened to you, absolutely anything. Whatever you learn about yourself, whatever you learn about psychology, psychiatry, sociology, chemistry, physics, the laws of thinking, the processes of moving people, community action, political activism, not to mention design, architecture, lighting, acting, directing, how to balance a budget, and how to sell ideas to people, and it doesn't hurt to run a box office or to be able to clean a bathroom well—there is nothing in the world that is wasted.

I came from a multiple of interests and forces. I was once a pre-medical student, I was an English major, I graduated from Cornell with a major called "Russian Language and Literature," at which point I met Chekhov for the first time. I acted when I was eight years old, maybe younger—I think five. In college I wrote plays. I've had a great number of influences, none of which seem to me in my position (which is extremely miscellaneous) to have been wasted. And, as a matter of fact, I feel that I'm very grateful for all of those things that were not craft-oriented, that fell into my life quite by accident, or not so much by external accident as by the accident of my own human nature. I was politically active in the '40's. I learned how to organize an event from A to B which, strangely enough, seems to be a very important and somehow elusive skill. If you are at A and want to get to B, then how do you get there? Now the impulse of many people is to go ask somebody else how *they* got from A to B, but that was *their* A to B. The best way is to analyze immediate data, sensorially, to take part in and experience the world which is immediately available to you. This is a method of basic scientific research; it's even a method of analyzing literature, of being a literary critic. It is a method of personal creativity. Start with your own experience and relate it to the world which is around you. So be wary in collecting information in all of these seminars! Understand that you are collecting highly biased and personal information which you must, *must* screen and use only as it is useful to you. That doesn't mean bullshitting, that doesn't mean being any less rigorous in your own thinking about your task. It means you have more responsibility, for example, if you are going to be a producer, to analyze the community in which you are in by immediate perception—not by getting a poll taken. It means if you are going to be a director, you have to have a very strong world view. You have to know how to interpret material according to where you come from. If you are going to be an actor, you have to know why it is you want to embody another character so that you can give some direction to your own career, so that you can identify one acting school from another. If you want to be a designer, you have to have an attitude toward space and toward finding the relationship of this primary art to the environment around it. You have to have an ecological position. You have to be a total human being to be a total theatre person.

My accidents are really nothing, except they tell you that at one time I could read and speak and write Russian, which is very good, which is going to come in handy now because we are going on tour to the Soviet Union. But that's twenty years later. I didn't know that was going to be useful. I had some work in psychiatric and social sciences, which helps me inordinately. During college, instead of reading my textbooks, I read all of Freud, just because I was interested. Then I had marvelous English professors who tuned me into being able to evaluate the written word and to revere the written word; and my work is strongly colored by literary orientations because of that. You know, being open and having a goal and collecting all of your stuff as you go along is very, very important. Since other people have learned things, you can learn them, too, if they are available to the human mind. When you need them, you can always find someone else who knows what you *don't* know. The great lesson is that you cannot be renaissance people today. There is too much to know. The day of the renaissance man is over. You can know a partial corner of the truth, and you can surround yourself unjealously and unpossessively with people who can fill in for what you don't know, which is a very important lesson.

Our theatre came along on August 16, 1950, when we opened in a reconverted movie house. We started very small: wee, miniscule, struggling, on the edge of death! It continued this way for many, many years. We were a non-professional company for one year and then we became a professional company. We opened in an old, run-down, abandoned movie house in the skid row of Washington. We ourselves, we loyal few, scraped the chewing gum off the bottom of the seats, hung some lights, staked out an area sixteen by twenty feet in the middle of some bleachers, which we constructed, and we opened a theatre with Oliver Goldsmith's *She Stoops to Conquer*, followed by *Of Mice and Men*, followed by a miscellaneous repertory ranging from new plays to old classics—seventeen productions in the first season! We did fifty-five productions in five years, and then we closed because we couldn't support ourselves even at a hundred and *ten* percent of capacity.

The theatre was then a terribly revolutionary idea. That one should, in 1950, think that an audience would come to see a troupe of actors (I think we had ten in the acting company and some very good people whose names you might know—Lester Rawlings, George Grizzard, Marian Reardon, Frances Sternhagen, Pernell Roberts—all of us were doing everything) was a revolutionary idea. It was revolutionary to collect a permanent company devoted to the maximum expression of the life within each given play, do non-commercial plays, compete with the road house (which, by the way, didn't exist then because it was closed on the segregation issue, but was soon to come) *and* to get an audience to come. It was looked at as "community theatre," meaning faintly second-rate. The road was long and hard and there were times we played to eighteen people in a two hundred and forty-seven seat house. Over the five years we built an audience. We had no subscription yet, we closed for a year and a half. We reopened in a five hundred seat re-converted ice house of a brewery and someone named us "The Old Vat," after the Old Vic, because we came from a brewery. We were there under a two-year lease and we stayed for five. In the course of this time we changed our structure from a profit to a non-profit institution. We started out the only way we knew, we raised fifteen thousand dollars in hundred dollar units of stock, five of us each put in a thousand dollars. We spent twelve of that renovating the building. We had three thousand when we opened and we lived that way for five years. Then we became non-profit. In 1957 I got a call from the Ford Foundation, a man by the name of Mr. Lowery asked for me and he said, "I'd like to talk to you about money," and I said, "I'm terribly sorry, I haven't got any at all!" Now that's the truth. That's how naïve we were then.

Anyway, the Ford Foundation entered slowly, cautiously into the arts. By now they have given away something like three hundred and fifty million dollars in the arts, thirty-two million of which has gone to theatre. They have become the largest givers in the history of civilization, including the popes and the Medici. Since that time, too, government has entered the arts, starting in 1966 with one million and seven hundred thousand, up to now where it's many more millions in giving to the arts, so you see what has happened. When it came time in 1960 to tear down our building, we built one; we built an eight hundred seat arena, and three years ago we built a wing to it which has another theatre which we named the Kreeger because David Lloyd Kreeger gave us two hundred and fifty thousand dollars toward what was a million-three adjunct to our building, and he got his name on it. So, we now have a complex of buildings which is quite useful, not very fancy, very functional, and is the end of our building. We have now a subscription audience of about seventeen or eighteen thousand, which is large but very small, it should be much bigger. It's small because it's in Washington with a population of just over two million, and because a city which, when we opened, had only us, now has fourteen professional theatres, including those in the Kennedy Center—the second busiest theatre town outside of New York.

It's suggested that I make some comments about my present position and present organization. I am called "producing-director," and my opposite number is my husband, executive director, who was an economist. He was an economist with the Twentieth Century Fund and he worked on many projects, one of which was the book called *America's Needs and Resources.* So he's an accomplished economist. When we went into the latest phase of our building about thirteen years ago, he left his job and he came in to be executive director of this, by now, very large project. My position is more or less that of an artistic director, except that I do stick my nose in every area of the theatre because I believe that every area is a reflection of the generating impulse of an arts institution. I am interested in the lay-out and wording of every brochure, I am interested in the ticket policy, I am interested in the parking lot, I am interested in the cleanliness and aesthetics of the building. I am interested in how late we start the performance because there's rhythm to beginning a performance, and if you wait too long, the rhythm's gone. I am interested in how long the intermissions are, how hot the coffee is. I am also interested in how money is raised and in the community relationships and in the kinds of services that we offer. So my function spills over into other areas besides those which you might suspect by the title "artistic director," those of choosing the plays, the final say on the company, the designers, the technicians, and directing some of them myself. We have a large organization. If you do a cross-section of it, it can vary because we have two theatres operating. We might have sixty actors employed, but we only have a small permanent company nucleus which is fifteen actors this season. And the rest is production staff, technical staff, promotion staff, box office staff; a round number would be about one hundred, which is not astronomical. There are theatres with larger and as large. Our weekly payroll is about two-thirds of the budget, which is good. We're spending a lot on people and a lot on lumber, because the cost of lumber is more than can be believed. We once bought out a lumber yard that was going out of business and that's how we balanced the budget that year; that is, balanced it with a deficit. As of spring, 1973, we spent one million, three hundred thousand a year and we had a deficit of approximately four hundred and fifty thousand. We take in between eight hundred and fifty and nine hundred thousand a year, which is over ninety percent of capacity at a moderate price scale.

Let me say this, for the purpose of running things the staff is organized under the two heads, so that promotion, publicity, box office and house management will fall for administrative purposes under Tom Fichandler, and matters of the productions *per se* and all that that entails will fall under me. But there is a very close and symbiotic relationship between the two. Do you know what "symbiotic" is? One can't live without the other. You can't rip them apart, you can't do it on a table of organization. Any good institution should be *unable* to be reduced to a table of organization, because people should be crossing the lines all the time. Do you know the marvelous story about the guy in the restaurant who says to the waiter, "What time is it?" And the waiter says, "I'm sorry, it's not my table!" That's a *non*symbiotic organization, and an arts institution cannot run that way because then there are no impulses, no synapses going between the two, and it becomes sterile and it dies.

Technicians have to be able to pick up a hammer if they need to and not say, "Will somebody go get me a hammer?" And I have to know how to do almost everything, which I don't anymore. I used to know how to do everything, I don't anymore. I couldn't fill in for a box office person anymore, for example. But the less separation there is, the better. And the teetering between cleanliness of organization and looseness of organization is that which makes it alive, so to teeter is to live, just like out in the real world.

How do you define the difference between a producer and a manager? Well, in my way of thinking (and I'm like the Red Queen, when I use words they mean exactly what I mean them to mean—no more, no less) in my way of thinking, as the Red Queen, they don't belong in the same category, they're two different functions. The producer does what the title says. He or she leads out, leads forth, leads through. The producer is the total organizing human being who generates the impulse from the organization: what direction is it going to take? When is it necessary to move in another direction? The style of the work; are you going to do only new works? Are you going to do only female playwrights between the ages of forty and forty-five? Are you going to do only dead playwrights? Who can come to rehearsals? Are you going to increase your deficit and say, "To hell with it, let's see what happens?" Are you going to cut costs? Are you going to have two theatres? Which twin has the Toni?—all of the big questions. The manager, it seems to me, has a very important function. But the manager works within the compass design, works within the full circle to manage whatever area. We're lousy with managers—we've got a box office manager, a house manager, a theatre manager, a production manager. A manager is an executor of the design set by somebody else, in my view. You'll hear other opinions, thank goodness!

My advice to aspiring producers-arts managers? I'll take that to mean producers, just because I can speak better to that point. I don't know what the state of book-learning is now, but I don't think anybody can get too much of it. There is a wealth of human experience codified in pages of books, much to be learned from Aristotle on up about the way of thoughts and the way of progress. There is what one German radical called "the long march through the institutions," which is to be learned; how change occurs in society—none of this is wasteful. No activity that you engage in, even if it's organizing something on campus, is wasted. I think I started by saying this and I think I've come full circle.

No personal experiences are wasted, because they tell you more about *you*, more about how the other guy works, and how you can work with him. And, of course, the most smashing training in the arts that you could possibly get is an apprenticeship on the lowest level, to a great mind. That is worth ten years. Had I been able to apprentice myself in a theatre, like the one that I run, I would have saved ten years of labor, and I mean that very seriously. There was nobody to apprentice to and to sit and listen to including the dull moments. You have to have the patience to listen!

Commentary by *Adrian Hall*

Artistic Director, Trinity Square
Repertory Company, Providence,
Rhode Island

There's an old joke that I can never quite remember, but it's about a lady and a psychiatrist and the tag line is, "*Kiss* you? I shouldn't even be in *bed* with you!"

I have a little bit of this same reaction now. I don't really think of myself as a producer, although I suppose that I do produce plays. I certainly don't think of myself as a manager, although I do manage a theatre. I suppose for a very long time in my life I thought of myself as a director. But that wasn't really what it was called. I was producing-manager.

My beginning was strange. I grew up on a farm in Texas and—oddly enough this feeds so well into what Zelda has said—I lived about seventy or eighty miles from Dallas, Texas. When I was in high school, a lady came to Dallas, Texas, to start a repertory theatre and her name was Margo Jones. I got to know her quite well and came under her influence at a very early time. After that, I went out to Pasadena, California, where there was a very fine man in the theatre who might be categorized as a regional theatre leader. His name was Gilmore Brown; he was very, very important in that whole early history of what the theatre is in this country today. You'll find that when Zelda talks, Peter talks, I talk (we talk a great deal), we talk in the framework of the regional theatre.

There was a man who died recently, Bob Porterfield,

who ran a theatre in Abingdon, Virginia, for a very long time, the Barter Theatre, which was also one of the very early professional theatres outside the framework of the commercial theatre. I didn't know Bob until we were all trying to band together to make some kind of specific identity for ourselves as regional theatre, as opposed to these various titles that you've heard before.

Later on, after Pasadena Playhouse and Gilmore Brown, I came to New York. I had been through the university by that time and when I came to New York into the commercial world, I came under the very strong influence of a lady in the theatre named Stella Holt, who used to run something down on 13th Street, the Greenwich Mews Theatre. I worked there for a number of years in the '50's, the late '50's and early '60's, when I was first into the commercial theatre. It was a very long time and it took me a very long time after I moved out of the realm of the commercial theatre to not continue to long for it, and to not continually gauge things in relationship to what they might mean in the commercial theatre. I still thought of material in terms of whether it would be successful commercially, or succesful in the mass media so that it would get a movie sale, or would get some kind of television rights, or something. Gradually—which might be coming of age, or it might be disillusionment, or the loss of innocence—gradually, I began to realize that that wasn't where the battle was—finding the play, or the right kind of material that would lead into some kind of commercial acceptance. That, for me, has happened only in the last three or four years of my life. And so that would be a very complicated subject to talk about, how I finally arrived at that place, and what it means, and am I at the end of that cycle? Am I looking at the last part or is something else going to open up for me?

Let me say that my training in the theatre was training, very unfortunately, not unlike yours. That is, certain professors influenced you in certain ways, and so you immediately became a disciple of Stanislavsky, or you immediately became a disciple of Grotowski, or you immediately became a disciple of someone who had a point of view. *Working* in a situation, you finally are able to cut off all the extraneous things, like the lure of the commercial world, like the incentive to achieve certain things—other people's goals that have been set *for* you. Ultimately, when you're able to cut all of those things off, you find yourself wondering, for instance, "What kind of influence did Lee Strasberg have on me?"

It's taken me years, you don't know how many years it's taken me, simply to be able to say that! At one time I genuflected in front of Stanislavsky and in front of the American "Method," the way that all of the people of the '50's were doing. Regardless of what they tell us now, that's where it was and that's how we were doing it at that time.

Now I'll move to the Trinity Square Repertory Company. It is located in Providence, Rhode Island, not in Provincetown, Massachusettes, as is sometimes said. It is a theatre that is nine years old. We began in very much the same kind of humble beginnings that most of the theatres in the country began with—in a church, the second floor of a church in Providence. After two years, we had attracted a certain amount of attention, the time seemed to be right. People were wandering around the country, principally Roger Stevens and Gregory Peck, who happened to come to Providence, Rhode Island, for the National Endowment. At that time, the National Endowment had some kind of agreement with the Office of Education in Washington, where they came together to see if they could find some way to introduce the young people of this country to the theatre in a way that would be, as they say in government circles, "ongoing." In the commercial theatre we used to laugh quite a lot about all the student programs that were always evolving. But, if you look carefully, every time Mr. Merrick or a really successful management announced that they were going to develop student audiences, they always began with plays that were failing at the box office. So you suspected in your mind that perhaps that was a way to get audiences into that play. It seemed ass-backward, and it didn't seem a way to really introduce a young person to what the theatre is and to the arts.

We were doing a new piece at that time, a short Dostoevski novel called *The Eternal Husband*. Roger Stevens and

Gregory Peck were very impressed with this and said, "We would like you to organize some kind of program in connection with this kind of theatre with the Office of Education and with the National Endowment." They gave us quite a lot of money and we organized a program which was loosely called "Project Discovery." It was funded by the Office of Education for three years, it was heavily funded, it allowed us to move from a small theatre, from a three hundred-and-fifty seat theatre to two theatres offering two kinds of programs; one, a kind of experimental program, the other a larger, more accepted classical program. And so that's what we've been doing up to this time. We have currently purchased an old movie house in downtown Providence. A large building, four stories high, and it will be ready this fall. It's a theatre that will have eight hundred seats in one theatre and three hundred in the other theatre, and it will have a number of performing spaces where we're able to break through and open up a little bit more.

I don't know, truly, how my theatre differs from Zelda's theatre, or from Nina's [Nina Vance, founder of the Alley Theatre in Houston] theatre, or from Peter's theatre, or from any other theatres around the country. I mean, I could say that the outside of the building is different, and so it is, and so what? Most of the regional theatres that I worked in prior to Trinity Square share the same problems; that's going to bring me to the core of what I wish to say to you. It is this: the problem, or the pride, or the challenge, is not with the method that you use to achieve your production goals, and not with your own personal development as an artist—these are things that will come about naturally if you're in there fighting, and if you continue to try to be in touch with yourself and stay alive—the real problem is something that is so simple as to be absolutely uninteresting. How do we in this country give people some kind of choice about art in their life or *not* art in their life? You see, we go bumbling through our whole way, and we grow up, and we either grow up in a place where there is a theatre or there isn't a theatre, so then by the time we get to college we say certain things. We say, "Oh yes! I saw that particular play," and then later on, when we're out on our anniversary, we come to Broadway and we see a commercial play, and so forth. All I can say about that kind of lifestyle and that kind of development is that it's very sad, because the person never had a chance. We give balm to ourselves with all kinds of clichés, one being that if you get them in the theatre once, they'll love it, they'll come back again. Well, that's a crock of shit! You *know* that's a crock of shit! Why should they? It's a complex art, it takes endless kinds of conditioning for it. You don't learn to read by looking at it one time, you don't. A cathartic art experience can take *years* to get to. The reason that we're so prone to sexual attitudes is that it's easier, right? A good hour of hard work sexually and something usually happens! It's not true in the arts, and so for me the challenge has been a way to make possible art in the lives of the people in our country.

I think there are always (and I certainly don't mean this as any kind of put-down) I think there are always Zelda Fichandlers, I think there are always Margo Joneses, I think there are always Gilmore Browns and Bob Porterfields. What now, it seems, that we must do is somehow to take hands and say, "This is one of our rights, this is one of our basic rights as human beings." And that can be done! But it can be done only by finding the area wherein there is the most resistance, the most hostility, the most indifference to what the performing arts are, and go like the evangelists of the Nineteenth Century went, and do it, convince them!

It seems to me that what I'm talking about is a kind of art that is indigenous to who you are. If it doesn't relate to you, or doesn't speak to you, put it in a museum! You understand? So I feel about plays, I feel about dramatic literature as we know it, that it is a piece of the theatre experience; it is not *the* theatre experience, you understand?

In the last year I've had two or three overwhelming, wonderful things happen to me. I went to Nashville, Tennessee, to see the Grand Ole Opry—very difficult getting in to see the Grand Ole Opry, I don't know if you are aware of that or not. I can only say that it was the most harmonious art experience I've ever been involved in. One just leaves it trembling, because there is so much rapport and give and take between the people who are the viewers and the people who are presenting the thing. God damn it, it happens! You know, it's exactly what Grotowski is talking about, it's *exactly* what he's talking about. We as craftsmen in the theatre and as people dedicated to the art can only bring it all together, you see, and we can only put it there, right? But it doesn't happen unless you've got somebody that's willing to meet you halfway and *have* it happen. Well, does a tree make a noise when it falls in a forest if there's nobody to hear it? I don't know. I suppose there could be an extraordinary art experience, but if there's no one there, it's the same thing. O.K. The Grand Ole Opry was the experience that *I* had in the last several years. In the last two days in New York I've had very good times. One was going down to see a play by something called The Shade Company down in the Village, an Israel Horowitz piece called *Dr. Hero*. In a little small theatre some kind of scaffolding was built and you sat around the scaffolding with your feet hanging off, and it was all very clubby, and it could have been very arch. But what happened that night was that there was a theatre party of City College professors—Israel Horowitz teaches at City College, I think, teaches playwrighting there. His associates had come to the theatre that night. There was give and take and it was wonderful, so they let that experience happen. Last night at Judson Memorial Church I saw Al Carmine's play, *The Faggot*. Wonderful, interesting, exciting piece! But it wasn't the polish or the shine or the technical perfection of the piece, it was the combination of the people who were there, so that it could *happen*.

My advice to aspiring producers and arts managers? I don't think I really have any!

Commentary by *Peter Zeisler*

Director, Theatre
Communications
Group, New York City.
Earlier: founding director of The
Minnesota Theatre Company at
the Tyrone Guthrie Theatre,
Minneapolis, Minnesota.

Back in the early '50's I went to London to The Old Vic and walked into a performance of *Henry IV*. I had been working in the commercial New York theatre for fifteen years; I had never in my life seen a production of *Henry IV*. During the first intermission, two little kids, thirteen or fourteen, sitting next to me—nice little public school boys in their blazers—had a very interesting, actually fascinating discussion comparing this production of *Henry IV* to the last *two* they had seen! This depressed me so that I just wanted to jump off the London Bridge, because here were two kids taking theatre for granted and having it accessible—something that none of us have ever been able to have and certainly, as a native New Yorker and one who's lived here all my life, if it's not in New York, it ain't no place! It was the big difference, up until recently, between the major European countries, especially Eastern Europe, and America—theatre was just not possible here. Also, there is this constant misconception between theatre and entertainment. They're two different animals; there are actors and there are performers, and there's a big difference. There is an endless amount of wasted verbiage and emotion over the commercial theatre on the part of many of us in the noncommercial theatre, more so now than formerly. I just think you have to remember what you are talking about. Are you talking about theatre, or are you talking about entertainment? One doesn't negate the other because, if it is not entertainment, it's not theatre. But it *can* be entertainment and not be theatre. There's nothing wrong with aimless, slick musicals, absolutely nothing at all. What is disturbing is when people feel, because we have been used to believing it throughout the tradition of the commercial theatre, that that's *all* there is to the theatre.

I am a rare animal because I changed worlds in midstream. I spent fifteen years in the Broadway commercial theatre and I am glad I did, because you learn a respect for craft which is simply staggering. Very often, or *usually*, what you are expending your craft on is hardly worth it. There was one hideous period when I was a stage manager and I did four productions a year for seven years, twenty-eight consecutive flops! I spent an entire year on a train between New York and Philadelphia. And with the exception of two, because I really analyzed this at one point, with the exception of two (twenty-six out of twenty-eight) there were at least one or two absolutely first-rate artists involved, be it a director in one, or a designer in another, or an actor or two actresses. So it was not a waste at all for me.

I think the greatest problem Americans have is always wanting easy answers. We always think that money is going to buy everything, or that you can bull your way through to an answer. But when you're dealing with the arts, it is just not possible. I think there has been a terrible omission in our attitude toward craft in this country. It's partly because it is so difficult to establish viable criteria or parameters around the theatre. If you are a pianist, you have to be able to play the four books of Chopin. You *have* to do it. Your fingers have to do it. Anybody can say they're a director, anybody can say they're an actor. There are no established criteria, therefore it makes for a very muddy business. It can get very messy. I think only in the last eight or nine years have we started to establish criteria about the theatre; we are beginning to understand craft. There was a whole period of about twenty years in this country resulting from two people, who should be nameless, who went to Russia and came back with Stanislavski's first book. Unfortunately, the idiots came back with the wrong book! They came back with one book rather than two books. They came back with *An Actor Prepares* rather than *Building a Character*, because they thought the entire Stanislavski system was endless contemplation of navels, and ignored the second book which had to do with the craft aspect (the voice work, the movement work). If you go to any decent acting conservatory in Eastern Europe, which is really the only place in the world where there are good acting conservatories, you will see the kind of physical work that you would see if you went to Ringling Brothers training school in Sarasota, Florida. You would see kids spending three or four hours in acrobatics and juggling, six days a week, for an entire year. You would see boys and girls taking not only fencing, not only foils, but sabers, epee, the entire armory, and becoming incredibly adept at it. You would see an enormous concentration in physical craft. We in this country, for so long, have been led down the garden path into thinking that if you think good thoughts, it is all going to come out right. You have to have the techniques that are required in all the performing arts, and the theatre is no different. We are only beginning to learn that now. No singer spends a day in his life without vocalizing. I come from a family of pianists, so I know whereof I speak. No concert pianist, regardless of whether they're concertizing or not, would spend one day of his life without an hour on that piano—unless he's Rubenstein, who never practiced in his life, but he is the exception that proves the rule. They're at it every day. Every dancer, whether performing or not, does his bar work each day. All the performing arts are the same, but for some reason until very recently we lived with that romantic myth, perpetrated by the whole Barrymore myth, that you can drink all night and sleep all day and get up at eight o'clock and do a performance. It won't work! We are beginning to learn what is involved in it.

I think you are very fortunate to hear both Adrian and Zelda. There are only three criteria, one is commitment, one is passion, and the third is discipline. God knows, that's what both of these people have, and that is all that's necessary, but they're all-encompassing. The basic problem with the noncommercial theatre for many years was the lack of a point of view—a lack of a *particular* point of view.

I am reminded of Martha Graham, who received an award some place years ago. I remember the address very well. She said, "When people write me asking, 'should my daughter be a dancer?' I write back and say, 'no.' However, if they write me and say, 'my daughter is going to be a dancer, where should she study?' Then I'll take time to answer the letter."

You've got to have the commitment. What drives me crazy in this country are all the fence-sitters. You don't find fence-sitting in any of the performing arts except the theatre, because of the lack of criteria. Nobody says, "Well . . ." they're going to be a concert pianist. *They're going to be a concert pianist!* But some people in the theatre say, "Well . . ." they're going to be a director, they're going to be an actor, and if they can't, "Well . . ." they'll sell shoes or run the FBI. Only in *this* art form does that exist.

One last point that I plead with all of you about: I feel passionately against this terrible tendency I find all over the country toward generalists in the arts. I find that an absolute obscenity. This is a degeneration of the art form. I don't understand "arts administrator," which means somebody who is sort of a "utility fielder," equally adept in ballet, opera, visual arts, the theatre. There's no such thing, there's no such thing! You've got to make a commitment. Look at any kind of success in the theatre—they have the guts to go out on a limb and stay there. It's the fence-sitters who don't make it, and I find the same tendency now working in the area of arts administration—in this great, gray area where a smattering of ignorance qualifies you for everything. I think it takes a very special kind of passion, a very special kind of drive, and an enormous amount of personal integrity.

Questions to *Zelda Fichandler*
Adrian Hall
Peter Zeisler

QUESTION   Mrs. Fichandler, what is your policy about bringing productions from the Arena Stage to Broadway?

MRS. FICHANDLER   Well, there's no code of ethics on this, there's no handbook yet: each one is its own experience and I haven't collected them all. We've had only a few that went to New York and they were all different. The first one that went to New York was *The Great White Hope*, which started out as a very embryonic piece of work and evolved over a number of years and then was done at Arena Stage. We just did our production and then all of a sudden, rather unbeknownst to us as a matter of fact, it was sold to the movies and then there was a production of it. It was surprising to us. In fact, we read about the movie sale in the *New York Times*. We *did* know that there was something cooking about a New York production, because we had all kinds of people suddenly visiting us. But it built gradually; the initial reviews on this play were not all that smashing. We kept working on it after it opened and it got to be awfully good and eventually it was taken to New York. We had no participation, in fact we had a great deal of antagonism because we felt that out of the vast amounts of money that were made on it, that our own institution should have realized something. But, since we had not protected ourselves in that way, there was nothing legally dishonest in the way that it was handled. It was just a great moral lapse, I felt, and it was also very rude, since we'd been part of it. It was taken to New York, it was advertised as a Washington production, it was not advertised as an Arena Stage production because of the fear of libel suits, and because of circumstances. That one just happened that way.

Then there began to be a great thing about bringing productions to New York. *Indians* was submitted to us with a producer, and we were very careful to say that as long as our productions were kept separate and that we could produce them with our own independent decisions, that would be all right. We achieved for ourselves at that point five percent of the profit, because we feel that if we are going to evolve a work and lose thousands of dollars on it, then, if there are any profits, our work should be subsidized by commercial success. There was no profit realized on that production, it was a failure in New York, or a quasi-failure.

The next thing was *Moonchildren,* which, again, we did totally improvisationally. I read the play on a Saturday morning, I hadn't gotten dressed yet and it had been submitted to me by somebody who represented the play in England—a friend of mine, Martin Rosen, who had produced it in England—and he had called me and said, "This is a play I think you should do." When it got very good notices, including the *New York Times,* I was personally not terribly interested in it going to New York because it disrupted our company, it meant I had to recast the whole season, which I did. But I also don't like to keep people who want to do something from doing it, and it was a very warm company and a very happy company and they all believed in the play and in Michael Weller, who was with us in residence. It went and it closed. David Merrick produced that; we didn't produce it. Our arrangement was very minimal because of certain economic tie-ins that the play had with it from London, from the Royal Court where it was first produced. So there was no money to be gained there. I'm very interested in taking things to New York that will make money to feed back into Arena Stage, though not at the disruption of the organization, but one always has to balance these things out.

When we did *Tricks* we were in rehearsal for a new musical, a rock opera, and it fell apart. We had to substitute something in two weeks. We'd been working on this rock opera for a year and it just fell apart. We brought in something from Louisville and mixed it with our own company and did it in two weeks, which was really just to save our skins, and it was very popular. A lot of our actors were invited to go with the Broadway production. They didn't go because they weren't in love with the material. But had they all wanted to go, it would have been very foolish of me to say, "No, you cannot go with this production."

We live in changing times and it's only recently that the axis has switched from New York for the creation of new material. So we don't know how to juggle all of this, except from one instance to the other. My philosophy is that, if it's good for the theatre, New York is a region, too, and there's no reason why it's not entitled to theatre.

MR. HALL   One of the things, technically, that seems to happen a lot with regional theatres is such a strange distrust among commercial managements of what Zelda Fichandler is. That's something that I don't totally understand.

MRS. FICHANDLER   Neither do I!

MR. HALL   No, I just used you as an example!

We've all, in our beginning days, worked for commercial managements and I must say that some of my best friends are commercial managers. But there is a funny kind of feeling that, even though this play worked in Providence, Rhode Island, if it comes to New York then we really must *get* somebody and do it *this* way. I mean, I have no resentment of that and, of course, I'm very happy to say, "yes, I really do think that Abe Burrows is absolutely right for this," or something. But it goes back to a feeling that it can't have happened in Providence first, because New York won't take that.

MRS. FICHANDLER   There was a recent article in *Variety* which said that it's been proven now that those things that are successes in the regions are no good in New York, because in the regions they've been supported by locally conscious critics and even *The Great White Hope* had to be goosed up, or "hypo'd"—that's show biz language, "hypo'd," or strengthened. That I read in *Variety*.

Five years ago, when they discovered this great fertile territory for finding out if a strange play would work before they had to spend any money on it, then it was something else. Now that a couple of things have bombed in New York, they're beginning to get a little more suspicious. Their attitudes are essentially opportunistic, since they're essentially based on making profit, not plays—I mean, you have to start with that premise. New York exists not to make theatre necessarily, but to make profits; making theatre is a way to making profits, so that one can only make improvised value judgments from that point of view.

Until just a minute ago, I used to think that Broadway was terrific. I'm beginning to wonder. They've made such stupid decisions lately I'm beginning to feel they make really bad artistic decisions. Like with *Indians*, why do you have one hundred Indians; because it's bad for the play. And why do you take *Moonchildren*, which is fragile, and put it into a great big barn where it isn't going to work, and it closes in three weeks? Those don't seem terribly competent decisions; they seem short-sighted, partial vision, part astigmatic, I think is the word.

MR. ZEISLER   Well, in the first place you have no producing companies like you used to. When I worked for the commercial theatre, I worked for over ten years with the Playwrights' Company—*one* organization. It was the same as resident theatre.

MR. HALL   Yes, and the old Theatre Guild was the same thing.

MRS. FICHANDLER   And there was a taste that prevailed in those kinds of organizations.

QUESTION   Mr. Zeisler, could you describe the functions of the Theatre Communications Group.

MR. ZEISLER   Yes. The Theatre Communications Group is a service and informational organization. It was started in 1960 by the Ford Foundation to help the residential theatres, at that time, to at least discuss and learn common problems. Zelda, who was then in Washington, Jules Irving, who was then in San Francisco, had never met, didn't even know each other, and this country, being the size it is, the sharing of common problems seemed terribly necessary. I think that enormous explosion of resident theatres that occurred in the '60's would have happened anyway. I think it happened more neatly, more efficiently, and certainly a lot faster, due to the central information and service organization which TCG runs.

About two years ago, Zelda was on the Board of TCG's group; she and some others were very concerned that there were whole areas of the noncommercial theatre that were really not being serviced by this organization, that did not have the advantage of this kind of central framework. And the organization was thoroughly reorganized. It now consists of five separate sections. There is a resident theatre section, the principle function of which is a central casting service. There is an experimental theatre section; we're in the process now of setting up a touring service for them. There's a black and minority panel section, which is aimed primarily, at the moment at least, at getting increased visibility for black playwrights—black technicians and administrators, not actors. And there is a professional training group.

QUESTION   Then has TCG helped to establish more resident theatre companies—ones that will last, like the European theatre companies?

MR. ZEISLER   That's not really practical in a country of this size, and especially with the increased importance of television. It's very difficult to keep actors far from the source of television production. It is a fallacy to accept European models as a perfect example. Let's face it, The Royal Shakespeare and the National Theatre would not be able to keep the actors they have if the studios weren't located seven miles right outside of London. If the film studios in London were the equivalent of Los Angeles, they would not keep those actors.

I spent a year in Eastern Europe two years ago. The National Theatre in Warsaw, which is where every Polish actor aspires to go, has a modest company of one hundred and thirty-seven actors, all on five year contracts. The year I was there was the first year that the senior actors were refusing to sign five-year contracts. Why? Because television had finally come to Poland. The idea of "the company" was not to be in America. The relationship between training and production is absolutely essential for any sort of continuity in the development of art; in Europe it comes out of conservatories attached to the theatre, but that was not to happen in this country. Yet, in the last ten years there has been a very definite shift toward professional training programs. The other performing arts have always accepted this commitment to craft. Nobody concerns themselves about whether a violinist has a great knowledge of political science, or knows how to dissect a frog! God knows, no one thinks that of a dancer. But everyone takes it for granted that an actor has to know all these things, whereas with the best training programs all over the world—*outside* of the United States—the myth of the liberal arts education just doesn't exist. In any of the European schools they spend four years in a conservatory learning craft subjects, just as in this country a musician will spend four years in a conservatory, or a dancer will spend ten years in a conservatory. I now work more closely with the training program, trying to close the gap between the producing companies and the training organizations.

MRS. FICHANDLER I just want to lift out something that you've said to underscore a point. Administering an art has something to do with knowing it, and you can't in general produce and administer *any* art form whatsoever. I think for the people who are thinking about arts administration that this is very important. It's the same as a hospital being administered by somebody who's not a doctor, which happens often. It's very bad. And there are calls now for arts administrators; we get them at the theatre, you know, like, "Come and run this arts complex." To administer an art sensitively means that you have to understand the need for the artist, the need for the art from the *inside,* so that your administration is experiential, not abstract.

MR. ZEISLER If you are seriously considering a career in

administration, for God's sake go out tomorrow morning and buy a hair shirt and go to the nearest hospital and have a lobotomy operation to get rid of the ego! The biggest single problem I find with administrators, with managers, with producers, is this terrible ego thing. Just by the way the cards fall, they're in a position of enormous power because they control the money. It gives an unfair advantage to administrators and I've seen it being used unwisely and unjustly time and time again, really because of ego. Remember, *you're* never the guy out there, *you're* not the one who has to get naked on that stage; it's the actor or the director, not you. You're there to serve them. The big problem with many organizations in this country is that everybody gets their priorities screwed up and it's exactly backwards. You're there to help *them*, they're not there to help *you!*

QUESTION   Mrs. Fichandler, what kind of administration did you have—of what quality—when you were a non-professional theatre?

MRS. FICHANDLER   We were only nonprofessional for one year and we had nothing so fancy as administration, believe me. We were self-administering and self-run—into the ground! I slept on the floor in the lobby, on the floor of the theatre. I used to design the mailing pieces and go to the printer and direct every other production. Administration was a luxury, just like budgeting was a luxury. There's a slogan that says, "Save up for the things you want;" well, you can only save up if you have enough left over after eating. I always think that is a really marvelous example of the American psychology of money; that everything is available if only you just plan right, live right. And, as a matter of fact, administration is a great luxury; for things to proceed in an orderly fashion means that there has to be enough money. To assign someone to see to the orderly progress of events means there has to be a salary. The first Ford Foundation grant that I personally got was ten thousand dollars, and I was very jealous—ten directors got it and they used it for going to Europe or they used it for doing special projects. I used mine to buy administrators. I used to be the only one on for the summer. I'd open the mail, answer the calls, file the resumes—I type very well, marvelous thing to know, by the way. (You know I'm not kidding—a very practical thing to know. I still type my own notes when I'm directing because I can't keep anyone up as long as I can stay up and it's very helpful, I save rehearsal hours that way.) The first money I got was to buy administration, because when you buy administration, you release creativity. And that's what administration is about. What happens is, administrators forget what they're about, they think it's about them. It's not about them—they're enabling devices, they're empowering devices, the thing that they empower is creativity; but usually they stifle it like cholesterol in the blood veins, they clog it. You have to sign eighty-two papers to get to a pencil—by which time you forget what you wanted to say or write.

So to answer you, we just took care of things, helter-skelter. We'd say, "You do that, you do that, and you do that." Then we got a little better and we said, "Now, you just do *that*." It happened gradually.

QUESTION   How do you select people for administrative positions at Arena Stage?

MRS. FICHANDLER   Well it's very funny, because every good arts administrator is an artist. Scratch the skin of any good arts administrator and there's an artist. There may not be a performing artist, but there is an artist—somebody with sensitivity and taste, empathy, talent—they're usually people who know something about one art or the other. Our business manager has a very important job—a young lady in her early thirties, she was an administrative intern with us and she moved up through the ranks, she didn't move from acting. But our box office manager, who's been a box office manager for thirteen years with us, was an actor, though not with us. We don't have a lot of administration. We've got two people and a secretary in the promotion department, three people in the business office, which is very small.

MR. HALL   I think it's just in the last three or four years in the theatre that we really knew about theatre administra-

tors. In the old days everybody was really in the theatre because they wanted to be an actor. Everybody wanted to be
an actor and so they went into the theatre, and then eventually they became stage managers or directors or administrators.

MRS. FICHANDLER   Well, my production manager, a new
post for my theatre—and now I've moved him up to associate producer—was a zoologist; but before that he had been
a circus performer. That's what I'm talking about, everything being miscellaneous—he was a circus performer, he
was an IBM computer analyst, he has an M.A. in Zoology,
and he was a stage manager, an actor at the Charles Playhouse, and he moved into production managing. I wouldn't
have at Arena Stage somebody who would be an isolated
systems analyst, who just came in and said, "Oh, well, at
U.S. Steel what we would do is we would take ten percent
of each of the staff across the board, lop them off and you're
rid of your deficit! What you've got to do is you've got to
spend one thousand dollars less on every set!" I mean,
that's how they come in and do a budget analysis, because
they have no internal awareness of the pulse of the patient.

QUESTION   How did you raise the original funds to build
the Arena Stage?

MRS. FICHANDLER   There were five of us; five of us lost a
thousand dollars because we bought a three hundred and
twenty-seven foot riverboat. It was going down the Poto-
mac, we were going to make a theatre out of it, we couldn't
moor it anywhere and the floods came. We spent three
weeks trying to find a place to berth this thing in the flood
and there was an option on it. We had to give it back and we
lost the money. And then we put in a little less the second
time. Then we sold one hundred dollar stock dividends. At
the end of ten years, we asked them to take their bonds, plus
their overage, and turn it into contributions, which they all
did. They just turned it into non-profit donations. That was
a very historic meeting. It was a unanimous vote, something like fifty people turned back their money as non-profit
donations.

QUESTION   What do you have to say about the relationships between the artistic directors of a nonprofit theatre and the board of directors or trustees?

MR. HALL   All of my experiences with them have been bad! And not just with me, I might say, but right across the country.

The idea that there should be a superimposed group of well-meaning community laymen who act as a bureaucratic structure and take care of the artists, because they're babies and can't really take care of themselves, I think, was imposed on this country in the early days when the Ford Foundation first began to help the theatres. It seemed that that was the way to tie you into some kind of respectability, into the community, and into your region. So a kind of concrete cookie cutter plan evolved in which you would go out and get a board of trustees and that board of trustees would take care of your deficit. I got down to that kind of simple thing. Funny things began to happen within twenty minutes; artistic directors began to be fired, real confrontations began to happen, and so forth. And I found, personally, that some of the toughest battles in staying alive and in trying to stay in touch with yourself, trying to do your work with what have not been your own kind of identity battles or your own artistic battles, has been trying to politically maneuver away from some kind of top-heavy bureaucratic structure that does not work. Everytime I say this there are a hundred people who raise the thing, "But I know at Lincoln Center that so and so bailed out such and such," for example. For every example that you could give me of the places that it worked, I can give you a concrete example of the places it didn't work. I, being an inarticulate person sometimes out of my own choosing, have managed to devise certain ways in which I—how is it you say in your country—keep my board of trustees in line! And most of that comes from being able to talk louder, faster, and meaner and having a certain kind of survival snake skin. I think it is not a good thing!

MR. ZEISLER   You've opened up a can of worms. I think you have to remember that, outside of opera (which is a whole different animal), theatre is the most complex of the performing arts because it requires the most disparate kinds of talent, all of which have to be on the same wave length for anything viable to occur. The reason that the batting average in any good theatre is as low as it is, is because only occasionally is everybody going to be able to transmit a central thought into a central action; the designer, the director, the actors, the musicians, all have to flow into a kind of central unity. That occurs very, very seldom.

I remember talking to Peter Hall just before he left the Royal Shakespeare, having finished doing eighty-seven productions at the Royal Shakespeare. I asked him how many of those productions he was really satisfied with. Seven. Pretty good batting average. Only with seven was there the kind of unified cohesion of action possible, or did it occur. Now, when you realize the problems just among the creative artists in the theatre and add to that the problem of ten, thirty, forty, fifty people who are in fact providing you the wherewithal to do this, and having to constantly win their approbation and assent, you have an untenable position.

It's very significant that the majority of the major performing arts statements that have been made in the world have been made by people who can work individually. Ingmar Bergman could never function in the Hollywood system, he's got to be his own boss and no one is going to tell him what to do. It's very significant that the New York City Ballet got as far as it did as fast as it did, because George Ballanchine had only one man to answer to, Lincoln Kirstein. But when you take us poor slobs in the theatre, where Adrian's got to answer to thirty or Zelda has got to answer to forty, you find you're dealing with a ludicrous situation. Why is that the model? It's the model because it was the model used by the only other performing art in which America has any kind of track record, the symphony orchestra. Now what the hell possible conflicts are you going to have with a symphony orchestra? The only time they're going to yell is if you start programming too much done after 1812 or 1814! But a board is not going to have any clout, because the organization is making no demands on them.

I was one of the people who started the Guthrie Theatre. When we got to Minneapolis, I found that there were two enormously wealthy families in Minneapolis that were making no contribution to the Guthrie whatsoever. One of them owned Pillsbury Flour Mills—billions of dollars— and I went to this lady and no, no, she wasn't interested in the theatre, she couldn't give any money to the theatre because she was giving all her money to the symphony. She invited me to go to the symphony that Friday night and I went with her. She sat down and promptly slept through the Egmont Overture, woke up briefly during the third movement of Tschaikovsky's violin concerto long enough to start writing notes to all her neighbors who would be waiting for her in the lobby, so she could conduct her little seance in the lobby during intermission, then had a great social time during the intermission, then went back and slept for the rest of the performance! Of course she is going to be willing to provide money for this, it's not making any demands. If you're going to a good theatre, that theatre better be making demands on you; you can't sleep, it's going to make you angry, it's going to upset you, if it's any good at all.

MRS. FICHANDLER   I just want to say that we have absolutely no board problems because we were self-supporting until very recently, which is hard to believe. Deficits have become accepted as part of theatre. But we've been self-supporting most of our history, I think it's seven years that we have not been; so that our board was a more or less formal thing. Also, I've been at the theatre from the beginning and I, with other people, started it. The board came later, the board was invited. And I think it was before the Ford Foundation said, "We'll give you money if you get money from the community," as Adrian pointed out. So that this form of organization is really much more natural for theatre if a group of people say, "Let's have a theatre," and then whatever board you need legally, you have. When a big daddy gives you money and says, "here's a quarter, if you get another quarter from the community, we'll know they want you, and then you'll get another quarter from us, then they'll give you a quarter, and we'll give you fifty cents, and they'll give you a dollar, and we'll give you two cents, and they'll give you five dollars, and then we'll go away, and then they'll carry you;" that is essentially the formula of the Ford Foundation. It's the "carrot" formula. And so they leave behind a community which is supposed to support you. But we are now entering into the great question mark period of the resident theatre—will, indeed, the communities support these theatres, once the Ford Foundation has withdrawn? This has not been answered. But the objective was to create community organisms that would with their loving tentacles cradle these new-found cultural phenomena once the Ford Foundation had withdrawn and had turned to social matters such as poverty, education and supporting backward countries, as you've read in the *New York Times* editorials.

MR. HALL   One of the interesting things about that, too, is that you never see anybody on a board of trustees in a regional theatre who doesn't know an awful lot about the theatre, and is quick to tell you he doesn't know anything about the theatre, but he knows what he likes! You know, *that* kind of attitude. It's a different problem than the hospitals face, for instance, or the museums face, an entirely different problem. We've just had an enormously successful capital fund drive, about one and a half million dollars we've raised in the last ten months. Now that's staggering, that's not from the Ford Foundation, that's not from any foundation, that's from the people of Rhode Island. A million and a half dollars! Just yawn at that, if you will. That's an incredible feat! It was principally done by one very interesting, driving, very successful man in our state, he's a doctor. But I don't know what that man wants from this. Does he want what our theatre's about? Does he? I don't know. So it's a very dangerous, dangerous time. Zelda is a smart lady because somewhere along the line she got off the trolley, or she never got on the trolley.

MRS. FICHANDLER   No! I'm in great trouble because I *don't* have a board to raise the money that we need.

QUESTION   How do you raise money, other than box office income and grants from the foundations?

MRS. FICHANDLER   There's a basic, unresolved dilemma here because foundations are not set up to support anything in perpetuity, and it's quite normal for any foundation to pull out after a while—that's what they're there to do. The government is getting in by degrees, but then you have inflation, so things keep spiraling. The government is getting in gradually, though not quite fast enough in terms of what we need in our spreading deficits. But you don't want all government money, one doesn't want all government money. It's nice to have a mix of support, I think, in this country.

MR. HALL   Recently, I proposed a program to five universities in our area: we would take twenty of their undergraduates a year and they would have some kind of involvement in the theatre for six weeks. The only requirement that we would make is that they would *not* give us drama students or English students, they would give us the students who, five years from now, were going to be doctors and who were going to be on these boards of trustees. In other words, we were trying to set up some kind of plan so that people could be brought into the situation for which, ultimately, they are going to assume the responsibility. You see, you, as people who are going to be *participating* in the arts, will not be the people who have control. You will go into situations where it is organized, where there is bureaucracy. You're going to have to deal with the question of how do you take the money from their hand and turn around and bite them! It's difficult.

QUESTION   Mrs. Fichandler, you mentioned the importance of apprenticeships. Do you operate any apprentice programs at Arena Stage?

MRS. FICHANDLER   We have a lot of informal and formal apprenticeship programs in the theatre. One of the best programs we've had, which is not funded anymore but we're trying to set it up again, was a production intern program where people in the technical areas of the theatre would apprentice. In four years we turned out people who are working all over the country. We have director internships, and next year we're setting up with Boston University an internship program in administration, directing and technical areas. The acting apprenticeships are an ambiguous area because of certain union problems.

I happen to hold the particular opinion that, after actors are very well trained at a place, that carrying spears and being in crowds is extremely counter-productive for them. They should be playing parts in small theatres and growing that way. So, until we get a small laboratory theatre or until some other way is found, I don't like taking acting apprentices, because about the middle of the year they get very unhappy. And I don't believe in apprentices playing for children because I think, as with education, I think the younger the child the more expert the teacher should be and the more damage the teacher can do; so, the younger the child, the better the artist should be. I think actors, adults, can pass on destructive experiences, and a child isn't ready to select. So I don't have a junior company.

QUESTION   Mr. Hall, how did you raise the original capital for your theatre, before the foundations came along?

MR. HALL   We were formed in 1950. We paid for everything out of box office money until about 1968, and we did that with very low prices, by careful budgeting, and by actors and staff taking very, very little money. It was literally subsidized by the artists themselves.

MRS. FICHANDLER   Now as the economy gets more and more inflationary, there is a problem for the arts which is very critical—you can't raise ticket prices any higher than is logical, you can't raise them to ten or twelve dollars a ticket. People can't afford twelve dollars a ticket, that's an expense account audience, that's some other kind of audience, that's the Broadway audience. So the deficit is inevitable as costs go up and ticket prices can't reflect it. And, by the way, I think something should be done about preserving Broadway in its more adventurous forms without raising tickets to fifteen dollars. There have been some very good Broadway producers—I think the tickets are fifteen dollars for *Two Gentlemen of Verona*. I think that's too high.

QUESTION   What kind of step-by-step process would you recommend for creating a theatre today?

MR. HALL   That can't be answered quickly. I feel very strongly about the choice of material. You work with the material because you have to do it, you have no choice there. As far as establishing a theatre someplace, I could only talk in very general terms. Peter made the point that theatre is a communal art. It is not the- kind of thing where you sit in the attic and write the play and then it's sifted down to the interpreters and they do it. I should think, first, that there would have to be people like you who share a common need, right? Then, out of that common need, has got to come the audience. You cannot continually do plays in a vacuum. I think there should be an area where it's possible to ignite, if you will, excite, turn-on, get committed to. If you find that you're only interested in restoration drama or in medieval morality plays, well then I shouldn't advise you to go to Houston, Texas. But there are certainly places in this country where certain kinds of restoration plays might very well work in. the context of that region. I think the two biggest problems facing you would *not* be how to raise the money, not that kind of problem at all. There *is* money to be had, if there are people who are dedicated to the common cause, and if there is somebody who needs whatever you've got.

QUESTION   How can you determine whether or not a restoration comedy will go in Houston, Texas?

MR. HALL   I don't believe that one can make blanket statements about people in a certain economic class not appreciating Shakespeare, or that kind of thing. I think, for instance, in Houston, Texas, if you have John Wayne and Bob Hope do *The Rivals* you'd sell out every seat! The material has got to do with the input *into* the material and into the region.

QUESTION   How do you, then, go about selecting a season of plays to perform in a particular region?

MR. ZEISLER   The first year of the Guthrie Theatre we picked four plays: *Hamlet, Death of a Salesman, The Miser,* and *Three Sisters.* My board of directors was terrified; why would all these upper-midwestern Lutherans be interested in Chekhov? So I scheduled exactly fourteen performances of *Three Sisters,* because obviously nobody was going to come. But we felt it was important to do, we felt it was terribly important for the company to work on. By far the most successful production of the season was *Three Sisters.* If it's good, they're going to come, if it's not good, they're not going to come.

MR. HALL   Well, that kind of statement is not really a truth either. I just don't believe that statement, I think that statement is all cloudy. "Good?" What's "good" to you may not be "good" to me, right?

MRS. FICHANDLER   I have a better one. I have one that goes, "If people won't come, you can't stop 'em!"
    I want to disagree with you about something, if I may. I don't think there's a lot of money around right now, and I don't think new ventures are going to get a lot of backing. I think they have to demonstrate self-sufficiency to a large degree. I think that people who are thinking about setting up new arts institutions better be very well aware of this fact, that we're in a tight money situation. Before they set up general institutions, they'd better really look around at the population and see whether there's money there, whether there's interest. You don't get a long go at it anymore, you don't get ten years to accumulate yourselves, you don't get that. You can lose too much money too fast now; things cost too much. You may want to do what, say, André Gregory is doing; that is, work with seven or eight actors and a limited amount of space, with a limited budget—and, by the way, he gets a large portion of his expenses subsidized because he doesn't take in much at the box office. That's one set of problems. If you're talking about a wide community base

thing for which, I think, the winds are very negative at the moment, extremely negative at the moment, unless you can get in there and do what Adrian suggests—mesh with the tastes in the community, or what Peter did in Minneapolis. But you've got to smell that out. If you are going to Boston, for example, there are certain kinds of things that would turn them off. If you're going into a southern city, there are certain kinds of other things. I don't think just any "good thing" will work, but I think it has to be good of its kind. It has to be a good *right* thing! People could be terribly turned on, for example, by a circus-type theatre, a very extroverted, biomechanical theatre. Other people might be turned on by a literary theatre.

I would go back to something I said earlier: the environment has to be examined freshly each time and other people's experience, in the end, is not very good. Picking plays is difficult for this reason: to pick a season intelligently, you've got to know what's happening out there, *in* there, inside the people, that *they* don't even know about!

MR. HALL   Yes, absolutely. There's a whole world of history in the last seven or eight years in this country—astounding!

When Julian Beck and Judith Malina came back from Europe in '67, they really plowed right in, in a kind of frontal attack that would not, could not, happen today. And that is really very interesting, it was the right time and the right place. Now, whether it worked or not depends on your criteria for success. It certainly caused a great deal of controversy, it certainly caused a great deal of resistance on the part of the established values, and it certainly caused a great deal of talk. A few years ago the same thing happened when Grotowski came to this country: a great rush of followers: "This is the way!"

As Zelda says, perhaps the geography of the place is not important to you. It's very possible not to work in a large area, where there are staggering numbers of people. But then what you have to accept is the fact that you're not going to have a play run over a long period of time and have a lot of people see it. So those are endless kinds of decisions. Almost everything we're talking about here could be broken up into forty thousand different decisions. If you are unwilling to go into a kind of building that is a real fire trap, where you know that there's a danger of a fire, then it's also a possibility that you'd have to raise a staggering amount of money to go into a building that *is* fireproof. Endless decisions!

MRS. FICHANDLER   Did you ask that question of Marketa Kimbrell? They started with absolutely nothing, but they work with absolutely nothing. They work with the resources they can get from nothing. So if that satisfies you, that's a marvelous way to work—it might be the best way. In fact, one of our major institutions in this country, a theatrical group, is closing because of what's happened with what's called "institutionalization." Things were expected of them: they had to perform on a certain schedule, they had to raise a certain amount of money, they got locked into all of these problems you've only heard the edges of. These problems themselves have problems!

There are dangers whichever way you turn in this business called "arts administration." There are dangers in being small, there are dangers in being big, there are dangers in being too popular, there are dangers in being not popular enough.

MR. HALL   And there are dangers in being institutional and not being institutional.

MRS. FICHANDLER   Yes. Louis Jouvet said, "The first law of the theatre is success; without success there is no theatre." That's the only universal law; you can only be successful. Your work has to communicate because you're in a communicating art. So that's at the base of your question, really. What do you want? Do you want to communicate with fifty people? Or do you want fifteen hundred people to come to fourteen performances of *Three Sisters* in Minneapolis? The parameters have to be stated very specifically—at six dollars a ticket?—the minute you say eight dollars a ticket, you change it, or three dollars a ticket changes it.

QUESTION   Mr. Hall, how did you decide to locate your theatre in Providence, Rhode Island?

MR. HALL   Actually, I didn't pick it, it kind of picked me. I had a lot of my early conditioning in other theatres around the country. I somehow knew that eventually I would have to move into an area where I could work in a different way. Then they just called and had a swell idea about starting a professional theatre there, and so it actually began to happen. As people tell you in marriage quite often, "I never really believed that it would go on and on! It seemed like a good thing for a little while." Then, suddenly, there you are getting all kinds of money and people are talking about various things, and so you get yourself locked into little circles very easily, and it is spiraling—it really is backwards.

QUESTION   Would you say that administrative personnel contributed to the success of your theatre?

MR. HALL   Oh, yes! Yes, yes, yes! It sounded as if we're saying "down with administrators!" No, I would say they contributed a startling amount to the success of what we are. It's just that I think if you're working in the craft, let us say, I think you tend to be very suspicious of people who have voices of authority. Maybe it's just paranoia on our part.

QUESTION   Are you both the artistic and business head for your theatre, or are those responsibilities divided?

MR. HALL   Well, we have what we call (and most theatres do) a, what is that called? A producing-manager? No, a managing-director? No, that's what *I* am! We have a general manager. It's strange that Zelda said what she did about the corporate person, because we have a corporate man. He's only been with us one year now. He's from IT&T and his wife had worked in the theatre many years ago when I first started. He came back from New York wanting to live in a certain size city and in a certain way and he seemed like somebody who would really be able to sympathize with what we were doing. So we've taken him on and it seems very, very hopeful and encouraging. Occasionally he says,

those embarrassing things about "corporate structure," or
something like that, but otherwise I think he's good. I
mean, IT&T can't be *all* bad! (Cross that out—I didn't say
that!)

QUESTION   Do you use nonsalaried, volunteer staff people
at the Arena Stage?

MRS. FICHANDLER   We're just beginning to use volunteers, after twenty-seven years. We never used volunteers
because we never had time to use them creatively, we just
had too much to do. Now we're trying to get a group called
the Arena Stage Associates to help raise money and to participate in other functions in the theatre, because we can't
increase our staff any more. First of all, we're out of space
and, second of all, we're out of money. But the jobs keep increasing because that's the basic biologic law of evolution,
the cells get more and more complex as the animal evolves.

Off- and Off-Off-Broadway Theatre

Off-Broadway: *Theodore Mann*
Paul Libin
Off-Off-Broadway: *Ellen Stewart*

Commentary by *Theodore Mann*

Artistic Director, Circle in the
Square, New York City

The Circle in the Square was founded in 1951. When we
started, there were no Off-Broadway theatres. There was an
area known as Greenwich Village, which I had seen while I
was attending the New York University School of Commerce. My brother had told me that there were some burlesque houses there, but I had never gone.

We were all young people and we were floating around,
not knowing what exactly we were doing with our lives after World War II. A group of seven, including José Quintero and myself, decided that we would like to have a
theatre company in Woodstock, New York. At Woodstock
we did a series of plays in what is the oldest summer theatre
in America. It's a wooden structure, had a dirt floor then,
wooden benches and electricity—its only modern conven-
ience. None of us had ever been involved in the theatre,
knew nothing about producing plays or building costumes,
but we proceeded to do a season of plays. At the end of the
season we were the first company in Woodstock to have
paid all its bills. All of the preceeding companies had been
run out of town after the fourth week. So, reved up by this
great success, we decided to come down to New York and
continue as a theatre company. There were now twenty-five
people involved in the group.

We began to look for a place and I remembered my
brother telling me about those burlesque houses in Green-

wich Village, so I started to search. I thought some might be empty. There were many empty nightclubs then because of the Internal Revenue crack-down on prostitution and gambling in the area during that period. One of these was called The Greenwich Village Inn. It had been abandoned following a recent vice raid! We found out that the rent was $1,000 a month, which I thought was terrific. But we didn't have $1,000. I think we had $256 amongst the twenty-five of us. But we decided that we would like to take it. The landlord said we had to put up $7,000 security, which of course we didn't have. Finally, my father guaranteed the lease. He said, "Take it for a month and see how you like it," being positive, I'm sure, that that would end the matter and after one month I would be back doing whatever the family wanted me to do.

We started off with the necessity of raising money, starting with friends and relatives and branching out quickly from there. Later, we began to open the telephone book and point at names and I was elected to go visit these people. Out of this rose several very interesting experiences. One in particular had to do with a girl who was an orgone therapist. When I walked into her apartment, she had a big orgone box, which is like a huge refrigerator lined with steel wool! I gave her my whole pitch about how wonderful the theatre was and how it would be important for her to contribute and so forth. I was so agitated with the anticipation of getting money from her that she had me calm down by sitting me in the orgone box for about an hour. After that she did, in fact, give us some money. There were many experiences like that before we finally accumulated about $4,500.

We started to do the first play, *Dark of the Moon*, which ran for five weeks at this theatre which we called "Circle in the Square." The reason we called it "Circle in the Square" was that there are certain zones designated by the Building Department as being either residential or commercial, zones for nightclubs and zones for theatres. This particular place happened to be zoned for a nightclub, so we could not get a theatre license there. We could not call ourselves the "Circle Theatre" (it was a three-sided theatre with three poles in the middle) because "theatre" would immediately alert the authorities that we *were* a theatre. Our space was in the shape of a circle located on Sheridan Square. Chicken-in-the-basket was a very popular dish at that time and we were hunting for a name. Well, "chicken-in-the-basket," "circle in the square," that's how that name came to be! Somebody said it was a tough name to remember, but that's a good reason to have it.

The first play, *Dark of the Moon,* ran five weeks. After about three weeks we decided that we weren't attracting enough audience—we were only seating forty people a night. We decided to close that play and do another play called *Amata,* by a professor of architecture from Columbia University. I used to sit at the box office table in the lobby of this former nightclub and hear passers-by remarking, "Oh, that must be that snake charmer!" or, "Who is that dancer in there, Amata?" They thought that it was a person rather than a play. They passed us by in droves. Instead of forty or fifty patrons, we'd sometimes have one or two people in the theatre. Most evenings the cast outnumbered the audience.

When I think of it now, it was incredible what we did to subvert the law! Watergate was nothing! Because we were licensed as a nightclub, the code required that we had to have food and liquor. So we had these little tiny wooden tables constructed in front of every chair, and there was *one sandwich* at the bar for everyone! As far as the drink was concerned, we served grape juice and watered-down orange juice at twenty-five cents a shot. I remember a youngster came to see the show with his mother and said, "Mommy, this water tastes like orange juice!"

Because we were operating under a cabaret license, we couldn't charge admission, so we used to get up after every performance and make a speech in which we would ask the people to donate money. Then the actors would circulate through the audience with bread baskets from the old nightclub and people would put in their money, primarily dimes and pennies. I think if we ever got twenty dollars in one night we'd immediately eat it all up. Since we were living and eating in this abandoned nightclub, we immediately spent the profit on food. But we kept going and going.

After the first year, we toured the Borscht belt and we had many funny experiences. We did Christopher Fry's *A Phoenix Too Frequent* at some allegedly intellectual hotel up in New Hampshire. I thought that would be a place to sell *A Phoenix Too Frequent* and the manager agreed to pay us $150 to do it. The theatre was in a small room with the stage about as large as a sofa and only one exit in the room. *A Phoenix Too Frequent* is about forty minutes long, and about a hundred people came. The first line of the play is, "Oh, Zeus! Oh, some god or other!" Some guy in the audience said to his girl friend, "Zeus!" and started to go. Then in a very orderly fashion, throughout the forty minutes of the play, everybody followed him. By the end three people who worked in the kitchen stood there applauding vigorously. The next morning when I went to get the $150, the guy refused to give it to me. We became the first sit-down strike in New Hampshire, sitting in his office and refusing to leave until he paid us the $150.

The next season we played in places like Grossingers, where all during *The Glass Menagerie* the audience talked across the room. The following season we returned to the theatre downtown, which we had rented out during the summer, and started to do a series of plays again. I cannot for the life of me remember where we got the money. I guess it was what was left from the rent money. Somehow you manage to pay the more pressing bills and ignore others, thereby staying alive. In the latter part of our second season—May 24th, 1952—we opened *Summer and Smoke,* which had been a disaster on Broadway. We had Geraldine Page, who was then an unknown, former button factory worker. The only critic who came was Brooks Atkinson. All the critics on the other papers never came to Off-Broadway productions. But Atkinson came and gave *Summer and Smoke* a marvelous review. The next morning we were a hit. I mean, we didn't know what happened to us that night. We were just having the usual opening night party, and the next morning there was a line from where I always sat, out the door and down the block. Phones kept ringing all the time. We didn't have air-conditioning, so we had to accumulate several weeks of box-office receipts in order to buy an air-conditioning system. Finally we got it in late June. The play was a great success. It ran Off-Broadway for a year and I think it was really the birth of Off-Broadway. It showed that you could succeed, that it was possible to have a play the critics would attend and that you could draw a large audience. This spurred a tremendous amount of activity among the other theatres. All of this activity, which is now Off-Broadway and Off-Off-Broadway, I think, really eminated from that first success in the early '50's.

Now to bring you quickly up to date, over two decades later. About five years ago, Paul [Libin] and I were approached by Robert Weinstein in Mayor Lindsay's office who said, "How would you like to have a theatre on Broadway, an Off-Broadway theatre on Broadway?"

We said that two hundred and ninety-nine seats is too small for Broadway with the union demands and so on. Besides we didn't have the money to build one.

He said, "Well, supposing it was built for you?"

So we replied that it still would be too small and couldn't survive with two hundred and ninety-nine seats. I thought it was a joke and never even bothered to call him back. But he called a second time, and the third time he called, he said, "Why don't you just take a look at the plans?"

When Paul looked at them, he said, "Why would you only want two hundred and ninety-nine seats, why don't you have six hundred and fifty seats?"

The Lindsay representative said, "We thought that you were an Off-Broadway theatre and you would only want two hundred and ninety-nine."

"Not if we can have six hundred and fifty."

"Well, we could do that for you!"

Then we entered into a very lengthy contractual negotiation and formulated a lease in which they agreed to build us a theatre. At that point we had absolutely no money to undertake the operation of this theatre. They were going to build us a fully-equipped theatre, and it was then our responsibility to do the plays. The fact of that theatre coming into existence never hit us as a reality until about a year and a half later. We then attempted to raise money from the foundations. By May of 1972 we still had absolutely no luck. We had written letters to many foundations and had no responses at all. But we had a wonderful season scheduled—*Mourning Becomes Electra* with Colleen Dewhurst, *Medea* with Irene Papas, *Uncle Vanya* with George C. Scott, Julie Christie, Nicol Williamson, and Mike Nichols agreeing to direct it. We had all that, but absolutely no money. There we were a few months before opening, saying, "Yes, we're gonna do it!" only half believing it but thinking that all things are possible.

I am really telling you this because when you have something that you want to do in the theatre, you have to go ahead and do it. You have to find a method by which to do it. So there we were with this theatre presented to us.

Over that summer, which was the time we really had to hit some pay dirt, we began to get some support from the Rockefeller Foundation and then the National Endowment. These names may be unfamiliar to you now, but when you operate a theatre on a non-profit basis, they will be what you hear every day of your life, because institutional theatres petition them for support—National Endowment, Rockefeller, Ford Foundation, New York State Arts Council and so on.

So we have now done *Mourning Becomes Electra*, we have done *Medea* and *Uncle Vanya*!

Commentary by *Paul Libin*

Managing Director, Circle in the
Square; President, League of
Off-Broadway Theatres and
Producers

I had the good fortune when I decided to work in the
theatre to come to New York, which I think is essential for
anybody pursuing a career in the theatre. New York, unlike
any other place in the world, affords an extraordinary opportunity for people who are involved in any aspect of the
arts—to learn about it, to experience it and to become involved with it. I came to New York as a student while
completing my college education at the School of Dramatic
Arts of Columbia University. In the midst of my studies
and pursuing a professional acting career, I was drafted
into the Army. While in the service, I decided to venture
into producing and directing, which I began to do in the
Army, and when I came out, I completed school at Columbia and went to work in a professional situation, working in the offices of Jo Mielziner, who was then producing a
play. I became acquainted with a number of people and it
wasn't too long before we decided that we should join
together and produce a play on our own.

The first play I produced was *The Crucible* in a theatre
Off-Broadway which I now own and operate, The Martinique Theatre. We joined with a zeal, desire and energy to
become involved in the theatre, to do it the way we thought
was right, in a manner important and significant to us and

to the people we hoped would come to see the play. And through all my years in the theatre I feel *that* consideration is really the most important one. You must set goals for yourself, and reach for them, and even disregard the institutional regimes if necessary. I think it's important that you evaluate the system, its structures, taboos and traditions, and if necessary disregard them. Respect them only in the sense that they're there and absorb them where they're valuable and discard them were they are not.

When the Off-Broadway theatre began, when Ted [Mann] started it at the Circle in the Square in the old days at the Sheridan Square, there was a yearning and a need for the kind of expression in New York that didn't exist at that time. His initial efforts, and the success of the Circle downtown, inspired people like myself and a whole cadre of other people to go out and do things the way they thought they should be done—break down the barriers, the traditions, the bad habits, that the theatre had created, and concentrate on the essence of the theatre. The play, the actor performing, the director, the scenery, lighting and costumes were what was important. That's where the energy had to be directed and that's where the money had to be spent.

I can well remember the early days of Off-Broadway. The Circle was an extraordinary institution, it was mecca! It was representative of a special kind of theatre and undertaking that was looked upon with highest esteem. I remember one day going by the old Circle and seeing Ted—not knowing it was Ted until someone pointed him out to me—Ted was unloading the scenery for a production that had come to an end at the Circle, and getting the theatre prepared at the Sheridan Square for the next play. I don't remember the attraction, but it was probably a good twenty years ago. I was thrilled to see him doing that, because I had been doing that, too, and it was symbolic of the spirit Off-Broadway twenty years ago that, I think, nurtured it to what it is now—an important force in the American theatre.

Through the years, as you look back over things, you realize it was the zeal of a dozen or so people who started this movement, disregarding all the traditions and just functioning in terms of theatre, in terms of a play, in terms of the creative endeavor. They evolved, I suppose, a kind of organization, a kind of function that was important in order to support the theatre from a managerial and administrative point of view. But the essence of their undertaking was to deal only with essentials, you could never burden yourself with commitments to overhire—personnel who couldn't function on many levels, for example. You needed people who could be like a jack of all trades, who could be in the box office to sell tickets if whoever was there couldn't show up that day, and who could run to the advertising agency and change the ads, or who could move some scenery that night if someone else didn't come around, or run the lights, or be the stage manager that night, or a porter, or repair a toilet—whatever it was, you had to be able to do it and if you couldn't do it, someone else in the organization had to be able to do it, because you didn't have the money to pick up a phone and call a plumber. That kind of undertaking and energy all added up to a kind of unorganized discipline, because what happened was, as the Off-Broadway theatre developed through the years, every producing organization had people who were capable of these kinds of undertakings. All those persons who worked at management levels, who worked backstage, were committed to the theatre and they all helped to develop Off-Broadway. Their commitment was certainly something that was not financially rewarding. However, their accomplishments were of the highest order.

In those early years, as the Off-Broadway theatre began to develop, we inherited the kinds of problems that the Broadway theatre had been burdened by and overwhelmed with. Economics—including fund-raising, theatre rentals, labor unions, advertising, lawyers and accountants—contributed to the pains of growing. As the Off-Broadway theatre activities continued to increase, labor organizations wanted to establish their jurisdiction. It was about 1957 when the League of Off-Broadway Theatres began. We all sat down and, out of the need to protect our interests, formed an organization that made it its responsibility to "reply" to these organizations. When I say "reply," I put quotes around it because the essence of our philosophy was that we would *not* reply to these organizations, that whenever they confronted us with issues regarding labor contracts and representation and jurisdiction, it would just become apparent that we didn't exist! If they called us at one place, we weren't there. If they called us at another place, or if they came down, someone would run back and tell us that so and so from such and such a union was here, and everyone would disappear! The union representative would be told to wait for somebody to come back, but after an hour and a half he'd lose his patience and leave. This technique was very successful for many, many years. One of our arguments—and it was truth—was that we simply couldn't afford this kind of jurisdiction and, essentially, that's been maintained through the years. In the later years of The League of Off-Broadway Theatres we were able to convince the craft unions that Off-Broadway was not a place for their members, that a living wage was not the answer, and that we could not afford to pay a stagehand a living wage when we couldn't even afford to pay an actor one. That often created an atmosphere of cooperation with various craft unions. As the League continued and prospered, not in an economic sense but in its activity, occasionally a production would enjoy an extraordinary success. *The Fantasticks* was just such a miracle. These rare "hits" caused great problems, because unfortunately these successes were always used as the labor organizations' argument that we were financially capable of that responsibility. Of course, that was not the case.

Equity, which was very essential to the development of Off-Broadway and its origin, in our initial years accepted the philosophy that there was a tremendous collection of actors in New York who were not functioning and that Off-Broadway was a place where they could function. If they made a little money to supplement their other earnings, that was acceptable. But as the occasional successful play surfaced, it also became the erroneous criteria for the union to negotiate new contractual demands. The decline in Broadway and summer stock employment and the reduction of live television in New York helped to change the union's attitude. Now, Actors' Equity realized that Off-Broadway was one of the few places where employment opportunity existed. The union saw a need to increase this jurisdiction so that it could claim at least that it was securing a living wage for its members. So what has happened in the last few years is that, as Equity has changed its philosophy and attitude toward Off-Broadway and increased its demands, there has been a substantial decline in Off-Broadway activity. There were years when we presented more than one hundred and twenty plays. Now, fifty to fifty-five plays a season. Of course, this reduces the opportunity at every level. I'm convinced that that was not the only reason we had a theatrical decline in the City of New York, but it's certainly one of the contributing factors with regard to Off-Broadway.

I can only recommend that you come into the professional theatre with a passion to see what's there and change whatever has to be changed and not burden yourself with commitments to traditions. The theatre is an institution that will survive the onslaught of any kind of change. The important thing, I think, is to come to it with a passion to correct the things that are wrong and improve on those things that one can improve on.

The greatest problem the theatre has today, I think, lies in its relationship with the people who go to it: what do we do to make people interested in the theatre? What do we do to make it easier for them to go to the theatre? How do we market the whole idea of going to the theatre for people who live away and are removed from the core of the central city and the location of its theatres? From a management point of view I think that's probably the most essential problem you have to face, if you're going to work in the theatre and solve some of its problems.

And then, of course, the other essential problem from a management point of view is how to make the theatre productive beyond the three or four hours that you're presenting plays in the evening? What kind of programming, what kind of input can go into that theatre and help sustain it and help get the community involved with it and interested in it? What other programs, what other performing arts can you take into the plant of the theatre and present there, to exploit the resources you have with your theatre? If we can solve some of those problems in the Off-Broadway and Broadway theatre—and I think those are problems people involved in the management and administrative area of the theatre have to deal with—then I think that theatre can thrive and be healthy and increase its importance in our lives.

The theatre is an absolutely essential activity. I don't mean to sound clichéd, but the experience of the theatre is unique and special. For those of you who make the choice that this is where you're going to function as human beings for the rest of your lives, it's going to be difficult and hard. But if you come to it with a true realization of its excitement and also an awareness of its failings, then I hope you accept the challenge and that the theatre will benefit from your contribution. I think you will receive pleasure in the theatre as I have during the last twenty years.

It feels like only yesterday when I saw Ted taking the scenery out of the old Circle. I feel like a youngster, simply because there's still so much to do, so many things to change and so many projects with which to be involved!

Questions to *Theodore Mann*
Paul Libin

QUESTION   Can you elaborate a little further about how the new Circle in the Square theatre was given to you—you make it sound as if there really is a Santa Claus!

MR. MANN   Well, Mayor Lindsay and his administration had the notion that it would be desirable to revitalize the Broadway theatre area by stimulating new construction of buildings. There was much planning afoot for office buildings in the Broadway area, but no theatres were being planned. So they organized an incentive program for prospective builders. If they put theatres into their structures, they would have a waiver as far as the zoning regulations are concerned, allowing the structure to be built ten stories higher without having to go that many more feet deeper in terms of support for the ten additional floors. Other examples of the same type of planning are The Minskoff Theatre, The Uris Theatre and The American Place Theatre, all part of office buildings.

QUESTION   What do you pay in rent?

MR. MANN   Our rental annually is $27,500, which is about as much as we were paying in our mortgage payments on the downtown theatre. We pay about a dollar a square foot. But that's the commitment that The Uris Building made for the concept. In a sense it's an annuity or an endowment approach.

QUESTION   Mr. Libin, could you tell us a little more about *The Crucible*, your first professional production, and how a person begins producing Off-Broadway today?

MR. LIBIN   We decided to produce *The Crucible*, which I had seen on Broadway and felt had an important statement to make at the time. We wanted to do the play in an environment that put the characters in a crucible, where the audience would be wrapped around these people. At the time, Circle in the Square was the only theatre with that condition, and Ted was enjoying a good deal of success. Because we couldn't get into that theatre, we decided we would create our own environment for *The Crucible*. So, we went to the Martinique Hotel. There was a room that didn't have any pillars and I said, "It's terrific!" So we went to the owner of the hotel, who was very reluctant even to talk with me. But I pursued him and when I told him what I wanted to do, he said, "Get out of here. I don't need a theatre. Where are you going to get the money to pay the rental?"

I kept at him, but I couldn't make any headway. By this time we'd already optioned the play from Arthur Miller. At the time Miller was married to Marilyn Monroe. I had already told him that we had the theatre, although we didn't. Anyway, I suggested, "Why don't you come down and take a look and I'll show you what it's like and what we're gonna do to it?"

And he says, "All right if I bring Marilyn along?"

He arrived at the hotel with Marilyn Monroe. So I told the hotel owner I had the playwright here to look at the space, and I wanted him to come down to meet him. He knew vaguely who Arthur Miller was, because he knew he was married to Marilyn Monroe, but he never expected to meet her. So when we walked into the room, I introduced him to Arthur Miller and then to Marilyn Monroe. The owner couldn't wait to tell me afterward that it was a deal!

There was a door in the back of the theatre that had a diamond-shaped glass window. We were probably in that room for about half an hour. In that time every time I looked at that diamond glass opening, which was no bigger than a foot in each direction, there must have been at least fifty heads peering through that little opening! Therefore, much of what happened at the Martinique is really a strange tribute to Marilyn Monroe, because she was a very important influence in getting that hotel owner to say, "Yes, it's a deal!"

I remember when we got the theatre, we thought, "Well, you rent the theatre and that's it. You just open the door." But it was located at 32nd Street and Broadway, where there was an ordinance which prohibited a theatre in a retail zone. The only way you could circumvent this was to come before the Zoning Board or the Planning Board. First we tried to do this ourselves, which proved to be a disaster. Finally, we had to engage an attorney to do it. But the theatre had been running for eight or nine months before we even got our license. That's how long it took, but we just kept right on going. The fire and the building departments would come in and we would dance them around. It was really something!

You know, as I think about the beginning of the Off-Broadway theatre and some very famous on-going theatre operations, I can recall myself sitting in student seminars, listening with awe about the Group Theatre. I was certainly interested, amused and very absorbed with what everybody had to say. But I can remember what went through my head during those sessions, and that was, "Why doesn't somebody tell me a little bit about how *I'm* going to break into it? Forget about how *they* broke in, how am *I* going to make it?"

Well, there's no formula.

QUESTION Do you think that the New York theatre, or theatre in general, is on the decline?

MR. LIBIN I think that requires an elaborate or, at least, careful explanation.

I think really what's happened in New York in the last ten years—and the statistics will bear this out—is that the theatre has shrunk. I know that the theatre's not dying, and the theatre's not going to abandon the urban areas of America. But what has happened is many people have left the urban areas of America for the suburbs. The middle class, professional, college educated, young families that lived in New York ten years ago, fifteen years ago, were all actively attending the Off-Broadway theatres that Ted and I initiated and developed. However, the pressure of the central core of city living became untenable for a variety of reasons. I think economic pressures more than anything else pushed these young people to the suburban areas and changed their pattern of living. They still do come to theatres, but whereas before they may have attended twenty plays a year, now, they have to make many other arrangements. For example, they have to make a commitment to the ticket, arrangement for a babysitter, a place to eat dinner—there's a dollar investment. Now it may very well be that in shrinking, the theatre will translate itself into a healthy circumstance. What's happened in the last few years with the Circle is an example of this change. Look at Joe Papp's Public Theatre and its triumphant move to Broadway and to Lincoln Center, and the American Place Theatre. Ironically, I think that we are becoming the pillars of the *institutional* theatre! *That* may be the area where growth is established, where theatre can again make a serious cultural contribution. The serious theatre on Broadway twenty-five years ago was significant. But as economic forces exerted themselves, producers could not do plays of value, merit and significance because there was little money to make from them. The entertainment aspect of it started overriding the serious aspect of it. This generated our interest in doing plays that—I hate to use words like "important" or "significant"—contribute to the culture of the country in a serious way. As the entertainment phase of the Broadway theatre expanded and became more financially important, the other aspect began to disappear. So people like Ted started Off-Broadway. But now we've moved to Broadway and are saying, "Make room for us, we're gonna do it differently!"

I remember talking to the unions and explaining to them, when we put up our lighting equipment, that we're going to leave it up forever.

They said, "We take it down after every show and put it up again."

I said, "Well, *we don't!* It's up there and we're going to leave it up there!"

Well, they didn't like the idea, but I'll tell you one thing. In the theatre, if you have a reason for wanting to have something a certain way, and it's valid, the unions will generally agree. As long as you believe in it and can back it up, you'll fight because ultimately if you're right and strong and adamant, they will bow to you, because it is inevitable that it is going to be for their own good. Everybody likes to take advantage, but if you fight for something that you think is right, you're going to win. So we worked out our arrangements with the unions.

The change that's taking place now with our theatre, with the American Place, with Joe Papp, is going to happen more and more. Other groups are going to move because our society needs "serious theatre." We thrive on it, we live on it and we respond to it. And the institutional theatre is the answer to the performing arts in terms of its contribution to our culture. I don't mean to disparage the entertainment aspect of Broadway, because it allows the creative forces of the theatre to function and generate earnings so that they can pay for their rent and their food. It pays an actor to work in a musical for one season, so he can come and do a play for us! Our whole philosophy at the Circle in the Square in engaging people like George C. Scott and Mike Nichols, who are in such demand in the commercial branch of the performing arts, is to allow them to do the multi-million dollar picture as well as to function in the theatre, because they have grown *out* of the theatre. So the idea that George C. Scott can come back and work for three months, rehearse for a month and perform for three months, is exciting to him because he needs it and wants it. But what he *can't* do is come back to Broadway theatre and sign a contract that commits him for two years until the show pays back a quarter of a million dollars. Then he would have to return to Broadway and forget about any motion picture commitment for two years. And if the play opens on Broadway, gets bad reviews and closes in a month or two, he has abandoned his potential for big commercial earnings, of earning the livelihood he certainly deserves. By employing the short-run technique, we are able to get people like Cathleen Nesbitt, Irene Papas, Julie Christie, Nicol Williamson and George C. Scott. They're all people who have come out of the theatre. They're not the motion picture star of forty years ago, who happened to be wearing the right kind of sweater and walking in the right place at the right time.

These are people who have worked hard in the theatre, who developed their talents and origins here. They want to function in the theatre. So Ted and I have devised a concept that we feel can utilize these people and generate the audiences to come back to theatre.

QUESTION   You mention the fact that the Circle has become an institutionalized theatre, like other Off-Broadway groups. But look over your shoulder and there is Off-Off-Broadway with a constituency of over a hundred theatres here in New York. So there is an upward displacement. Is that the point?

MR. MANN   I think it's a very healthy thing that the theatre is going through a period of change, as Paul mentions. I think all that really happened is that the kind of low-level comedy that we used to get in abundance on Broadway has more or less ceased to exist. Also a very helpful thing is the fact that Off-Broadway has, in fact, moved into the Broadway area. Euripedes was never produced on Broadway before we did *Medea,* nor was O'Neill's *Mourning Becomes Electra,* or Chekhov's *Uncle Vanya.* When we asked Mike Nichols about a play that he would like to do, he replied *Uncle Vanya,* but that he could never do it on Broadway because no commercial theatre manager would finance it for him. What we and these other former Off-Broadway organizations are doing is, in fact, changing the face of what has been known as "the Great White Way." The Great White Way was made up of many bad plays, playing to a very mediocre audience that has now happily moved to television land!

QUESTION   To return to an earlier point, are either of you gentlemen saying you'd like to get rid of the trade unions in the theatre?

MR. MANN   Well, unions have come into existence to protect the individual worker, but I think that there are far too many instances where there are abuses that should be corrected within the parent body, within the union body. I think the actors need representation in their dealings with management and management needs its own organization, as Broadway producers have.

MR. LIBIN   There is a great deal of disenchantment within Actors' Equity. For some unfathomable reason at a time and place in our history when dissent is very popular, however, the dissent within the union is not directed to effectuate change. I think there is a group of people, professional actors, who belong to Actors' Equity Association who are responsible artists, who are concerned primarily about their ability to function as artists, and who consider compensation an essential and important aspect of it. However, this is not the most paramount consideration, and they are willing to make sacrifices. The union, I think, is there to protect its members from exploitation and, certainly, through history there have been examples of exploitation. But I think what is confronting the performing artist today is that in order to survive he must function. There must be programs that either arise from the union or from the professional culture of the theatre that allow the artist to function. I think there have been accomplishments Off-Broadway for many years and now an Off-Broadway actor earns $125 a week. In terms of the few years that Off-Broadway's existed, this represents a tremendous change. When Ted started, it was $5 a week! The current economic structure permits the actor to share in the economic success of a production. If you happen to be in a play that's very successful, your salary is then related to what the gross of the play is. As the play becomes more successful, the actor's salary increases to a maximum of $200 a week.

QUESTION   I would still like to know what I'd have to do if I wanted to produce a play Off-Broadway tomorrow!

MR. MANN   First, in order to produce a play you have to *have* a play, OK? It may be written by a friend and you decide you want to do it in an Off-Broadway theatre. So you have to find out the rent for that theatre; you draw up a budget and figure your costs. If it is being done as a commercial venture, you have to form a Limited Partnership and then seek investments from limited partners, starting with your friends and relatives and then, as I said before, branch out from there. You'll find out that the costs of producing your show Off-Broadway may be *way* beyond what you feel you're capable of financing. So you lower your sights a bit and say, "OK. I'm going to try to get this done in a coffee shop," or, "I'm going to try to get it done in an Off-Off-Broadway place so I can get an airing for it and get it seen. *Then* I'll stimulate some interest."

MR. LIBIN   The essential thing, I think, is that you set your sights high and not be afraid of cutting them down if necessary. Just keep moving ahead. Get the actors involved and get their energy turned on to the project. Get the director excited about the project, so then you have all the necessary support to give the project a reality.

MR. MANN   Before you decide that you're going to go to all this trouble, you've got to be sure that you really love your project. If you believe in it, you'll do it. If you half believe, it'll never happen. It should become part of your life, a necessity for you, and then you will somehow find a way to do it.

MR. LIBIN   Let me tell you something, just as a point of reference. *Godspell* started at Carnegie Tech as a student project. From Carnegie Tech it went to La Mama. Then to the Cherry Lane Theatre. From the Cherry Lane Theatre it moved to the Promenade, and then in about sixty theatres throughout America, into one hundred and fifty theatres around the world, and into a motion picture—all because its director and creator wanted to make a statement. He wanted to put it up there so people could respond. When Ted speaks of the passion of conviction, that blind love for what you want to do *will* make it happen, you'd better believe it!

QUESTION   How do you decide which plays you want to produce?

MR. MANN   The whole history of plays selected by the Circle have basically run along the same line. With some exceptions they are plays that have literary merit, and are naturalistic plays, (*The Balcony* being one of the few exceptions), dealing very much with the human condition. I read many plays and when there's something I like, I really like, that's the play that I choose. It's like a man who always marries or always goes with the same type of girl. You're always choosing plays of similar fiber. They may be in the form of a comedy or of a drama or a musical, but they have the same essential elements, because *you* choose them. Producing plays is very much a matter of personal taste. It *should* be that and it should *not* be what you think is going to be commercially successful, because nobody, *nobody* knows the answer to that, not even Clive Barnes!

There are so many examples of plays that have received great critical acclaim and have not been well attended and vice versa. A recent one is *See Saw*, which did near capacity business while not receiving particularly good notices, but the public went to see it. The public responded to somebody's original taste. They [the critics] thought *My Fair Lady*, based on Shaw's *Pygmalion*, was a terrible idea for a musical. But it had some essential ingredients and it had somebody behind it who said, "yes, I like that, and I want to do it, and I'm going to go ahead and get the money and find a place to get it done."

Get some people to put some money in, or get a co-producer, or find some way or other. You'll manage it!

Commentary by *Ellen Stewart*

Founder and Managing Director,
La Mama Experimental Theatre
Club, New York City

Note: This session was conducted about a year after most other sessions recorded in this book.

La Mama started because I tried to make a theatre for Paul Foster and for my brother. I didn't know anything about theatre. I thought that if you wanted to make a play, it was like playing house. You wrote the play, your friends were in it and you asked your friends to come and see it. I didn't know that you were supposed to have stage lights and sound equipment or, really, that you were supposed to have anything. I didn't think of it that way. Perhaps if I had known, I might have been frightened. But I really thought that you could just do it, and that's the way it started. I had no grand aspirations. The only thing was that they would write plays and, yet, never did it. So I decided that I would start a theatre so they could just do it! And that's the way it happened.

So far as how it evolved, it evolved simply because in those days we were considered by the municipality as being unlicensed and, therefore, illegal. We were harassed greatly and were forced to move, whether we wanted to move or not, out of the little places that we had built with tender love and care. Unfortunate though it might have appeared to me at that time—like a tragedy—each move was, in fact, a push forward, because we moved into a larger area each time. And from moving from a small space each time to a space a little larger, the playwrights with whom we were involved had to write for whatever space that we had to put on the play.

My own immediate background is vaudeville, because some of my own people were chorus girls and tap dancers and the like, and when I was very young I had a taste of it myself. But that's all that I knew about theatre. In fact, when I first came to New York, my brother took me to see *Streetcar* with Marlon Brando on Broadway and I hated it! I know that sounds crass, but I did. To me it sounded just like another soap opera that my mother listened to and that I didn't like either. So—since I didn't like that and this wasn't my idea of theatre, and I *did* like music and I liked a text that seemed to speak music to me, these were the things that I chose and that's how the play selection came about. I strongly encouraged everybody to try to use music with whatever they were doing, which is where our musical background has come from.

We were the first to produce Pinter in this country. I like his plays, you see, so I produced Pinter. Playwrights who seemed to write like he did were playwrights that I liked. The ones that everybody else liked and that were very big Broadway persons—this is not a criticism—I just didn't find interesting.

Now, I had no theatre then and I was not interested in writing or directing or being in the plays. But I was interested in *being* interested. Therefore, I tried to bring into our plays the elements that interested me and tried to encourage people to use those elements. The first person who believed as strongly as *I* did about these things was Tom O'Horgan. He came around in 1964. He has a strong musical background—he had extensive ballet training and he was a counter tenor, a singer, a concert artist. With these things that he had we tried music more and more, which has been constant at La Mama. The kind of play that I said felt like music to me is the play that I really thought of doing. And that has been our evolvement.

From that evolvement we started going to Europe in

1965—not for any grand reasons—the only reason being that no critics came to La Mama, and I believe strongly in our playwrights and I would send the texts to publishers to try to get them published, but they would send them back because they would not read anything without a critique. However, through some coincidence, I came to believe that if I could get the plays to Europe, I could get critiques. And if I got critiques, then maybe we could get some published. So we went away in 1965 on our first tour.

We took twenty-two plays and we did eighteen of those plays and I brought all of the critiques back—I didn't know you had to translate them! We didn't show the French critiques, because they were terrible, but we had beautiful Danish critiques and so I sent those Danish critiques to the publisher—in Danish. I thought this would help get them published.

I mention the tour because Brice Howard, who was executive director of NET, as it was then called, had been to La Mama and he liked our plays and he said that he was going to try something. He was going to try to make a program of our plays on that TV station, which he was going to call "Three From La Mama." And the plays that he liked that we were going to do were *Pavanne* from Jean-Claude van Itallie, *Fourteen Hundred Thousand* from Sam Shepard and *The Recluse* from Paul Foster. He said that, although he liked the plays, he thought that our actors were terrible and he would have to tell me that he couldn't use them in the production. I felt very badly about this, but I insisted that if he didn't use the actors then he would have to use Tom O'Horgan as the director of the plays or else we wouldn't do them. So that was the compromise. None of the actors would do these plays but Tom O'Horgan would direct them. And that is how "Three From La Mama" came to be televised. Since then, that particular program has come to be known as a classic and has been constantly rerun through all these years.

Well, with his telling me that our actors were terrible is how I got the idea to start a workshop wherein we could develop actors who could really work in the theatre. And subsequently I have learned through the years that the playwrights who had the advantage—and it was an advantage—of working with actors who had had this particular kind of training, seemed to be the playwrights that became the best known and got the most rewards. Tom O'Horgan and I got these workshops going and in the workshops the actor was trained in singing, he was trained in dance, he was trained in music. Added to that, we have gone to Europe (and we've gone every year, which is a long, long time) and we met many people on an international level—so we are very international. What has been a great benefit is the exchange into the workshop of many masters and many persons. We've had Japanese training, we've had Eastern training, we've had Korean training, we've had African training—we've had a wide, wide spectrum of different directors or troupes that come on our kind of exchange and participate within the workshop. So our actors are exposed to all of these different elements, they work within them, they travel, they go and they are interested in countries as well as in learning their techniques. So fortunately, the development of the actor is continuous, it's a continuous evolvement—La Mama continues to evolve *and*, I think, this has been the greatest asset for the playwright, because he finds in the actor an instrument or somebody that he can truly use for his craft.

In a backwards sort of way I think that explains our evolvement.

Questions to *Ellen Stewart*

QUESTION   Do you think that a young, energetic producer today could establish the kind of theatre organization that you have established?

MS. STEWART   I never call myself a producer. Really, I don't think I'm a producer because I don't think I know how to produce. I'm part of this place. That's all. I'm part of this place, part of the work we do, part of all the people. It's a together thing and I'm like a member of the club.

QUESTION   Does La Mama, perhaps like the Open Theater, evolve plays with the actors and playwrights creating them as they work together in the workshops?

MS. STEWART   No, I didn't say that. This was the home of the Open Theater. This is where they worked for their entire first year in developing and so on. At *that* time they worked with playwrights and with the text. It was only after that when they were not here—and certainly they are doing very well with what they want to do—that they don't work with the text. They evolve the play. La Mama is still a playwrights' theatre. We don't evolve the text. The playwright writes his text and that text goes into workshop and the actors, the directors, work upon that text, but they don't evolve it.

QUESTION   How does that little speech go that you make at La Mama before the curtain goes up?

MS. STEWART   I say, "Good evening, ladies and gentlemen, welcome to La Mama, ETC—Experimental Theatre Club—dedicated to the playwright and all aspects of the theatre," and that's what it is.

I think that playwriting is a very special art and it takes a very special person to write plays. Our part, the part that we contribute to the playwright, is the contribution to the playwright and for the playwright. That is what we do.

QUESTION   You spoke of your sense of musicality in reading scripts, and you were the first to produce Pinter in this country. How do you equate that?

MS. STEWART   Because for me, when I read the text I hear the music—my kind of music in the words, the rhythm and the way that the man puts the word on the page. And not very many texts have that for me.

QUESTION   But it was seven or eight years later before most people discovered Pinter.

MS. STEWART   Well, I don't know if they hear the music that I hear, you see. But I hear the music. It's all in the words. Again, you see, I was forced to listen to those soap operas. My mother had a radio in every room and she turned it on and she turned it on *loud!* You couldn't stay in the house, you had to leave because you couldn't escape it any other way. Those things went on from whenever they started until the last one. And—I love my mama—she lived every one of those stories. We didn't have a room where you could go and close the door, because we couldn't afford to have that. I had what was called a day bed and that's where I slept, and so I heard it—everywhere, those soaps! Maybe I react too strongly, maybe it is some kind of rebellion, whatever you call it that a person goes through from a parental standpoint, but I *hated* those soaps! So that is why La Mama has never, ever been a home for the so-called traditional theatre, because I can't abide it, just cannot stand it. On occasion I have *forced* myself to do that kind of play, because I never want to be so narrow that something is absolutely not acceptable. But we don't do very much of it.

So without knowing anything about theatre, the way Pinter put the word upon the page appealed to me. And, mind you, I had just begun doing plays then.

QUESTION   What has been the relationship between La Mama and Actors' Equity Association?

MS. STEWART   With Actors' Equity I feel that a large part of the problems have been in the lack of communication, because most persons involved with Actors' Equity—particularly at the time when I had so many problems—had never been to La Mama or didn't know anything about what this Off-Off-Broadway was. So they had no concept of the work we were attempting to do and very little respect for it. For them, and I think I understand, we were always some kind of renegade or maverick place that was always breaking the so-called rules that had taken them for whatever lifetimes it's taken to build and to settle a creative union. They just thought that to do theatre one must abide by their rules. Again, since I didn't know anything about theatre, I didn't know what Actors' Equity was. Their rules didn't apply to me because we were just playing house, as far as I was concerned. I was greatly surprised when I learned that Actors' Equity felt that I was a threat to commercial theatre and harrassed me. I couldn't imagine how I could be a threat to anything, because I didn't know anything about the commercial theatre— I never went, I didn't see it. We all worked hard at La Mama and we didn't have any money and we just made our plays, so I couldn't see what was the big deal. But we managed to get those things straightened out and we've managed to get along.

We use the Showcase Code, which was written for La Mama to enable us to function within their jurisdiction. That's how the Showcase Code was evolved. Now it has been applied to others.

QUESTION   How important is the audience to La Mama?

MS. STEWART   Well, there's no theatre without an audience.

QUESTION   How dependent are you on box office?

MS. STEWART   Dependent! We're dependent on every penny that we can get because we never, ever break even. We're always $100,000 in the hole and so everything that comes into the box office helps. We get subsidy of various kinds, but we're still always $100,000 in the hole because we are not fully subsidized. All the agencies have been helpful. We've been helped by the National Endowment, the Ford Foundation, the Rockefeller, the New York State Arts Council, the Shubert Foundation, the Kaplan Foundation and so forth. And we've had private donations. So we've had help, for which I'm very grateful.

QUESTIONS   What do you think about some of the Off-Broadway groups, such as Circle in the Square, Joe Papp's group and the American Place Theatre that have moved uptown to the Broadway area?

MS. STEWART   Well, with Joe Papp, I told him that he was going to move uptown and that he was going to be the hit of Lincoln Center, which he didn't believe at that time. I didn't tell him when he worked here (yes, he *did* work here) I told him after that when we were on a TV program together—I told Joe that was going to happen to him. He still wonders how did I know. Anyway, I'm very happy for him.

I think the kind of work that Paul Libin and Ted Mann were presenting—particularly the classics that they work with—was some of the finest that's ever been seen in New York, and certainly whatever they've gotten from their move uptown I think they deserve. As far as the American Place and its move uptown, I think that the more moves in *any* way is healthy. And I think it should be encouraged.

QUESTION   What if the Mayor of New York offered you a theatre space on Broadway for a dollar a year?

MS. STEWART   Well, they just gave me a very dilapidated one for a dollar a year, for which I'm very appreciative because we've made it into a beautiful theatre. But what would I say if he'd give me one for a dollar a year? I'd take it!

QUESTION   Then you don't feel especially tied to the East Village area of the City?

MS. STEWART   No, because I think that perhaps in seventy-five percent of the Broadway and Off-Broadway things you will find a La Mama person. So, in essence, we're there anyway, because the people that are associated with La Mama work in all places, which is what I think that they should do. I think that with Off-Broadway and Off-Off-Broadway—and maybe there's going to be an Off-Off-*Off*-Broadway—with all this I think that Off-Off-Broadway has been able to make a rise in the prestige of the American theatre. Heretofor, the so-called American theatre was really the Broadway musical. The things that we do are going abroad—the Open Theater, André Gregory, La Mama—our names are passwords or by-words in Europe.

QUESTION   How have you arranged these trips and where do you play?

MS. STEWART   We get invited to come. Not so much in our own country—very little in our own country—but in Europe a lot. I guess it is by the governments, since European theatre is subsidized by the government, but they are free to do with their subsidy what they choose and they invite many of us to come and play.

QUESTION   Was that how you started in Bogotá?

MS. STEWART   I always felt that I had an obligation as far as Bogotá was concerned, because Bogotá greatly influenced our first going to Europe, in this way: in 1964 there was a festival there in which Paul Foster's play, *Hurrah for the Bridge,* was chosen by a group of actors in Bogotá to present for the festival. They translated it and this play was subsequently invited to go to Erlangen in Germany with the Spanish actors. In Erlangen a group of Danish actors saw this play and they wanted to know where did this kind of play come from, and could they get in touch with the persons responsible for it. The kids from Bogotá gave the name "La Mama" in New York and the Danish people contacted me and told me that if I would let them do the play they would get critiques—which is where, as I said, I got the idea that we could get critiques in Europe if we went. The Danes promised that they could get critiques. Now, because the kids from Bogotá went, I always felt that they were responsible to a large degree for whatever has happened for us. They were part of the university set-up and, once they had finished at the university, they couldn't continue the work. So we decided to fix a place where they could continue to do the work, not only our plays but also develop their own playwrights.

QUESTION   Can you tell us more about the European theatre festivals? Who decides which companies and plays are presented there?

MS. STEWART   The Europeans select what they want to come. They will contact somebody here or they will contact us directly, because they constantly send people to see what we're doing. That's how we're invited to perform in their festivals. *They* select what they want to come. Certain productions are invited to come, which is quite different from when we started. When we started, I would pick what I wanted and we would send it because we were invited to *play*, but not invited to come. When we got there, they gave us the stage and they would give us room and board, but that was all. So we had to find a way to go to Europe ourselves. Now they invite us to come and they buy our transoceanic ticket and they take care of us while we're there.

You see, there's a great festival interest in Europe which Americans wouldn't know anything about because we don't have that here. But on an international level the Europeans have fantastic festivals to which we get invited. We'd been playing those festivals, getting there as best we could, but the first time that anybody gave us any money was when we went to Germany. We were invited to a festival in Germany and they offered to pay our way—one way—we had to get one way ourselves. The other times we went before that, we had to get there the best way we could. But beginning in '67 we got tickets to come, plane tickets. I remember that first boat, the first boat was in 1965. But since then, we get flying space. The Greek plays that we just finished doing [*Medea*, *The Trojan Women* and *Electra*, directed by Andrei Serban] have a tour that begins when we leave here May 30th and we don't return until October 30th. We've been invited to play a month in Holland, and then either we will go to the Spoleto Festival or to Zurich, and from there we will go to London and from London to Lebanon and from Lebanon to Iran, then to Yugoslavia and then to Berlin and then we will go to Brussels and from Brussels to Paris, where we will open a festival. We've been invited to play in Peter Brook's new theatre for three weeks.

QUESTION   I remember seeing the Yugoslavian production of *Hamlet* here. Did you originate that production?

MS. STEWART   As I say, we have these cross-currents. They come here, they must get their own ticket here because we don't have funds to invite people like they have funds to invite us. But they come and they work with us, so we have this workshop sort of exchange. You saw the Yugoslav *Hamlet*, what you didn't see is that they trained with us two years previously, and the work that you saw is a result of that training. They were here and then with the training they received they went home and evolved *Hamlet*. When they came *here*, they used American actors. But the different directors and many of the troupe members come here often. In residence here at La Mama now are people from East China, from Lebanon, from Korea, from Tokyo, from France.

QUESTION   What do you mean when you speak of a La Mama "troupe?"

MS. STEWART   Well there are some groups that have special identities in that there is a nucleus that is always constant and that works together, although they work from time to time within other troupes as well. It's like an exchange—also, they work on Broadway and every place else. For instance, the black troupe at this moment is not rehearsing anything together, however, Lamar Alford, who is a member of the black troupe, is working with the repertory troupe, the one that was doing the Greek plays. The repertory troupe is directed by Andrei Serban, a Rumanian, and there's a constant group of people in that who also work from time to time with other troupes. But all the troupes consist of persons who are particularly identified with La Mama and they have a constant director. For instance, ETC Company, which is directed by Wilford Leach and John Braswell, has a little nucleus to which other persons are added. They can be people from other troupes, if that troupe isn't busy with its own project, or from open auditions. But when ever you see the ETC Company there are some persons whom you're always going to see when they perform as a company.

QUESTION   Do I understand that you have a troupe in Tel Aviv?

MS. STEWART   I have a group in Tel Aviv. I've worked in Tel Aviv very, very often. The mayor gave me a shelter which we fixed into a La Mama. He told me that if I could prove to him that Israelis would work for nothing (because he said they didn't have any funds) and that they would study and would really try to learn the techniques that we were proposing, if at the end there was a constant group, then he would give me a space. But when the war came, it was necessary for them to take the shelter, because they used it for the war. Subsequently, most of the Israeli kids are right here with me. Somehow, they all managed to get here. The same thing with the Filipinos—with the problems that exist, a lot of my Filipinos have come here, a lot of my Koreans have come here. With the war and all, some of the Lebanese and the Israelis came here and for the first time they actually worked together. Almost all Israelis speak Arabic, so Arabic is the language they speak with one another. Now with a gun, perhaps they will kill. But here they sit at a common table and they work and they explore, which is what La Mama is about.

We've always had this exchange. We just had an incredible East Indian workshop in dance techniques. Two masters with whom I work in India came here for twelve weeks at which time they gave a workshop to which La Mama people could come and learn. We've been doing Indian workshops off and on since 1966. In 1962 I started producing Korean plays. The Japanese workshop began in '66 when one of the first of the Japanese came here. Working with the repertory troupe, directed, as I said, by a Rumanian, you will find the Lebanese, the Israeli and the Japanese. It is a learning experience for them. It sounds very complex, but it really isn't.

I believe very strongly in one world, and everything

that we do at La Mama is very much associated with that. In the best way we can and however we can, the kids are always going across the seas. A very unfortunate thing—I remember Martin Brenzell, who was the leader of La Mama, Canada. He gave workshops in Germany, in England, and then I sent him to Israel and he drowned while he was working there, which was a terrible thing—he was only twenty-seven years old. We haven't really had a leader in La Mama, Canada, since.

I'm trying to explain that we are not the only ones going and teaching. If you go into the workshops, then you will see the persons from other countries. Within the acting workshops—like the Korean workshops—they are giving brilliant techniques to the repertory at this time *and* at the same time they are learning how to speak English. But the kids know very well how to communicate with each other to a degree. They know words. They have to, you *have* to be able to communicate with people here.

QUESTION   Do you think it's a responsibility of theatre people such as yourself who are working with new plays and new forms to elevate the taste of the general audience?

MS. STEWART   Elevate? No, I think that is patronizing— and *beyond* patronizing. One would have to be an absolute manic egoist to think that he could elevate anything! One can make a contribution, one can hope to broaden, to introduce elements—like tasting another dish that you're not accustomed to eating, it is just one more thing that you know what it tastes like. And, if you like it, maybe you will eat it again. But that's really all we are about. I don't like the idea that we are supposed to "elevate." I don't think that anybody should ever underestimate man's God-given mental abilities, the thing that he is born with. He has these things. One has but to recognize and to respect them from one's own environmental premise.

QUESTION   What do you think about commercial theatre?

MS. STEWART   I think that any person who is interested in commercial theatre has a valid interest. Commercial theatre is valid, it's part of theatre and I don't think that one should be condemned because he wants to make a living or even make a lot of money in doing theatre. If that is what you want to do, you should go about doing it. My only criticism, if you would call it that, is that one should try not to hurt his commodity. He should try to find the *best* ways by which he can produce commercial theatre. A man can be lauded because he sells automobiles; the fact that a man sells theatre or art of any kind does not mean that he has lowered himself. Great artists who were commissioned and sustained by kings and queens lived as perhaps we never will live. Think about Michaelangelo, my dear, and the monies that he received. You have but to go and see what he was able to do, because he had the monies to do it. But you can't put a measure upon what it costs. Many people buy air transportation to go to Pisa to see the leaning tower or go to Florence to see the David—that's commerce!

QUESTION   What do you think about people, such as the Becks, who seem to be trying to make theatre into a militant or a political force?

MS. STEWART   That depends upon your interpretation of politics. I think there are many ways of approaching political issues. My way of approaching a political issue is what we do. I don't think that anything could be more political than La Mama. We try to do something about living with and loving one another, which is what politics presumably is. Everything is political. The very fact that you go into a room and sit next to a person whom you don't know and with whom you have a conversation which could be illuminating for the both of you is politics. I think that if all environments could be like that, we could have a human being association! Lack of communication makes the extreme blight upon this world. Many people who speak about hunger or about war simply don't know what they're talking about. They haven't been to see the war, they haven't been to see the fighting. They haven't done anything about it beyond a placard. And a placard is not very much. But when one goes and tries to join hands—brother to brother—with *somebody,* then that is politics!

I know that when we went to the ITI [International Theatre Institute] Conference in Russia—all the Communist countries came as well as the Western countries, the whole world was represented there—you saw that all people are exactly like one another.

We're accused many times of *not* being a political theatre. But I don't really think there's any theatre more political than we. I really don't. We are communicating with one another around the clock in just about every part of the world, not all countries, however. We are communicating with the people in Malaysia. I'm going to go to see the people in Cambodia this April, I have a lot of people in Cambodia that I work with. I *go* to Java, La Mama people go, we are in Indonesia—but it is not proselytizing. We're having workshops and we're learning what to do with the eyes and the fingers and how to breathe and what to taste and how to listen, which I think is fantastic, because you *grow* from that. It's a sprititual growth as well.

QUESTION   What have you learned here that might be helpful to commercial producers?

MS. STEWART   I think that within *my* budget, if I were going to do this, there would always be money for a workshop production of the property being considered *before* it goes on to the commercial level. One of the great things that Michael Butler did when Tom O'Horgan was doing *Hair* was that he allowed Tom to have a workshop with the actors for about six weeks before they went into rehearsal, which I think accounted for a lot of the magic of *Hair.* The workshop techniques that Tom developed here were applied to the actors and that cosmic thing that you felt certainly made a contribution. I think it's like a kind of insurance. One should take the property being considered, put it into a workshop and take a look at it before you go into the so-called four-weeks-rehearsal-and-open syndrome. I think automatically that should be a budgetary consideration. Ultimately, it is not nearly as costly as a disaster. The moment that the disaster happens, you'll wish you *had* put it into a workshop first.

QUESTION   What is your official title at La Mama? Do you consider yourself a producer, an artistic director?

MS. STEWART   I'm Mama! This is really true. It's what everybody calls me, and I think they mean it in a sense. I'm not a producer because the kids actually produce, *they* are doing it. Maybe I have a way of providing a little guidance, but it's my part to try to provide an environment in which they can function, rather than the product. I'm concerned with how the product is going to get made.

QUESTION   Don't I remember reading a book in which you are referred to as "this illiterate black woman who is working miracles in the theatre"?

MS. STEWART   I've got a degree in electronics! But somehow, for whatever reasons, it was someone's fantasy that I am a mammy type with a bandana on my head and that I can't read or write. Somehow this happened. But for my mother's sake and for my papa's sake—because they asked me after *they* had read that—I tell people that I *do* have a little education, and I do. That's all over the world—that book, but it's simply not true. I can read and I can write!

But whatever success we have comes from the enormous input of the energies that sustain us. When you've got an around-the-world heartbeat, you've got something! We've got people all around the world who are wishing that we are doing all right. That's something—that positive kind of input that's in the air everywhere. Clive Barnes told me about when he was in Australia; he said, "Ellen, I went there and people wanted to know how's La Mama and what is La Mama doing?" He found that they have a La Mama in Melbourne. He said it was really something. Their first book of plays—new plays—came out of that troupe a couple of years ago and they've been going strong ever since. You know, that's mighty nice!

You can go down in Karala, the deepest part of India, and you'll find people who want to know what Mama is doing and when is she coming or when they are coming. At least it's a word that they are familiar with. It's lovely to go into Poland and not know anything and say, "I come from La Mama," and they know La Mama, and then little things start happening for you. It's beautiful!

QUESTION   Do you think that someone else, coming along today, could do something like you have done?

MS. STEWART   I don't see why not. Of course! All you have to do is just to love doing it. That is all that is necessary—somehow all the rest comes through.

Broadway Theatre

Alexander H. Cohen
Morton Gottlieb
Warren Caro

Commentary by *Alexander H. Cohen*

Producer

I think you have to equate producing on Broadway with a commitment to any institution. Broadway is dedicated to continuing commercial theatre. If you're going to ask anything about why Sam Shepard isn't produced on Broadway, we'll cut the crap right from the beginning! Broadway is a commercial institution—it has nothing to do with pretentious notions. It's there to make money. We'll have none of those questions, because you're not going to put me on and I'm not going to put you on!

Broadway has a collateral function to television: television is an advertising medium. If anybody tells you it's a communications medium, they're full of shit! Television is an advertising medium, it was invented as a communications medium, and it was adjusted to the problems that exist in this society, and it's used as an advertising medium—a commercial medium. It has no other function that I know of. Regional theatre has another function that I know of, or have heard about. College theatre and, perhaps, the kind of theatre that you will be able to create may have a different function. I function in the commercial world. I have to live in the commercial world, I have to finance the productions I do—not by writing a check on what Mr. Ziegfeld left me because he knew I was coming, but by going out and hustling to get the money to produce plays on Broadway. Mr. Prince does it, too, Mr. Merrick does it, Mr. Whitehead does

it, but they don't "bottom line" like I do. They say they
have subscribers, I say I have to hustle the money in order
to keep a commercial institution viable. So let's start right
there, having put it out on the table, then we'll work backwards from that point. Within the framework of that commercial institution we'll try to determine how one can do
good work.

I think I started in this business twenty-seven or twenty-eight years ago. I came from a not well-to-do, but from a
middle-class family that was well-off and I didn't have any
education to speak of. So where else would you go? I think
that's probably true about a number of guys who got into
the business around the middle '40's. I spent some time in
the United States Army. When I got out, the theatre would
accept anything. In the mid '40's virtually anything that
was put on the boards was successful. That was the expense
account era, I was brought up in the expense account era of
theatre when virtually anything was successful, and I say
"virtually anything was successful," but in point of fact, *I*
wasn't successful. It seemed that everything I touched in
those days was the exception that proved the rule. I did a
play (I'm trying to remember the first things that I did to see
if they can be any help to you in later reference) I did a very
sterile play by Jean Kerr called *Jenny Kissed Me*. It's the
first play that Jean wrote. I'd gone to Catholic University to
see it, which is the subject of a separate lecture. Walter Kerr
was then the resident professor of drama at Catholic University and Jean had written this charming little trifle
which in 1947 or 1948, whatever year it was, seemed just
exactly right for Broadway, and wasn't. But I did have the
pleasure of producing her first play and of meeting both the
Kerrs, who are really rather remarkable people. I think anybody still in the theatre in 1973, who was in it in 1948, is remarkable.

Then I decided to take it a little bit more seriously, and
an actor named Louis Calhern decided that he wanted to
make a serious effort, and he presented himself to me as
King Lear. This was around 1950 and I was twenty-three
years younger then, and I thought that was possible. All
things are possible when you're twenty-three years young-

er! So, in fact, we did a very interesting *Lear*. It was interesting on several levels. It was conceived by Calhern, who simply wanted to play it. That's every actor's dream. It intrigued me because it meant having an association with a very important star. As a matter of fact, I guess you don't know who the hell Louis Calhern was, or some of you do and some of you don't. He was a very interesting actor who had spent a lifetime in the theatre and did achieve a rather interesting performance of Molnar's *The Play's The Thing*, and played *The Magnificent Yankee* on Broadway. Anyway, I was intrigued with Calhern.

I've always been somewhere to the political left of Eldridge Cleaver, and in the '50's even more so. Therefore, we determined at that time, as a gesture of our own defiance, to go anti-blacklist. So we cast the production of *Lear* out of a casting directory called *Red Channels*! Nobody who participated in that production of *Lear* was not listed in *Red Channels*. Calhern played Lear, Everett Sloane played the Fool, Edith Atwater played Goneril, Nina Foch played Cordelia, Martin Gabel played Kent, Arnold Moss played Gloucester, John Houseman directed, Marc Blitzstein did the music, Ralph Alswang designed it. I produced it and I remember, even, interviewing the heads of the departments: the electrician, carpenters—at that time we had a choice. In any event, in addition to being an interesting presentation for me, it had the unique distinction of being cast as a counterpoint to the blacklisting that was going on in show business at that time. Those were the days of very serious blacklisting in the business—blacklisting which really caused enormous human suffering and in some cases even death. I think Mady Christians would have lived many, many more years if she hadn't been blacklisted. There are those who are terribly sensitive to having their patriotic motivations questioned, and then there are others who, like myself, thrive on it.

Lear was the longest-running *Lear* ever staged, though it didn't run all that long. I think we achieved something like eighty or ninety performances over a ten or eleven week stretch. It was a very interesting production and, historically, well worth analyzing in and of itself. It lost all its money, because I was still proving to be the exception to the Broadway rule. But I went on to make several other interesting attempts, and almost made it a few times but didn't, until I decided that I had to make adjustments to the commercial theatre, and for the last fifteen years I've been able to make those adjustments and, I think to some degree, judge effectively what the public will have, and have presented these last fifteen years perhaps a hundred productions here and in the West End in London. I would say perhaps half of them were successful, which on the average in our business is very good. Most of them have what I would call a limited success—they have made some money. Incidentally, in the theatre a success is something that makes a buck, which is also a commercial definition which may or may not intrigue you, but I'm here to talk about the Broadway theatre and that's part of the reality. Therefore, "success" means "dollars," and you have to equate it that way.

During that period of fifteen years, I began to find for myself that there is an equation between what's good and what succeeds, and that's what I'm going to try to prove to you here.

I do a lot of *shtick*. I present Dietrich and Chevalier and Victor Borge and Yves Montand and John Gielgud's lecture, *Ages of Man*, and all that stuff, and it's all beautiful and it's all *shtick*. But it makes money. And I've always believed that it was good entertainment. I mean, Marlene Dietrich may be "camp" but she's "high camp," a kind of perfectionism within its own context which is awfully good stuff. It's the best of what it is. But I have found during that fifteen-year period of over-productivity—because no one producer should produce as much as I have in the last fifteen years—that I have never had a reservation about a property that didn't prove to be a valid reservation. If I said to myself, "this material really isn't any good, but I'm going to do it because it's commercial," it ultimately turned out to be no good and not commercial. And if I said to myself, "I will do Harold Pinter's *Homecoming*, because I think it's brilliant but it will never be commercial," it turns out to be brilliant *and* commercial!

So, ultimately, what I hope to impress you with is that

the commercial theatre shares something with institutional theatre, and that is, even on the commercial level, *what's good succeeds*! When you do little contemporary pieces which you think will get you a season—and getting a season is an important consideration to the fellow who pays the bills—you might get the season out of it, but you really won't make a dollar and you won't make a contribution to the theatre—you might as well have held out to find the piece of property that is practical for the Broadway theatre, and that you respect enough and love enough to do. Now part of my business in the last fifteen years has been what I call an "exchange program"—in a sense it's very rewarding, in another sense it's very unrewarding. I export American products to London and import London products to America. So, London has had the "privilege" of seeing Arthur Miller's *The Price*, and you have had, conversely, the privilege of seeing Richardson and Gielgud do David Storey's *Home*, because I got into the area of bringing some important attractions to America. Another example would be the Royal Shakespeare Company in Pinter's *Homecoming*. The converse would be taking *Plaza Suite* to London and showing them the success of the Doc [Neil] Simon material. So I have done that, and that has proven successful on one level, unsuccessful on another. Successful critically, successful commercially—unsuccessful because you ultimately find yourself in the import-export business and not in the producing business. And too many producers in the Broadway theatre say "I produced," and they'll tell you the name of the show, when in fact they *presented* it. There's an enormous difference between producing and presenting. I had hoped that Roger Stevens would be here, because he's a friend of mine and a man for whom I have great admiration. But, he has never produced a goddamned thing in his life! All he does is "present" what other people have produced at various points in their lives. That's what I find unrewarding about an exchange program. I don't feel that I'm producing anything. I feel that I'm in the import-export business and, frankly, if you're going to be in the import-export business, there's more money to be made in piece goods.

What I find is that producing plays today—and when I

say "today," I talk of the last decade ending in the 72/73 season—has become as difficult as you've read and as you've heard and as you have perhaps suspected. The urban crisis contributes to some degree, and the inability of the Broadway theatre to reach the younger audience. I suspect that there are some of you who are interested in the theatre but not my world of the theatre: you're the shoppers. It has become necessary for me, in order to maintain the size organization that I do, to work in television in addition to working in the theatre so that I can afford to do some of the things that I want to do in theatre. But the nature of producing in the theatre during the last decade has become almost literally an obstacle course.

Would it be of any interest to you to know the steps involved in producing a play? It starts with reading. You have to find the material; how do you find the material to produce a play? Well, there are several ways. Of course, you can have a creative head, as I have. The gentleman who accompanied me is Richard Hummler, who is our creative head. You'll notice he's young. I stole him from a publication called *Variety* about three years ago because I used to read his reviews and wherever he was writing on the subject of a play that I had seen, I found that his views were collateral to mine, so it seemed intelligent that I ask him to come and work with me. Richard and I and others in the organization read. We read everything that's sent to us; it doesn't make any difference where it comes from. It can come in the mail—though you're less likely to find something coming in the mail than you are likely to find it coming from a reputable agent who knows your taste and knows good writing. Fundamentally, a producer finds his property either sent to him by reputable agents who understand his own particular beliefs and drives, or from an editor of one of the publishing houses who has the same understanding, or by reading galleys, or passing a bookstore and rummaging through it. There are all kinds of ways of finding material but, primarily, it's the agent, it seems to me, who's responsible for seventy-five percent of the stuff that winds up on the boards.

Having found a piece of property, assuming that it's in

script form (obviously, if it's not, you're going to have to make fundamental decisions with your property, like who's going to do an adaptation), and it's a simple play to produce, that it takes place in one or two settings, has a cast of anywhere from nine to twelve, you then set about the business of producing the play. The first thing you need is a director. There are half a dozen directors who are in consistent demand because they're hot at the box office. Being hot at the box office has the great additional value to the producer of helping him in the financing of his product; it's not unlike the motion picture business in that sense. So you attempt to marry the right director to the right piece of material and, if you're lucky, it may be someone whose experience or reputation is also helpful to the financing of the play. But you better not be too influenced in that decision by the fact that he's hot, or you're liable to make your first mistake and it's the *last* one you'll ever make, because with the wrong director you're in the crapper no matter *what* you do after that that's right! You put the wrong director on a project and then cast it brilliantly with a couple of stars and a good supporting cast, get up all the money, route the show, merchandize it, publicize it, and have the wrong captain on the ship—to use a cornball expression—and you're sure to have a guaranteed failure.

Now how do you make that determination about a director? Is it enough to have seen his work? Isn't it enough to say that you've seen three or four productions and they all seemed workable and playable and well done to you? On the face of it that would seem to be good. But I think that you have to take that director and find out if you can wed him, if you can marry him to the author. You've got to put them together and be the catalyst in what hopefully could be a very successful working relationship; and if it is, it means a kind of success for you and it also means a lot of money for everybody concerned. But if you make a mistake here, you have a pretty difficult row to hoe. A mistake is very easy, because a writer is terribly anxious at that point to have a director, and a lot of directors are terribly anxious at that point to have a job. And now comes the romance of all time: when you go to the meeting and you listen to the director tell the writer how brilliant his work is, and you hear all the stock phrases tripping out of the mouth of this director, whose work you very much admire on stage, and then you hear the author tell the director how much he admired all the productions that he's seen the director do. They're like two dogs—they sniff at each other all afternoon, but they never get down to business. I'm always suspicious of that, I'm very suspicious of directors of contemporary theatre, because they are the real bullshit artists. And that's why I narrow it to half-a-dozen. I think there are only six directors who function in the contemporary theatre who know a goddamn thing about it—which means that there are a hundred who don't. That's a pretty broad statement, but that's how I feel. So I think it's a matter of getting down to cases with a script and a writer and a director, and dealing with specifics and not with vague explorations of social ideas, attempting to determine whether they get on personally together. It's very difficult to find a writer and a director to whom you're offering employment who don't get along personally together, only to find three or four weeks later that the director doesn't quite understand what the writer was writing about and is a homosexual, and the writer doesn't like homosexuals, because he doesn't quite understand what he's all about himself! Now don't misunderstand me. I am not putting down writers or homosexuals. What I'm saying is that unless you get to the meat of it, you're not going to produce a play, you're going to produce a circus, and if you come up lucky, you'll come up lucky.

Ed Sherin is a fellow whom I worked with this year on a play called *6 Rms Riv Vu*, which is a decent play and it got me through the season all right. Ed Sherin is a brilliant director in my opinion, interested in analyzing the material, he wants to get his head into the material. I first discussed a play by Joe Orton with him, which I was interested in presenting in this country while the author was alive. Then, tragically, he died or was murdered, I'm not sure which. The play was called *What the Butler Saw*, it was presented in London at the Queen's Theatre by a friend of mine in one of the worst productions I have ever seen. Nobody in the play had any concept of what the play was about and,

most particularly, neither did the director. So I, not knowing Sherin but having seen a production of his called *The
Great White Hope*, which I very much admired—theatrical
bullshit, but brilliantly directed—asked him to come to
London, and we discussed the potential of an American
production of *What the Butler Saw*. We didn't do the play
because the author died. We didn't want to do this play
without the writer. But there remained some relationship
and Sherin came to me, I guess about a year ago, and gave *6
Rms Riv Vu* to Richard, whom I think to this day thinks
somewhat more of it than I do. And Richard brought it to
me and said, "Here's your season for you." And he was
right. I would like to say that he also brought me *That
Championship Season* and that I turned it down. And
another play which he brought me that I turned down was
Sticks and Bones. We'll get to that. I mean, we will evade
that a little, but we'll get back to it! And he said, "That's a
piece of shit, but Ed Sherin will direct this play."

And I said, "That gives it an intelligent reason to me."

And Sherin came in and explained how he would like to
approach the play, and explained why he thought the play
had meaning and why he thought it had texture, that Jane
Alexander would play it and that Jerry Orbach would do it
and I thought, well, let's give it a shot.

Now, let's qualify what is "shit," because I think you
may be misled by what I'm saying. I'm saying that it isn't
Arthur Miller's *Creation of the World and Other Business*,
which is shit of a different kind. I'm saying that it doesn't
have a social point of view, it isn't dealing with a problem,
it doesn't address itself on the public forum to the nature of
our society, like *The Oppenheimer Trial*, which I admire. I
admire people who come into the theatre and do *The Trial
of the Catonsville Nine*; I'm all for that kind of theatre. I'd
like to do "The Watergate Follies"!

Joe Levine (who's a marvelous guy no matter what you
read about him, take my word for it, he is a marvelous guy)
walked into the William Morris Agency ten years ago and
nobody knew who the hell he was, and he stuck his hand
out and he said, "How do you do. My name is Joe Levine
and I am a purveyor of shit!"

And he was one hundred percent right, in his terms. And he's made a fortune because he has a view of what he's all about. All I'm saying is that I hope I have a view of what *I'm* all about. But what are you doing when you're not able to find *The Trial of the Catonsville Nine* or *That Championship Season*, or you weren't smart enough to latch onto *That Championship Season*, which I think has a very important base? All I'm saying about the other piece (*6 Rms Riv Vu*) is that it *doesn't* have an important base: ergo, "shit."

So now you find a capable director who's doing that kind of work, and a capable producer who is doing that kind of work. But *why* are they doing that kind of work? Where are the plays? Why were only twenty-two plays presented on Broadway this season? Twenty-two plays presented on Broadway in *one season*? Theoretically, you ought to be able to turn that out in a drama class this season. Theoretically. How did we come down to that; how did it all filter down to twenty-two plays? And why? Is it enough to say that in the last quarter of a century the theatre has declined in direct inverse ratio to the ascension of television? That's interesting, by the way: direct inverse ratio. I think it's important to acknowledge that since post-war '47, television made enormous inroads. In the early '50's we had Uncle Miltie every Tuesday night, and it used to murder the theatre. One hour of Milton blacking out his teeth and doing the same blacking out of the teeth fifty-two weeks of the year—that eliminated Tuesday! You are now competing with something which is global, which is effective, which is free of cost—but, although it's free, you pay more for television than you do for theatre tickets, but nobody's ever constructively analyzed that. Remember that eight percent or ten percent that's tacked onto everything you buy from the advertiser, that's the television budget. Remove that and you could eliminate part of the basic problem in this country. But they're not about to do that, so there's no point in opening the discussion. Anyway, the fact remains that the theatre has decreased in inverse ratio to the ascension of television over a twenty-five year period. That's one of its problems.

The second problem is the inroad of the motion picture with the elimination of a practical kind of censorship, so that the screen can now deal with mature material. I'm not talking about crap. I'm talking about dealing with important material which I think the screen does better than we do—it is capable of presenting *Paper Moon* and X-rated material like *Last Tango in Paris*. This gives the motion picture industry a very wide range. The consequence is that, if you were to make an individual determination about what you were going to do tonight, how many of you have a play that you would go to this evening in preference to a film that you also haven't seen? It's valid to ask that question. We figured out that all of Broadway plays to five, six, seven million people a year—less than the 11 o'clock news on one night. Think of it! Take that 8 o'clock show that Shirley Booth was in, *A Touch of Grace*; one of its weekly episodes played to more people than our industry plays to in fifty-two weeks! That is where it's at. So we have to recognize the global force of television and what its ultimate meaning is when it is turned over to people who will know how to deal with it.

Now let me tell you something about a guy named Martin Starger, who runs the American Broadcasting Company and makes program decisions. If I live to a ripe old age, I hope that I'll be as good as he is at his job. There's a guy named Fred Silverman who runs CBS and there's another fellow named Herb Schlosser who runs NBC. Those three fellows really, in effect, run network television programming. Your first instinct would be to say, "My God, if those are the three guys who run it, let's go get them!" But boy, would you be wrong, because, given their own free hand, they could make it work as well as you can and as well as we can—better! They know what they're all about. But you have to understand what they're about. The networks are not like what you hear. There's no license granted by the federal government to a network, only to a station. A station is licensed, not a network. A network's function is to supply those stations with a product that advertisers want to buy, that's the name of the game. And then you, in turn, buy what the advertiser sells you. There is a validity in that, in the system, in our system, but it is also destroying writers—taking them from the theatre.

Now we're coming to a cycle, now we're coming to why there are twenty-two plays in the year instead of one hundred and twenty-two plays a year; and that is that a fellow has to eat—while he works he somehow gets hungry, when he gets hungry he gets this urge and he has to satisfy this urge, or he cannot get back to the typewriter. Television can help him satisfy that urge because it eats material. Tonight there are, what, fifteen or twenty dramas and tomorrow there are fifteen or twenty other pieces of material and the next night there are fifteen or eighteen variety shows, and it goes on and on and on. And now it goes into the morning. It used to stop at ten, but then prime time went to eleven, and then they figured out what to do between eleven and eleven-thirty, that became the news, and then they figured out how to add ninety minutes to the night and go to 1 A.M. They've got Carson to do it on one, they've got Cavett to do it on the other, and they've got films to do it on the third. *Now* they've figured out how to go from one to two. And you know what they're doing today, while we're sitting here, they're figuring out how to go from two to three—they are! That's the biggest assignment at the networks—what do we program between 2 A.M. and 3 A.M.? Why? Because it is an advertising medium and from 2 A.M. to 7 A.M. they'll work it, they'll make it work. And *you* somehow, some years from now you will be on a new sleep schedule. You will go to bed at 6 P.M. and you will get up at 2 A.M. and you will watch the goddam thing from 2 A.M. to 6 A.M., because they're going to program you that way! And in a sense that destroys what I'm doing and what you want to do. Television has an enormous need. It needs writers. If your future relates to working, to getting a job, television is your bag, if you don't specifically care about the end results. And, incidentally, I don't denigrate television, I understand it. I insist that I'm the only one who does! I'm positive that you really look at it at times and think it's a means of entertainment, and others of you look at it and say whatever it is that you say. But I'm sure that every time you look at that screen you do not automatically accept that you're looking at an advertising medium. But you cannot label it any other way. To do so is to delude yourself.

Mobil was giving a million dollars to present some regional theatre on Public Broadcasting, which is less effectively in the advertising business but nevertheless *in* the advertising business. We could do a separate session only about Public Broadcasting and the BBC. That would be interesting because public television, I maintain, and the British Broadcasting Company, are full of more crap than the networks are. But how does all this affect the theatre? What does it mean? It means that there are millions and millions and millions of dollars of advertising money going into a medium which is directly competitive to the theatre in terms of the audiences' time and the writer being forced to equate writing with eating. The writer says, "What the hell, I know I can get $4,000 for that job, and I don't know that I can get a $500 advance in the other area." And he's writing in television with some very, very competent people, and more than capable and more than competent people are functioning in the television industry, to the detriment and in some cases the direct elimination of the theatre. Now that's the second problem, because we did admit that the first was the urban crisis and its effect on theatre attendance.

And now somebody's going to say to me, "What about all those rotten plays? Doesn't that have a lot to do with theatre attendance?" You bet! Absolutely. But I try to equate the fact that we don't have the amount of product because of the inverse ratio theory.

So you've produced your play, and you have it on, and you succeeded in taking all the steps which I've outlined on the briefest level for you. And the director of your choice has been the right director and he has taken the property and achieved for the property the degree of success that is there to achieve and it works and it's up on the stage. And Clive Barnes says it's a wow: "Go see it tonight," and you quote that in your ads for the rest of the season. Did you ever notice how the only one who likes plays in the ads is Clive Barnes? Did you ever look at the ads? You merchandise what you have, and you get your season. But you no longer are able to make enough money in that season. Equate that with the twenty-two shows presented (and two of them are successful and twenty of them either fail or run a bit or lose eighty percent of their money). Again, remember the equation of what is "success" in commercial theatre. If you make *one dollar*, that's success. Invest $100,000 and get back $100,001—good! So with that equation, and having one of the two hits of the season, you have now made money and you go the route again. Do you know anything closer to a crap game? The odds are ten to one— there are two hits out of twenty-two and you roll the dice on a crap table at ten to one odds. You can walk across the hall to a Black Jack table and get two to one—better odds. So, therefore, who functions in the theatre today? I can only speak for the producers. They share one, perhaps two or three general descriptions: they're all egocentric, they're all misfits who couldn't find anything else to do, they're all independent impresarios, they're all the last of a breed, they all want to defy the odds—that's one description. Or, they are people who are dedicated and feel that it's worth it to them to spend their lives in relative insecurity, not poverty and certainly not anonymity, because they do make some money and they certainly do have exposure and publicity— "relative poverty" in so far as the odds are concerned, if you're functioning in an industry where two shows can come out in the black in one year—I'm not talking about two thousand. But there have to be a couple of thousand *television* shows in a year, I suppose, and there have to be a few hundred successful *motion pictures* out of a few thousand films—not material that you necessarily want to see, but creations that make *existence* possible. Not so for the theatre. Therefore, you must go on one of two assumptions—either they're egocentric nuts or they're dedicated human beings who have developed a philosophy about existing in the arts. Now we're down to it. You can make your own determination about what I am later. I think that I straddle that fence—I think that I'm absolutely an egocentric nut and I also think that I'm terribly interested in wanting to see an area of the world survive. It is both a social drive and a need of mine to exist in that business. I know that's a fact, because I could make a fortune anytime I want to get out of it. And so can every other guy in it, and I want to impress that on you. The days of *Hello, Dolly!* have passed, but I can't imagine how David Merrick could make less than ten times what he makes doing anything else he wanted, because he's worth it. I think Hal Prince could make a million dollars on anything he wanted to do. There's a reason why people have dedicated themselves, there's a reason why they won't get out, there's a reason why Jean Kerr keeps coming back. That was 1948 I told you about, this is today—and, incidentally, I didn't mean to diminish that kind of writing, I think there's a place for that in the theatre.

You can have several careers in the theatre. You can have them on a semi-facetious level and be involved in the convention of the Broadway theatre; you can have them on a more serious level and be involved in commercial theatre or regional theatre; you can have them on a more realistic level and be involved in theatre for television—which has to come. Or, you can try to straddle the fence as I do and have it all, which you won't manage because I'm going out of style—quickly! But if you're to exist in this business you've got to create your own attitude about it or go stark raving mad.

Questions to *Alexander H. Cohen*

QUESTION What difficulties have you encountered in bringing foreign artists to work in the States? Doesn't Actors' Equity Association try to prevent that?

MR. COHEN   I have never been refused permission by Actors' Equity to bring people here, nor have I been refused in London. But that is because they are usually stars of enormous magnitude. In spite of what appears to be my genuine vulgarity, I am the man who presents John Gielgud in virtually everything he does, and I get along very well with a whole stable of stars who really want to work with me in the theatre. The consequence is that in this country we never deny a star's application to work. In England they are more liable to let in lesser-known performers.

QUESTION   We frequently hear the unions criticized as a counter-productive element on Broadway. Do you agree with that?

MR. COHEN   You're thinking about "featherbedding." Perhaps in very inexperienced theatrical organizations the unions will get away with featherbedding, but they certainly won't with us or with Merrick or with Prince or with organizations that know how to staff a production.

Now let's define "featherbedding." A friend of mine is a guy named George Banyai, who used to be general manager for Gilbert Miller. He's now about eighty years of age, but a very vital eighty. I live occasionally in the south of France. When I've had a good season, I stay almost three weeks. But George Banyai has had a lot of good seasons so he *lives* in the south of France. To keep his hand in, he runs a theatre in Madrid and another in Barcelona. About three weeks ago, when we were sitting having lunch, we were discussing his present situation and he was asking me if I had any plays that would suit his theatre. By way of conversation I asked him what he had at the moment, and he said, "In Madrid we have *Butterflies Are Free,* which is now in its third year."

I have been terribly interested, lately, in curtain times, so I said, "By the way, what time is your curtain?"

He said, "Well, we play at seven and ten."

So I said, "Oh—meaning on matinee days you play at seven and ten."

He said, "No, no! Every day we play at seven and at ten."

I said, "What is every day? You mean six days a week you play at seven and at ten?" "No! Seven days a week we play at seven and at ten."

I said, "You mean to say you play fourteen performances a week?"

He said, "That's right. You got it!"

And I said, "That's astounding. So you pay all the actors double scale?"

He said, "No, that's what the Spanish theatre is. You play twice nightly, seven nights a week." Then he said—now get ready for this—he said, "Backstage we have one man, he is the electrician for the house. That is, he turns out the house lights. When he's through doing that, he turns up the show lights, and when he's through doing that he pulls up the curtain, and when he pulls down the curtain for the intermission, he rearranges the props. If we have to change a set, he does it, because he's the carpenter. He is also the stage manager and the assistant and the prompter."

And I said, "What does he do during the show breaks?"

He said, "He goes out front and counts up!"

Now we analyzed this together, over the longest lunch I've ever had. One guy runs the backstage and in the interval goes out front and counter-signs the box office statement. The same show in New York took twelve people to do those particular functions. Now are we featherbedding in New York, or is there a lunatic loose in Madrid? Everything is relative. Does a Broadway theatre need a house electrician? Guess so. You have to turn on the lights when people come in and before the show starts you turn out the house lights. House and show are separate. There's a house electrician, a house curtain man, a house carpenter, and a house prop man. Are those four people essential to a play? I don't think so. Is it essential to this industry to pay those four salaries? I *do* think so. Now how do you explain that? I guess it's one man's view of the structure of an industry.

When we did *An Evening With Nichols and May*, it seemed a simple enough thing to do. It was done in the context of the Nine O'Clock Theatre, which is a descriptive title which I hung onto a certain kind of presentation. We had Mike and Elaine alone on stage in a fluid, very fluid production which appeared to have been designed out of Bentwood furniture and looked terribly easy to work. A scandal developed because there were seventeen men backstage working that show and somebody said to *Life* magazine, "There are seventeen people working on that show." So they came and they saw the show and they looked at it and they said, "Well this is the greatest story of all time, let's get onto this, this is featherbedding!"

I thought I needed seventeen men, I could carefully and honestly maintain that seventeen men were needed to work what, to me, was theatrically valid for the show. It was obviously not economically understandable or translatable to these people, who were looking at it out front as audience. Could that show have been worked with twelve people? Under different union rules, yes. When you negotiate a basic labor agreement at the beginning of every third year, you have to live with it. When we have four musicians who don't play (and such a situation does occur), it is the result of a very carefully thought-out negotiation. We have four who don't perform with a small play and twenty-six who do in a big musical. It's different for *A Little Night Music*. It has a twenty-six man minimum in the pit. *That Championship Season* has four musicians and no music. Why do they have four? They have four because three years ago when we negotiated the agreement we were able to hold to twenty-six jobs in one pit by supplying four in another pit. Is that valid labor negotiation? I insist that it is. Other people insist that it isn't.

QUESTION What kind of role does the League of New York Theatres play in Broadway labor negotiations?

MR. COHEN   Well, the League of New York Theatres is a trade association of which I am a member. It includes all the Broadway producers except David Merrick, who occasionally gets his name into the paper because he's *not* a member, so that's enough reason for him! But other than that, everybody is in, and when it suits Merrick, he is in. This group negotiates just as any other group would negotiate within an industry and also it is allegedly charged with looking after the general welfare of producers and theatres. It's a pretty good bunch of guys.

QUESTION   How do you go about the business of casting your productions?

MR. COHEN   When you do a lot of plays, you departmentalize. Hildy, who is my wife—an ex-actress whose professional name is Hildy Parks, and she has been an actress for twenty years or so—Hildy casts almost everything we do, rather brilliantly and with enormous success. Her casting of *1776* in London was one of the greatest achievements in casting that I've ever seen, and *Applause*, which I'm presently presenting, is a brilliantly cast English company of an American musical. So my office is departmentalized, because we're a large producing organization. In another office the way to cast a play you are going to produce is to have personal knowledge of actors, presuming always that your fundamental judgement of what is an actor is sound. Then you have to have personal knowledge, you've got to watch everybody—you cannot miss a Broadway or an Off-Broadway play. My office is structured that way. I cannot see everything, that's not possible, or I'd never get to see my kids, or get a night off, or watch television. But you've got to see every play that opens on Broadway, Off-Broadway, Off-Off-Broadway, in colleges, in regional theatre. You've got to watch actors who are coming up on television whom you haven't seen before, and you've got to go to films endlessly. Now in my office that's split between five people, but don't forget we've been at it a few years.

For the individual who plans to produce a play, or who is producing a play, he just better be damn good enough to cover the bases, or call in a casting consultant who does the work and who *does* cover the ground and who knows. Most people who are really interested in producing, truly interested, are dedicated producers who cover the bases—like Morty Gottlieb. I don't remember when Morty Gottlieb has spent a night out of the theatre unless he was ill. That's why he's capable of casting his own plays or, at least, collaborating with the director. And the same thing is substantially true of the fellows who do lights in the theatre. I don't think there is anybody who lights plays on either side of the Atlantic whom I don't know about—although I was "taken" the other night. I went to see the revival of *Streetcar* at Lincoln Center, which I enjoyed. It was a little busy, but I loved it. I was so smug. I thought I knew every trick that Jules Fisher had in his book, only to find when I read the program that John Gleason lit the show! So I learn something new every day. Lighting is a magnificent contribution to that production and to most professional theatrical productions and I think you have to learn it, study it, breathe it.

It's sometimes very difficult to go to a play, you become so involved and passionate about what you're watching that you lose the individual involvement, and later on you hear people talking in numbers. When I go outside a theatre, and if I was standing in the same lobby as you, you might be talking about what a lovely evening you're having, and I might be saying, "It took twenty-two men to make that change in one minute and twenty-eight seconds," because that's what I'm watching to see—if the production stage manager is proficient at what he does—but after twenty-five years, you can do that in almost computer fashion.

What you have to do, to make determinations as you start out in the business, is to watch very carefully and to make determinations about whose work you like.

For example, how do you choose a designer? You choose him because instinctively you like his work. One of the great advantages of being able to produce in New York and in London is to see different productions of the same show. *Jesus Christ Superstar* in New York is one thing, lit by Jules Fisher. The same show, lit in London by Jules Fisher, is another show. He decided to go from scratch, he's got things in the London show that are so dazzling and so advanced technically, you wouldn't believe they could do them on the London stage, but they're being done. Anyway, it's important to see everything and then to be able to form opinions about relative values.

QUESTION Could you explain how the Theatre Development Fund operates; and has it brought new audiences to the theatre?

MR. COHEN Theatre Development Fund is administered by Hugh Southern. Public contributions and foundation contributions are used and administered by a board which decides that the Fund will buy tickets to a specific show as encouragement to that show, and then distributes those tickets in the marketplace to people who normally cannot afford to go to the theatre. Let's say they buy two thousand seats at five bucks and sell the two thousand seats at two and a half, thereby endowing the theatre ticket. How can you knock it? Their judgements are sometimes not the judgements I would make. But then, sometimes I wish they'd just give me the hundred grand and let me produce a play by Beckett. But I can't fault them. And, yes, it's gotten audiences in the sense that every first-time attendee is a potential second-time attendee. Get them in there once and, if they relate, you've got them for life. If they don't, they're worth losing anyway.

QUESTION But why expose a first-time attendee to something that is less than first-rate if, indeed, audience development is the objective of this organization?

MR. COHEN I remember when I was a kid I would go downtown on a Saturday and go to the movies which in those days, before one o'clock, cost thirty-five cents. You could see Frank Sinatra on stage and a feature film for thirty-five cents, if you got in before one o'clock. And boy, could you eat up a storm for another quarter—two hotdogs, two hamburgers and a coke! And if you then had sixty cents to your name, you could go to Leblang's Drugstore and buy a dollar-ten cent theatre ticket for sixty cents, but it was really half price—the dime was the tax, the seat was a buck and you got it for half a buck, plus the dime. And that's how

I started to go to the theatre. Obviously, the only things that sold at half price in Leblang's cut-rate basement were flop shows which didn't sell out at the regular price, right? I saw Constance Cummings in a play called *Young Madame Conti* and Osgood Perkins in a play called *Ceiling Zero*, and the two plays together lasted a week. And I was hooked forever, and I feel that with the exception of the rare disgrace, which the Theatre Development Fund has really not gotten into, that anything that they send young people to see has the potential of hooking them. They buy, or they attempt to address their funds to plays that they think need help, like *The Changing Room*, or other worthwhile pieces. Sometimes they're wrong. But they never come up with anything, it seems to me, which is reprehensible. So, I'm for them and if I had some money that I didn't know what to do with, I think that I would consider that a good place to put it. I think that people who really want to go to the theatre will find a way to go, including what we as youngsters called "second-acting"—you stand on the sidewalk until the act break and then you go in with everybody at the beginning of the second half!

QUESTION How do producers, who are so bright and sharp, get involved in putting on some of the stuff that opens and closes in one night?

MR. COHEN I'll tell you how. Did you ever have good friends, a husband and a wife, whom you know and who have a child? They tell you how bright and how beautiful and how courteous and formidable and deeply-concerned and extremely well-adjusted and how entertaining this child is—but you've *met* this dumb kid! Producers have "children" and they cannot see the faults of those children. I happen to be the one who is thoroughly objective about it, so I'm not going to use myself! I seldom brag, but I look at it and I say, "That's crap, get rid of it!" But most guys are absolutely unable to do it if it's theirs. It is their sweet little child. You know, I think Hal Prince to this day thinks *Superman* is a musical, or *Flora the Red Menace*. That doesn't detract from his talent, because he did *Cabaret* and *A Little Night Music* and *Zorba* and a lot of other things. But, there was this dopey kid called *Superman,* and it was *his.* These are things you nurse from conception and you refuse to let go. You're out of town and your best friend says, "God, that kid's dopey." And you say, "Not *my* kid!"

QUESTION   Can "merchandising" make a show into a hit?

MR. COHEN   I don't know. I once did a show called *Baker Street.* It goes back ten years. It was based on *Sherlock Holmes.* In any event, it was pretty bad, but we did a merchandising job on that show which was enormous. It ran for a little more than a year *on the strength of the merchandising.* Did it hurt the theatre? I don't think so. I think most of the people who saw it liked it. Is it good for the theatre to merchandise a show? I think so. I think the theatre needs a lot of pizazz, that's what I like about the theatre. I think that the great quintessential showman was Mike Todd. By the time you got out of a theatre where one of his productions was playing, you believed you'd seen a show. That has something to do with theatre—that *is* theatre in a way. How much does this have to do with the contemporary theatre? A lot. *6 Rms Riv Vu* without careful merchandising and hard work wouldn't have lasted until the intermission!

QUESTION   You mentioned Clive Barnes. Do you think that one or two critics can make or break a show?

MR. COHEN   I don't believe it and I think it's become an easy out, a cop-out, for every bum who produces a flop. Sure, the *New York Times* is a heavyweight newspaper, we've only got one newspaper in New York so what are you going to do? The *Post* publishes, but you can't call it a newspaper, and I would refuse to characterize the *Daily News.* So you have a one-newspaper city. But let's analyze for a minute whether the one newspaper, which *has* to be powerful in and of itself, is detrimental to the theatre. (Thank God, in light of recent developments, for the *New York Times* and the *Washington Post,* but let's not talk politics.) The point about the critical system is that I have never produced a play where in retrospect I felt the critics were wrong. I have never had occasion to say they berated my play. Nor have I ever believed it of anybody else's play. I think occasionally a critic may call a shot wrong. Now when I say "critic," wait a minute, let's qualify—who are the critics?

The heavyweight is Barnes, a major reviewer—and the *New York Times* probably made the most constructive theatrical-journalistic decision several years ago when it decided to have two major reviews with a Sunday piece by Walter Kerr. So on the *Times* we've got two major reviewers, and a man who is sound as the second stringer, Mel Gussow; and I don't mean to diminish him in any way by saying he's "sound." He's coming up—they've got some major reviewers there. On the *Daily News* they used to have a fellow who was a dear friend of mine named Jack Chapman, who couldn't find it in his heart in the last five years of reviewing to pan anything. Great friend of the theatre, cared about everybody in the theatre and consequently was unfortunately and unmeaningly hurting the theatre by liking all of it and thus diminishing the standards. Then Chapman died and was replaced by a heavyweight named Doug Watt, whom I think is a major reviewer. The *New York Post* has an aging gentleman named Richard Watts, who is a major reviewer. *Women's Wear Daily* has a man named Martin Gottfried who, if not a major reviewer, is a good, sound critic. NBC had the best of them all—the intellectual's gift to television—a guy named Ed Newman, who is no longer reviewing plays. And then you've got, peripherally, several bright people like Marilyn Stasio on *Cue* magazine, Brendan Gill in *The New Yorker.* Then you've got clowns like John Simon [*New York* magazine] who really, at the expense of anybody in the theatre, would like to grand-stand and create a controversy. His taste is questionable.

If I have a criticism of critics, it is that I believe that some of the majors are going too easy because they are worried about the theatre. They're worried about our business and they let you get away with something in the name of entertainment which really isn't worthy, and I am much more resentful of that than I am of all those poor sons of bitches who can't take a flop and come in and say, "Oh, Clive Barnes and those bums!"—that is a lot of nonsense.

These are very sound reviewers. It's a good system and if they err, they err on the wrong side—err by letting a piece of junk get by. I wish they were just a little tougher.

QUESTION   Do you think that things will get better or worse for Broadway? Have the foundations helped to offset the economic problems at all?

MR. COHEN   Wouldn't it be nice to finish this and say, "Well, it s going to get better." I don't think so, I think that the problems are so real and so difficult that the twenty-two will be nineteen next year. I don't know what to do. I don't know what the answer is. I did have hopes for things like the Billy Rose Foundation. You know, leaving all that money to be administered to perpetuate the name of Billy Rose—but they're not producing any plays that I can see. I had hoped that foundations might be the answer. I had hoped that somebody was going to bail the theatre out, but at the moment nobody is bailing, except those twelve or sixteen active, independent impresarios that I keep talking about. They keep bailing all the time.

QUESTION   Are there any new producers coming up?

MR. COHEN   Yes. This guy named Stuart Ostrow is hot stuff. Very good producer: egocentric, but he is good. There are Waissman and Fox, who did *Grease*. I think they're probably good. I don't quite relate to *Grease*, frankly, but there *is* another generation of us.

QUESTION   Do you think the commercial theatre will ever receive government subsidy?

MR. COHEN   Richard Barr has raised the question of subsidy for commercial theatre. What a dog fight that would be, if it ever happened! I hope it happens.

QUESTION   Is business as bad on the road as it appears to be on Broadway?

MR. COHEN   Well, from where I sit the road has become the haven of the big box office attraction. If you send out Carol Channing in *Lorelei*, that is brilliant producing—a rework of *Gentlemen Prefer Blonds*, which I was the man-

ager of in 1948, but it works. The road works for big attractions everywhere. *Godspell* works everywhere. *Hair*
worked everywhere—the young attractions. *Fiddler, Dolly,*
the big musical attractions. But there is virtually no road
left, as we knew it, for the little, simple play. You couldn't
tour a modest success, except in what we call our subscription set-up. The road now has become the key city subscription stands. There is an organization called The Theatre
Guild—American Theatre Society—and it attempts by subscription theatre to keep fourteen cities alive. When I came
into the business it was thirty-one. Four years ago it was
nineteen. This season it was fourteen and we are hoping
next season we are going to keep twelve cities on subscription. That area of it is shrinking, and yet the big attractions
can still go on.

QUESTION   Are Joe Papp's television attractions of his own
productions going to hurt those shows at the box office?

MR. COHEN   I don't know. Joe said when he closed *Much
Ado About Nothing* that the television had hurt the box
office of that show on Broadway, which was just a lie—
nothing more. He was just lying. The fact is that in the three
or four preceding weeks it did no business and he copped
out and closed the show. As far as the television *Sticks and
Bones* is concerned, I have seen it and it stinks, and I think
CBS had two motivations in not running it. So CBS made a
lousy deal with Joe Papp, and they're stuck with him or it.
Joe Papp is a very good producer. He has done a great deal
for writers and a great deal for the theatre. But he didn't do
so good for CBS; he made a television show that got on and
got lousy ratings.

QUESTION   How do you go about raising money for your
Broadway productions?

MR. COHEN   In order to get money you have to be person-
able, charming, handsome, intelligent—just like me! Go
around with your hand out, and people give you money. I
don't have the answer. That's a creative function of a producer. I get it, but it gets harder. It gets harder as the econo-

my of the theatre diminishes. When two out of twenty-two are hits, you think it's easy? It gets harder. I get it because (A) I am good at it, (B) I work at it and (C) I have some reputation over the years. But it gets much harder. It's much, much harder.

Commentary by *Morton Gottlieb*

Producer

Note: This session was held in Mr. Gottlieb's offices in the Palace Theatre Building in Manhattan several months after most other sessions recorded in this book.

The question is always asked, "How did you become a Broadway producer?"

It all started in the mid-1920's. I was very fortunate in that an uncle of mine owned the Lyric Theatre on 42nd Street, which is one of the grind houses now, but in those days in the '20's had such musicals as *The Coconuts* with the Marx Brothers, *Rio Rita, Fifty Million Frenchmen, Three Musketeers* and many, many big musicals and plays. By the time I was six years old I'd been to the Broadway theatre, say, seventy-five times. Between the ages of four and six I used to go virtually every Wednesday and Saturday and would see all the musicals in town, not just those at the Lyric Theatre, but other theatres as well.

My great-uncle would get us passes—in a box, usually— and I'd go with my mother, my brother, if it was on a Saturday matinee since he was already in school, and my aunts, and so forth. Certain shows I would see two, three, four times. I liked them. I saw *The Coconuts* three times, I saw *Rio Rita* three times, I saw a couple of the *George White's Scandals* a couple of times. When I started going to school at the age of six, I went every Saturday matinee. My father, who's a lawyer, just thought it was amusing, and my mother sort of enjoyed it. Also, we always went to the local movie theatres every Friday night and possibly Saturday night. That was from the time I was three years old; so by the time I went to school I was seeing virtually every movie and also many of the Broadway shows, and that was part of my life.

At the age of four or five I decided that I wanted to be a producer. During intermission I'd sit out front in the box office watching how they were selling the tickets, listening to the problems; and then I would go backstage a bit. Although there was a certain kind of fantasy about being *on* the stage, I liked sitting out front. So everything all my life was towards being in theatre and working in movies. I love movies! And when I went to school I was always involved in theatrics. When I went to Yale I was in some of the plays. And I did arrange, along with a couple of friends, for Yale College to allow us to major in drama—to take a couple of courses a year in the graduate Drama School and have these classes qualify towards an undergraduate major. I also founded the Yale Film Society, against the good wishes of the Dean of Yale College, who said to me one time, "Are you trying to imply that the movies are an art form?"

And I said, "Yes."

And he said, "Well, don't come here next week and try to organize 'The Yale Burlesque Society!'"

That was the attitude the university had at the time—movies were something which could not really be condoned as anything for the university to take an interest in. But I pushed it through with the help of William Lyon Phelps, who was a professor emeritus and the man who popularized Tennyson and Browning in America. When he started teaching at Yale in 1891 or '92, Tennyson and Browning were looked upon as pop tune lyricists. The idea of teaching them was as unheard of in the 1890's as was having a Yale Film Society in the late 1930's.

At any rate, everything I did at Yale was toward increasing my awareness of theatre and getting a background in the theatre. I not only took courses in the Drama School, but in order to satisfy my classical civilization requirement for a Bachelor's Degree, I took Greek and Roman Drama. So by the time I was out of school I had read every Greek and Roman play and some of the Roman ones in the original language. I also took British Drama and Dramatic Criticism in the English Department and Social Psychology in the Psychology Department, which dealt with movies, radio and advertising.

As soon as I graduated from Yale, I rushed out to Columbia Pictures with a letter of introduction to a top executive out there (which I'd got by pushing my father to push a friend to push somebody else to get me an interview in New York with Jack Cohen, who was corporation head of Columbia pictures in the East). And with that letter of introduction I got into the studio and refused to leave unless they gave me a job. Columbia Pictures created a job which was sort of "literary efficiency expert." What I did was to go through all the story properties that they had never made into movies and tried to resuscitate some. One that I found was marvelous. It came from a Broadway show by one of the world's greatest composers and they still haven't made it. This was 1941 and I tried to get them to make a musical and keep it in its period of the '20's, but they said, "Why do a musical about the '20's?"

It still hasn't been done. Anyway, it was a terrible idea to do a musical about the '20's in 1941.

I stayed in Hollywood until World War II was declared and then came back East, assuming I would go into the Army. I didn't go into the Army, but got into publicity. After a few years, I became Gertrude Lawrence's press agent and through her I really got into the theatre—always planning to use publicity as a stepping stone to becoming a manager. Along the way, I met Dick Aldrich, her husband, and at the end of the War when Theatre Incorporated was being organized, they had me come in and do publicity for Gertrude, who was starring in their revival of *Pygmalion*. So I did some special promotion for Theatre Incorporated and was the press agent for the first American engagement of the Old Vic. At that time, doing publicity for the Old Vic was rather interesting because the *New York Times* couldn't get it through its head that "Vic" was not spelled

"Vick" and I couldn't convince them of what the Old Vic was!

Then I got involved with the Actors' Studio. I'd been around the Actors' Studio from before it was organized. It was organized, really, by [Elia] Kazan, Marty Ritt and Bobby Lewis—Lee Strasberg came along later. I knew all of them in 1947 when they were organizing it and the various actors who were part of the group—Maureen Stapleton, Marlon Brando, Beatrice Straight, Arthur Kennedy and so forth. Some years later, when they wanted to expand, they needed money to buy the building which they now own. I got conned into running the first Actors' Studio benefit, which was the premiere of *East of Eden* with Julie Harris and Jimmy Dean. They wanted to have just five dollar and ten dollar tickets for the premiere and raise a little money and I said, "Nobody is going to buy a ticket to a movie for five dollars to benefit something that isn't even a disease!"

Nobody actually knew what the Actors' Studio was. Warner Brothers publicity department kept sending out releases saying it's for the benefit of the "Actors' Alliance." They couldn't even get the name right! So it was a matter of publicizing the Studio at the same time as trying to sell the tickets for the first benefit. Well, I decided the only way we could sell the tickets was by raising the price to fifty dollars a person and try to make something special of it. We'd make it a kind of glamorous evening. No premiere, no ball, no charity event had ever charged fifty dollars per person at that point. It was the first time. It would have been a hundred dollars a couple, and I figured the more you charge the better it would be, and the more special you could make it. And we threw something else in, we got the Hotel Astor to give us the Astor Roof and the food and the waiter services for nothing. We got the French champagne industry to give us all the champagne we needed for nothing, and Warner Brothers to pay for all the printing material and the mailing and telegrams. I got usherettes of star status to come and show people to their seats and the whole thing was to convince people that all of the fifty dollars was going to the Actors' Studio, and no portion of it was going to anything else, including the orchestra. I got someone to contribute the money to pay for the orchestra.

Then we planned a big entertainment. The head usher was Marilyn Monroe, who had not been in New York at all. She had just walked out of her contract at Fox. She was here for the first time, and through Leonard Lyons and through her agent at MCA, I got them to "deliver" her to me, which they did. They presented her to me at the proper time and we had her pose for a picture showing Robert Anderson to his seat. It was that night that Lee Strasberg met Marilyn Monroe at the dance afterwards, on the roof of the Astor Hotel across the street from the Astor Theatre where the premiere was. It was a rather gala event. I had wanted Marilyn Monroe and Carol Channing and maybe someone else who had played Lorelei, to sing "Diamonds Are A Girl's Best Friend" together. But Marilyn Monroe didn't want to do that. She said she would dance on the dance floor with somebody, but she wouldn't entertain.

The nature of the entertainment was going to consist of various composers doing some of their own things: Arthur Schwartz, Abe Burrows, Harold Arlen, and Comden and Green; but when Marilyn Monroe said she wouldn't entertain (this was a week before), I decided we'd better get another additional entertainment. Through the William Morris Agency I got a group Kazan had never heard of, nor had Arthur Schwartz, who was helping out, and they wouldn't allow this group to go on last. They insisted I put them on next to last and have Abe Burrows follow with some of his songs. Well, the group was the Will Mastin Trio starring Sammy Davis Jr. It was the first time any one of the smart folk in New York had ever seen Sammy Davis Jr., and poor Abe Burrows had to follow the "debut" of Sammy Davis!

Anyway, enough of the Actors' Studio for the moment. I was trying to illustrate that all through the years I've always been touching base with many, many things. I was a press agent way back in the '40's, I'd been Gertrude Lawrence's press agent (first for her radio program in 1943) and then I went on to other publicity offices and on and on until I got to be a business manager. It was Dick Aldrich, her hus-

band, who let me be the General Manager of the Cape Playhouse at Dennis, Massachusetts. I got some initial experience there and then convinced them at the Playwrights'
Company that I was responsible and became the assistant
to Vic Samrock, who was the General Manager of the Playwrights' Company. We worked on *Joan of Lorraine* with In-
grid Bergman, *Dream Girl* and a number of others. The following summer I went back to the Cape Playhouse, and the
following autumn I was General Manager for a play for
Theatre Incorporated. We did a play that never got to New
York, called *The Big People*; Marty Ritt directed. It closed
in Philadelphia after one week and this was shattering to
me because, up to that point, I had only worked on productions that were giant hits, like the Old Vic engagement or
Joan of Lorraine. At the Cape Playhouse every seat was
sold, including some which were put in the aisle. So it never occurred to me that a show which I was working on
could be a flop. But *The Big People* introduced me to that.

After I went to work as a manager, I got into the Association of Theatrical Press Agents and Managers and was one
of the first and youngest members of ATPAM, but a full-
fledged company manager. I managed a play called *East-
ward in Eden* about Emily Dickinson, starring Beatrice
Straight. Right after that, I went to work with New Stages
down on Bleecker Street, which was planning a production
of *The Lamp at Midnight*, a play about Galileo. We took
over an old movie theatre that hadn't been used for years. It
was across the street from the Mills Hotel, a glorified flop-
house. We installed a stage and when I went down to get a
license, I discovered that if you didn't have a permanent
proscenium and an asbestos curtain, you couldn't have
more than two hundred and ninety-nine seats. So I came
back and I made them rip up all the additional seats above
two hundred and ninety-nine, and out of that formula—or
out of that predicament with the Building and Housing Authority—came the formula for Off-Broadway. Subsequently, in union negotiations, two hundred and ninety-nine
seats constituted an Off-Broadway theatre. Well, we opened
with *The Lamp at Midnight*, which got raves from Brooks
Atkinson and a snow storm from the weatherman! We did

practically no business. We were just biting our fingernails and trying to keep alive and I was paying last week's bills with next week's box office take.

Now the thing about New Stages was that it was the first time that a completely all-professional compliment of people worked Off-Broadway. Not only were all the actors members of Equity, but there were three I.A. stagehands, a union ATPAM manger and press agent, and a union treasurer. The only people who were not union were the ushers, who were various friends of mine including the unknown Maureen Stapleton, Felicia Montealegre Bernstein, Arthur Cantor and Paddy Chayefsky. I got other people to come and help sew costumes, but we did have union designers. It was a very precarious existence, trying to create an all-professional Off-Broadway theatre that gave eight performances a week. New Stages was financed by actors buying stock in the corporation, plus various other people whom I conned into buying stock, like Ruth Gordon, Garson Kanin, Gertrude Lawrence and Dick Aldrich, but most of the stock was owned by the actors themselves.

Now what happened in the case of New Stages was that we couldn't afford to pay the actors any money, so we gave them empty payroll envelopes, after making the government payroll deductions, and sold them more stock! I *did* put the tax money into a tax account and those were the only bills that were really being paid, because we weren't taking in enough money at the box office—just enough to make the payroll taxes. Nobody was getting paid except in more stock. Equity knew about this because a good many of the Equity council members were members of the New Stages company. And we did establish all the ground rules for Off-Broadway then.

The second production was a double bill, an Irish play called *Church Street* and Sartre's *The Respectful Prostitute.* At that time there was such a shock reaction to the title that the *New York Times* was considering not handling our advertising. As a matter of fact, the advertising agency that was representing us *refused* to represent us any more! Some people even stoned the marquee to break the glass lettering of the title.

The New Stages Theatre is currently the Circle in the Square Theatre [downtown]. In those days of 1947 Bleecker Street was not what it is today and that area of the Village was living in the memories of Eugene O'Neill and Edna St. Vincent Millay. There were only two places in the entire Village where we could get a cup of Capuccino—that was the kind of area it was. The Mills Hotel across the street was the clubhouse where most of the winos in the area lived. They didn't necessarily harass the patrons, but they really felt displaced by the fact that the theatre was in existence, because the theatre had been closed for three years or more and the winos used to sleep under the marquee. It was very interesting and odd and strange, having all these people coming from uptown to see the plays and the locals feeling infringed upon.

Well, when *The Respectful Prostitute* opened, it got rave reviews and it became an instant hit. We jumped from being this place that nobody could find, to a spot on the map. The day the reviews came out there were two hundred people on line waiting for the box office to open in an area they couldn't find a week before! It shows you if they want to see a show, they'll go anywhere and they'll find it. So much so that the second night after the reviews came out, there was a line of limousines. And at intermission all the people, the two hundred and ninety-nine of them, would crowd into these terrible bars on the street where whisky sold for ten cents a glass. It didn't bother them at all, you know, getting their drinks next door at a bar along with the winos from the Mills. And so New Stages took off. Although it had the good reviews with *The Lamp at Midnight,* it was *The Respectful Prostitute* which really established it. The play ran six weeks and then moved to the Cort Theatre and ran eight more months. I was one of the people who raised the money to finance the move to Broadway and it made a great profit for New Stages. The corporation still exists and has amassed profits from *The Respectful Prostitute,* including its share of the movie rights. The movie was made with Yves Montand and Simone Signoret some years ago in France. There are still accounts somewhere belonging to New Stages. I'm told that nobody can find the seal or the list of the stockholders, but the money from *The Respectful Prostitute* has been there for twenty-five years, and it's *still* there!

Anyway, the following September I became Gilbert Miller's general manager and we did *Edward, My Son*, starring Robert Morley. Well, I've always been star struck, always loved working with stars and always got along well with them. Actually, that's why Gilbert Miller hired me in 1948, because he was going to bring over Morley, whom he had brought over ten years earlier in *Oscar Wilde*, but had not got along well with him, and Miller thought I could handle him. And it was true, I got along very well with Robert Morley and subsequently went to Australia as his manager when he did *Edward, My Son* there. I virtually became a member of the Morley family and godfather to their youngest child.

When I returned from my round-the-world trip, I returned to Gilbert Miller, who then did *Gigi*, Anita Loos' dramatization of the Colette novel. He called the girl he brought over to play the lead (the unknown Audrey Hepburn), he called her "Gottlieb's folly," because I prevented him from firing her on the fifth day of rehearsal. He said that she couldn't be heard and that she wasn't going to be good and he hated her and he hated the whole show.

But I was always able to sort of smell superstars. There was one I'd known since 1945, Marlon Brando; I knew Marlon around New York and I'd become very friendly with him. Then he did *Streetcar* and became a big, big star and went to Hollywood and did *The Men, Streetcar, Viva Zapata* and so forth, and we still remained friends. In 1953 when I was planning to leave Gilbert Miller, Marlon said he would go back on the stage and do a play and that I should find a play and he would let me produce it. Marlon Brando did *Arms and the Man* so that some of his friends could have acting jobs—and I could become a producer. And that was the first thing I did produce!

Along the way, I did a couple of other things that weren't so successful and then I went back to managing. I was the general manager of the American Shakespeare Festival in Stratford, Connecticut, '56 and '57, and then went back to company managing more plays for Roger Stevens, Freddie Brisson and others. I was the manger of the Cambridge Drama Festival in '59, which did *Macbeth* with Jason Robards and Siobhan McKenna, *Twelfth Night* with Tammy Grimes, Siobhan McKenna, Zachary Scott, Fritz Weaver and others. John Gielgud, Maggie Leighton, Michael MacLiammoir did *Much Ado About Nothing.*

I was involved in regional theatre but always wanted to get back into producing and managing other plays. Then, out of nowhere, came Helen Bonfils, whom I had known slightly in my Gilbert Miller years. She had been an old friend of his and decided she wanted me to be general manager of *Sail Away,* and I said, "Yes!"

She liked the way I handled it all and later said, "Why don't you find a property to produce and I'll put up all the money?"

So I read a play called *Enter Laughing* by Joe Stein, from Carl Reiner's autobiographical novel, and decided to produce it. Helen Bonfils put up all the money for it, it played over a year on Broadway, made a star out of Alan Arkin, it's been done in practically every summer theatre and little theatre, became a movie and now is being made into a musical. And that was the beginning of my going back to being a producer. Helen and I did a succession of other plays: *Chips With Everything, The White House* with Helen Hayes, *The Killing of Sister George* with Beryl Reid and Eileen Atkins, and *Lovers* with Art Carney.

Around the time I did *Enter Laughing,* I thought it would be wonderful to do a mystery play. I didn't think there were many mystery plays and I thought the public wanted them. But they just had to be better than television. So I started reading mystery novels hoping that I'd find one that I could get Joe Stein to dramatize. And those we liked either weren't available because the movie rights had gone or we felt they weren't dramaturgic. So we never found one. But I kept asking every agent I knew. When we were doing Joe Heller's *We Bombed in New Haven,* I asked Robbie Lantz, who was Joe's agent, if he had a mystery play. He said, "Yes. Peter Shaffer's twin brother, Tony (whom I had met when I had been company manager of *Five Finger Ex-*

ercise, which was Peter Shaffer's first play in America), has just written a mystery play."

It was called *Anyone for Tennis,* and I loved it! Three minutes after I finished reading it, I spoke to Robbie Lantz and I said, "Yes, I'd like to do it."

Well, the next day he found out that Michael White had been reading it, too. They decided they would divide the American rights to me and the British rights to Michael White and, although we thought we might do it first in America, we later decided that it would be better to shake it down first in England. *Sleuth* opened there and we decided to bring that production here, and the rest is well known. It's the highest grossing play in the history of the American theatre. It has already grossed over eleven million dollars as a play in America—not including the movie or in any other place in the world, just in America. Now this isn't to say it is the most *successful* play ever in America. You might say *Tobacco Road* or *Abie's Irish Rose* or maybe *Barefoot in the Park* were more successful, but just on the basis of dollars and cents at the box office, I would say *Sleuth,* because of inflation or the fact that *Sleuth* has played in larger theatres than *Barefoot in the Park* may have played, is the highest grosser. I don't think there has been a play that has grossed over eleven million dollars in first-class productions and in stock. And it's my guess that it's probably grossed about twenty or twenty-five million dollars as a play all over the world, which is really amazing.

Questions to *Morton Gottlieb*

QUESTION   How do you explain the great success enjoyed by *Sleuth*?

MR. GOTTLIEB   Well, the quality of the writing is quite high, especially for a mystery play—its sense of imagery, its choice of language, its humor—and it happens to be brilliantly plotted. And it came along in a period when young people had not seen a play with a beginning, middle and end. This is really one of the reasons why the movie was so successful in universities and colleges and among high school students, because teenagers had not seen movies with a beginning, middle and end. That intrigued them. I mean, they didn't go to *Airport*—their parents might have. But *Sleuth* does have a marvelous, intricate, sound structure, and it's one of the best of its kind because the quality of the writing is much higher than most plays and certainly higher than any other mystery play. They don't have that kind of choice language.

QUESTION   Aside from the language, what do you think it is that makes a good play?

MR. GOTTLIEB   People in conflict. A play is conflict, otherwise it's an essay, or a novel, or a movie—it's "characters-in-conflict." That's what a play is to me. Two people are confronting each other and you have action and reaction. You see how they behave and you have to see the intellectual processes as a result of their behavior. But that's another whole philosophical discussion that we could get into.

When I want to do a play, I plan for the best time to get the best theatre possible. I decided *Enter Laughing* should come in in the early spring, when people are ready to have a belly laugh. There were no "belly laugh plays" at that time, so I wanted a belly laugh play. I said, "Let's come in in

March for that play." With *Sleuth,* I don't know, we just decided not to come in instantly in the early autumn, but sometime in the middle when I thought we would get the proper theatre parties. One thinks not only in terms of other plays, but also what is the proper timing and when is the talent available. You know, sometimes actors are not available for reasons of their own—they may be making a movie or on vacation with their family or whatever. But, generally, I prefer to come in in the early autumn.

QUESTION   Do you especially look for plays that have a lot of "tricks," as you call them?

MR. GOTTLIEB   No. But *Sleuth* happens to be a suspense play with tricks, only because that was the way it was written. I do think in terms of mystery plays that have tricks and suspense. Tony Shaffer's new play, *Murderer,* has more tricks than *Sleuth.* It has tricks on top of more tricks. I don't know how he thinks them all up. He's so ingenious, and quite remarkable.

QUESTION   What do you think about theatre parties? Don't they usually make very bad audiences?

MR. GOTTLIEB   They give plays a chance to stay alive while trying to reach their audiences. My guess is that if *See Saw* had had a lot of theatre parties in the period after it opened officially, it would have been a big commercial hit. A lot of the public wants to see the hit show and wants to see what they can't get tickets for. This isn't to say everybody, but that extra area of audience that makes a show pay off and makes it prosper very often comes from those theatregoers who dote on the unavailability of tickets. Theatre parties give you a cushion, meaning that you have a lot of seats sold and you have a lot of people coming to see your play. It makes the tickets less available and gives you an audience that goes and reports it. I think it's better to have seats sold in advance than *not.*

QUESTION   How would you characterize the Broadway audience these days, and what's being done to bring in younger audiences?

MR. GOTTLIEB   Well, it's partially people of the middle class and out-of-towners. It's people who love the theatre.

When we talk about getting a young audience to the theatre, the surveys have shown that about twenty-one percent of the audience is under twenty-five. That means that they are between thirteen and twenty-five. And it's been the same for twenty-five years. It may have been twenty-three percent in 1951 and in some other year it may have gone down to twenty-point-nine percent. But in the last surveys that I saw it is roughly the same. And it is essentially the same as that age bracket percentage of the actual, total population. I've always seen young audiences at my plays. But, you know, I don't want an audience that is going to be sixty percent under twenty at a play of mine, because there are certain values that I don't think are necessarily going to appeal to them. I want to do plays that have a certain amount of irritation, a certain amount of what I might call "sophistication." And I don't think that every fifteen-year-old from Brooklyn is going to like all of my plays. I don't want four-fifths or three-quarters of the audience to be a certain age. I want it scattered around. So when you talk about who comes to Broadway, it's a mixture.

Most of my plays, except for a few, have appealed to minority audiences; that is, non-lowest common denominator audiences. I always knew *The Killing of Sister George* would never appeal to the broad public and I did it knowing full well that two of the four daily newspaper critics hated the play. I did it predicting that it would be a "nervous" hit. But, I said, I want to do the play anyway, and I'll do it as inexpensively as possible and try to keep the costs down. Well, as you know, it ran for a season. Beryl Reid won her Tony Award and we got a tour for another season and a movie sale and stock productions. I don't know if it would do the same today. Coming before *The Boys in the Band* I think it paved the way for that kind of homosexual play of irritation and nonsentimentality. It was less sentimental than *Boys in the Band,* but I think if it had come after *Boys in the Band* it would have been more successful. I think some of the critics would have been less nervous about it. Two of the critics even said in their opening paragraphs that they hated plays about lesbians, therefore they couldn't possibly like this play. They had both seen it before and I thought they should have disqualified themselves from reviewing it. Anyway, that was not a play that was going to appeal to the lowest common denominator, just as *Chips With Everything* did not appeal to the lowest common denominator, nor *Lovers*.

Now, if you asked me, "How do I plan a play?"—Brian Friel's bittersweet *Lovers* was a play I did not want to open on Broadway opposite *Plaza Suite* and *Hello, Dolly!* So I figured out a more "cultural" approach for a play that might not console the average audience. I talked to Art Carney, and said, "Carney, would you like coming back on the stage?"

Art was unemployable at that point. It was after he had left *The Odd Couple*, unhappily, and gone to a rest home, got out of the home, divorced his wife, remarried; and nobody would give him a job in the theatre. He didn't even have the confidence to go on stage. I had to talk him into it and encourage him to do the play. And I took over the Vivian Beaumont at Lincoln Center because I thought that kind of atmosphere would be the best place to do this kind of play, and not try to compete initially with the Broadway audience. I did it in the summer as a festival production, so to speak, and then transferred it to Broadway. Then *Lovers* went on tour for five months and it did very, very well. But I think if we had even thought to open cold on Broadway, we would have had a certain kind of reaction from the press. Not all the critics loved it. Clive Barnes, who did not review it, did not like it as much as Dan Sullivan, who reviewed it for the *Times* and did like it. Everything sort of worked. Lincoln Center was the right kind of atmosphere in which to present *Lovers*.

QUESTION Do you think in the long run that people who invest money in Broadway shows can still earn a profit?

MR. GOTTLIEB Well, if you'd invested in all my shows, you'd wind up with quite a bit of profit, partly because of *Sleuth*. What happened was that some of them made a fairly good profit and some lost mild amounts. *The White House* lost about $45,000. and *P.S. I Love You* lost, oh I don't know, $75,000, and *Come Live With Me* lost some money, too.

For most of the productions, Helen Bonfils put up all the money. In the case of *Sleuth* I was prevailed upon by a couple of friends who were very successful in this business—one was Audrey Wood, the agent, who's name you know, the other Joe Stein, who wrote *Fiddler* and *Enter Laughing*—who said *Sleuth* was the ideal production to begin to line up a coterie of investors in case Helen Bonfils died. So I went to her and she agreed to let me take in a limited number of outside investors, because it looked like it would be successful. And we did, and they're very happy about it. I limited them to certain amounts of investment and they had to be rather sophisticated about the theatre and be in a position to lose that money. Most of them are multimillionaires.

I was going to do a musical of *Enter Laughing*, but I wanted large amounts of money from a handful of sources. It wasn't coming along quite that easily. I really didn't want to do any musicals, but I thought I would like to do *that* musical. I instigated the musical and suddenly decided, no, I don't want to work even on that musical. Tempermentally, I am just not suited to work in musicals. I'd much rather work on smaller units of people in a play. So the week that somebody came in with three hundred and four thousand dollars for the musical version of *Enter Laughing*, I decided to drop out.

Further to talking about plays that don't reach the lowest common denominator—when I did *Enter Laughing*, I realized that it was not the lowest common denominator for the Jewish family play, because the usual kind of Jewish family plays are the Gertrude Berg ones. "Mother always knows best!" But the nature of *Enter Laughing* is that mother *doesn't* know best and father doesn't know best. That didn't satisfy the average Jewish, middle-class, middle-aged audience. They recognized instantly it was written from the standpoint of the young people. In that play it's the younger people who always know best, and that didn't make the average Jewish theatre party lady very comfortable! That's why they do it in all the schools, because the young people win out.

So I think a producer has to know the kind of plays he wants to do. Whenever I've done a play that I didn't really love, and I tried to make a million dollars out of it, it turned out to be a terrible flop. You have to know what you want. Now, this isn't to say that there is consistency in the kinds of plays that I've done. For example, *Veronica's Room* was a mystery and so was *Sleuth. We Bombed in New Haven* was a play which I felt I couldn't make three million dollars with, but it was the only play or movie at that time which dealt with war. Even in terms of revivals of classics that dealt with war, there were no such plays or movies at that time. It came a year too late, and a year too early, actually. It came in the fall of '68 after Johnson had withdrawn and just at the time of Nixon's election. If it had opened on Broadway a year earlier, when it was actually written, it would have been very bold because Eugene McCarthy had not come along and made his statements and caught people's imagination. A year later in '69 when people saw where Nixon stood on the war, it was even more timely. It irritated, because it came face to face with certain attitudes about war. We all want to make a statement. And in that sense the statement was not unlike *Chips With Everything.* You might say, yes, I was making a statement twice about the military.

I think a producer has to know what he likes. I'm not really interested, necessarily, in irritating the public. But I would like to make certain statements. Also, once in a while, I would like to entertain the public in that old Louis B. Mayer concept. As a matter of fact, I am beginning to feel that the headlines are more dramatic than most plays. But it is important for the theatre to probe the background of the headlines. I don't mean that I want to do just a political play. What I do want to do and what I'm always looking for and have been for many years is a play about the corridors of power, meaning a play about the larger-than-life people who manipulate, who affect our lives by what they do— those people who are in conflict with others and may be in conflict with us and with the rest of the world. Now what I mean by a play about the corridors of power could be *Macbeth,* it could be *Oedipus,* it could be *Edward, My Son, The Little Foxes, Watch on the Rhine, The Best Man, State of the Union, Born Yesterday, All My Sons.* It doesn't necessarily have to be a political play. What they do and what their conflicts are—whether at home or in the office or in the world—affect the lives of everybody, and this is what we are seeing these days in the headlines.

Such a play should probe and show you other facets of behavior—I'm not saying a play about Richard Nixon, I'm not saying a play about John Mitchell—a play about people who not only tread the corridors of power, but who also manipulate the mores of the corridors of power. C.P. Snow writes novels like that (and Helen Bonfils *did* produce *The Affair,* which dealt with university life and the corridors of power there). I just think that's what I want to see these days. Now these are plays that often deal with ideas, and are always dramatic and tell a story. Unfortunately, I feel that we lost these in the '60's for encouraging many of the Off-Off-Broadway and Off-Broadway writers to write plays that didn't have a beginning, middle and end. Maybe I was responsible for getting grants from different foundations for some of them. Lanford Wilson was one. I used to write to the Ford Foundation saying, "This is a very talented playwright who has not yet written a play that I'd want to produce or that would be produced on Broadway. Some of them have been produced at Cafe Cino and other places, and he needs the money. Otherwise, he's going to starve or waste his time waiting on tables. He should be writing and writing and writing." But Lanford and others were busy writing scenes and what very often passed as a play was really just a large, one-act play. And, very often, the one-act play was an elongated set of revue sketches—Terry McNalley's *Noon* (which I loved) when it was part of *Morning, Noon, and Night,* I always felt was a hilarious ten minute revue sketch for Fanny Brice! I think *The Sea Horse* (which I like) should run for forty-five minutes. I think *Hot L Baltimore* (which I also like) should run an hour and five minutes. You can compress. But many plays that came out of the '60's and started writers were against what we call "the well-made play," which is a dirty way of saying, "telling a story with character development." I feel the plays about the corridors of power should have stories because they should be about larger-than-life characters who are in conflict.

To get back to plays of irritation—yes, I like to make a comment about our lives, I'm interested in dealing with the circumstances that affect our lives. You see, I think that the themes of *Veronica's Room* were overlooked completely by almost everyone. The duality of the nature of our lives in regard to time, space and personality—the whole schizoid notion of our lives today. Most of the critics and the public just took it as a little melodramatic situation and, actually, Ira Levin was making other statements there. It may have been too obscure or maybe they were shocked because of the necrophilia and incest, but that was part of the melodrama of the play.

QUESTION   What are the most important qualities that you feel a producer should possess?

MR. GOTTLIEB   The ability to stay alive during the failures and after the failures!

It's very interesting, you know, that many people gave up producing because they felt they never succeeded or they couldn't take it or they weren't masochistic enough (I've always said that you have to stay plenty masochistic to be in the theatre; even if you're an office boy, you have to learn to take rejection). Most of the producers who gave up producing in the theatre and went into the lamp business or the family automobile dealing business or television producing, have become enormously successful. The theatre is the best training ground in the world for getting through life. In the theatre everybody always knows that you can be fired during rehearsal, or the show can close out of town, or fold after one performance on Broadway. The inevitability is unemployment insurance, if you're lucky. I go around lecturing at schools and they ask, especially those who want to be actors, "What is the best thing I ought to know about breaking into the theatre?"

I always say, "Well, you better learn to be a bartender and a waiter first!"

I really think masochism is the best attribute to keep you alive in this business.

QUESTION   What sort of permanent staff do you retain?

MR. GOTTLIEB   I have a general manager and a stage manager who generally work exclusively for me, though occasionally when we don't have a production they may take on another job. And a company manager, when we have plays running, and a press agent and a secretary. We do all the things ourselves. We work very tightly together.

QUESTION   As a producer, how much do you usually get involved in changing or developing the script?

MR. GOTTLIEB   Well, when I read *Sleuth*—when it was *Anyone For Tennis*—it was more than double the length that it was eventually on stage. That was a year and something before it was done in London. I brought Tony Shaffer to America and we talked about an American production first. We went through various things in the script that were eventually cut, some of which he made notes on, some of which he may have forgotten, some of which other people told him about later. What I very often am good at may have little to do with the script, although presumably I have a certain sense about that, too. But I'm very good at what I call packaging and marketing a show. In other words, what you do with a play after it is open, the point of view about this package and how you sell it.

In the case of *Gigi*, to go back twenty years, I worked out a campaign months before we opened and before Audrey Hepburn was in the cast. How were we going to make whatever unknown girl we hired into a star overnight? I worked on where and how we'd do it, and what we would do, and I worked this out with the press agent. It didn't get good reviews and it didn't warrant running, except that I had sold seventy-five theatre parties months before on the basis that it was Anita Loos' first piece since the musical of *Gentlemen Prefer Blondes*, and Gilbert Miller was producing it, and if it was good enough for him to produce, it was good enough for the organizations to take for benefits. With those theatre parties we were able to stay alive and make a star out of Audrey Hepburn. We publicized nothing except her. We didn't even have Cathleen Nesbitt interviewed, nothing else—only Audrey Hepburn. And that was the point of view in packaging and marketing that show— AUDREY HEPBURN! Similarly, with *The Killing of Sister George* we minimized everything and just predicated our existence on Beryl Reid and the discovery of this personality. *Sleuth* was very difficult to promote because you couldn't tell the plot and there were only two actors and there were no women. It was a matter of publicizing the "hit" psychology—"If you are going to a theatre once, this is the thing you should go to see, because you don't see plays like this anymore!"

So what does a producer do? Once the show is on, he has to keep the quality of the production alive and make sure that everybody comes to see it—at least everybody who has the money to buy tickets.

QUESTION   Is it true that you once considered doing *Sleuth* with female performers instead of males?

MR. GOTTLIEB   I still hope to do it, but it's not easy to find the proper actress whom I feel would be right for the larger-than-life nature of the characters. I wooed Joan Crawford for a while and she was intrigued with the idea. But eventually she decided, as she has for decades, not to go back on the stage. She hasn't been on stage since she was in the second line in the chorus, way, way back. Everybody felt she'd be marvelous: Joe Mankiewicz, who directed the movie and knows her well and has written and produced a number of her movies at Metro; Anita Loos, who introduced me to her and started the idea; and Myrna Loy—they all thought it was a great idea. Many, many people felt that she'd be marvelous if she could only muster the self-confidence to do the role on stage. I mean, it was difficult enough for her to do the Town Hall interview and discussion with John Springer. She doesn't mind being on the dais, or making a speech for Pepsi Cola, or going around the country doing any of those things, but she just has a certain fear about going on stage. Oh, she would be marvelous in *Sleuth* because she is right for the part.

QUESTION What is your opinion about theatre critics. Do you think they're doing more harm than good for the Broadway theatre?

MR. GOTTLIEB Well, I wish the critics were better. What bothers me, personally, is that their tastes are different from mine. I think they are trying to change the taste of the public and I've always felt that styles and tastes only change through the creative people and the public, not through the critics. The purpose of having critics is for them to assess whether or not the creative people have succeeded at what they have tried to do. I think one of the reasons why the theatre is in a very strange state is due to the critics' notion that they can change things. This has fallen very harshly on the public, because the critics are always *over*praising— because there may be some small degree of quality, but that doesn't really satisfy an audience. When they overpraise with "this is the best thing there is," the average theatregoer leaves the theatre saying, "If that's the best theatre has to offer, then I'm going back to television where it's cheaper, or it engrosses me more. It's not worth my time."

Often the critics do overpraise certain obscure or obtuse kinds of plays. Very often these plays are not gratifying either as theatre pieces or even as intellectual exercises. Of course, they're all right if they're part of a giant diet of going to theatre. For example, I saw *The Changing Room* in London and liked it very much and considered doing it here. But I just didn't feel like doing it on Broadway. It's a play which, if there were a dozen marvelous plays all of a different nature (as there were many years ago when we might have playing at one time *Watch on the Rhine* and *Native Son* and a couple of George S. Kaufman comedies like *The Man Who Came To Dinner,* and a Philip Barry comedy of manners and a Philip Barry metaphysical play, and other plays of different styles and qualities) and *then* we have a play like *The Changing Room,* which becomes greater as part of the overall banquet. But when *The Changing Room,* good as it is, lures certain people who say, "Let's go to the theatre, we haven't been in a long, long time, and these reviews are tremendous and they're telling us it's the best thing ever on stage," and they go and it *doesn't* satisfy them—it keeps them away from the theatre for another six months. That, unfortunately, results from the overpraising.

Now it's true that the critics often try to help that kind of play, knowing that it's never going to draw the largest common-denominator audience. It's a very strange thing about critics these days, because they want to do a good job, although some of them hate going to the theatre. Some of them become bored going to the theatre and they should really stop. There should be a "rotation of crops." I think the level of the criticism is not as high as it should be. But listen, I wouldn't want to go to the theatre every night, especially covering Off-Broadway and Off-Off-Broadway and Broadway and regional productions, as some of them do. It *has* to blunt some of their sharpness. I wouldn't like to do that every night—although sometimes I do go every night, but not as a critic.

QUESTION   What do you think about the Times Square discount ticket booth? Isn't that bringing more audiences to the theatre?

MR. GOTTLIEB   I have certain apprehensions about it because it's like another nail in the coffin. What it does is tell the public not to buy seats in the balcony because you might eventually be able to sit in the orchestra for less money. So how can you pay the bills if you encourage an audience to pay less?

I think one of the reasons that *Pippin* remained so strong is that its tickets were never at the booth. I think that if the ticket booth had been in existence a year earlier, *Sleuth* would not have run so well and so long because we probably would have given in and sold the tickets there and we would have lost whole sets of audiences. You see, why should you sit in the balcony for $4.50 or $3.50 if you could sit in the orchestra for $4.75 by buying the tickets there? It's somehow the wrong concept. Now the concept of getting people to Times Square who wouldn't ordinarily go to the theatre is very good. But, especially on matinee days, I see the most affluent-looking women from the suburbs on that line! And when they talk about the students: why *should* the students sit in the orchestra if they can't afford more than a few dollars? Let them sit in the balcony! They say it brings in the young people. Someone has to sit everywhere in the theatre in order to pay the bills, and you can't pay all the bills if you're going to live on that kind of cut-rate sale. It's all right for the play that has run a couple of years and is just perpetuating its engagement by adding a few thousand dollars more a week, but it's not good for the play that is struggling to get off the ground. Once the tickets are there, people are more reluctant to pay full prices.

QUESTION   Do you think that more flexible ticket-pricing would be a good idea? For example, selling tickets in advance at a low price, then taking the price up if the play opens and turns out to be a big hit?

MR. GOTTLIEB   There have been many shows over the years that have raised their prices once they've opened. There is no law against it. Everybody was urging me to raise the price of *Sleuth* to $10.00 right after we opened, but I refused to do it, because I figured in the second year, or a year and a half after it was running there might be a certain apprehension, a resistance to paying $10.00 at that point. And I couldn't reduce the prices then. But there is nothing that stops you from raising the prices at any time you want, if you think you can get it.

How does one get more people to come to the theatre? Well, there are many ways. One is to have a healthier point of view about the theatre and, of course, some more good plays would help, and some more stars coming back to the theatre, stars whom people want to see. Cleaning up the area, getting rid of the stigma that it's unsafe to walk around—part of that stigma is perpetuated by the television comics and used to be publicized by the *New York Times*. But I think many things have been done for improvement.

If somehow we could backtrack on some of the rising costs, so that we could stay alive with the play that isn't a sure-fire smash hit. If plays could pay off more quickly, that would help. You see, the public loves to talk about plays that earn a profit, and people love to see a show that is a hit, and a "hit" means a show that has paid off. If the costs could be curtailed, we might have more hits.

QUESTION   How could you cut back on production costs?

MR. GOTTLIEB   I think you have to do it in every area. I think you somehow have to find a way of holding down some of the salaries and percentages. That's not easy because everyone wants to grab. They demand it, and many deserve what they can get.

Costs of sets, like everything else, are going up. I think payroll taxes are too high. Stars' salaries are high.

You know, the difference between Broadway and Off-Broadway and Off-Off-Broadway is that Off-Off-Broadway lives on coolie labor, Off-Broadway is half-coolie labor. And people have to earn a living.

And newspaper advertising—much, much too high.

QUESTION   We're always hearing about how Broadway is dying. Is it?

MR. GOTTLIEB   Well, it seems to be happening all the time. There's no question that television has not only drawn the public away from the theatre, but has also drawn a lot of creative talent away from the theatre. I know somebody who twenty or twenty-five years ago would have been writing marvelous satiric comedies. Instead, he is writing, directing and producing TV commercials and has become a millionaire. The movies are complaining, except for the blockbusters. But there are always blockbusters, and there are always blockbusters in the theatre, too.

For a while the *New York Times* loved to report negative things about the theatre. I think when the *Times* takes a healthier point of view about the theatre, it always helps a great deal. The *Times* always used to claim that it was interested only in the artistic side and not in the commercial side. Yet, for many years there were constant articles about the low financial circumstances in the theatre. And they're not even on the business page! I mean, if they were talking about the low financial state of one of the publishing houses, you wouldn't find it in the book review section on

Sunday, you'd find it in the financial section. The theatre has always been for much of the press a marvelous whipping boy, especially since the '30's. For the last twenty years, the *New York Times* has loved talking about disaster in the theatre—you know, "the fabulous invalid!" But somehow, happily, that's changed a bit and the theatre (and theatre business) is looking better—even on the pages of the *New York Times*.

And I wouldn't be in any other business!

Commentary by *Warren Caro*

Director of Theatre Operations,
The Shubert Organization, Inc.,
New York City

*Note: This session in the series was
held in the Executive Offices of the
Shubert Theatre in Manhattan,
more than a year after most other
sessions recorded in this book.*

I'm pleased that we're able to have this meeting here in a
theatre building. Maybe a little later you'll be hearing some
of the music from *Over Here*, which is playing downstairs.
And, incidentally, I just saw Alexander Cohen, who has an
office upstairs, and he might drop in on us a little later—
after he returns from notifying his cast of the closing of his
current play, *Who's Who in Hell*, which opened only last
night and which stars Peter Ustinov.

So, let's begin: How did I get interested in the theatre?

I guess it goes back to the time when I was a kid. I had
always loved the theatre, though I never got into it directly.
After graduation from school, I went into law. I went to
Cornell University Law School and had a thirteen-year
span in law, always keeping the theatre as my prime avoca-
tion. I just *loved* the theatre and would go whenever I could
get tickets for ninety-nine cents at Gray's Drugstore for a
Saturday matinee. I followed the theatre in whatever ways I
could and saw all the plays and musicals I could.

Then there were the war years. I was in Washington at
the time Pearl Harbor took place and I enlisted in the U.S.

Coast Guard—in wartime a part of the U.S. Navy . Ultimately, I wound up as an officer in the Coast Guard in Alaska, and you can't get farther away from Broadway than that. But, interestingly, I more or less got my introduction to the theatre in Alaska from the Governor of the Territory, a man named Ernest Gruening. He was a New Yorker who had known a great many people in the theatre, both in the producing end of it and in the press. He had known playwrights like Bob Sherwood, and members of the Playwrights Company, and the producers at The Theatre Guild. It was his letter of introduction to The Theatre Guild that got me a job. The letter simply indicated that, having been a lawyer for some period of time, I wanted to change my profession. He understood my feelings because the same thing had happened to him. (Governor Gruening later became, by the way, the Senator from Alaska—he and Wayne Morse were the only two people who voted against the Gulf of Tonkin Resolution and he was one of the first spokesmen against the Vietnam War. So I always felt that *he* should have gotten the Nobel Peace Prize and not Kissinger, because he really fought against the whole involvement at a time when it was very unpopular to do so.) Anyway, his background was New York and he had been educated as a doctor (he graduated from Harvard as a doctor) but his interest was in journalism. So he didn't practice medicine but got a job on the *Boston Globe* and eventually moved up from a reporter to become Editor of the *New York Herald Tribune* and then of *The Nation*. Then he got into government service, which really seemed to fulfill his wishes more than anything else, and from the Department of the Interior, President Roosevelt appointed him as Governor of the Territory of Alaska. He was a marvelous man.

Being the senior officer in Alaska, stationed in the capital, I had the luck to be appointed as his Naval Aide and we developed a great fondness for each other. Eventually, he wrote this letter of introduction for me to The Theatre Guild. The Theatre Guild at that time was at the height of its successes. *Oklahoma!* had just been produced and was running, and *Carousel* was to follow. So The Theatre Guild was in the position where it was earning a great deal of money and paying a great deal in taxes. They felt that as long as Senator Gruening, who was their friend, had this kind of enthusiasm, they couldn't lose very much by putting on this young man who seemed so interested in theatre. So instead of paying taxes, they paid me a salary—$75 a week. That's how I got into theatre, through the back door from Alaska!

It was a matter of starting at the top rather than from the bottom. I mean by that that I was an assistant to the producers of The Theatre Guild—Lawrence Langner and Theresa Helburn kind of created the job. I was an Executive Secretary for them. Whatever would come in for them in the morning I would read and analyze and try to deal with as far as I could, or, at least, simplify it for them. Having had legal experience didn't hurt, because there were large contracts submitted. I'd attach a memo to a contract and say, "This contract seems to be in accordance with what you had worked out, except for paragraph so-and-so on page so-and-so," and this would save Mr. Langner from having to read a thirty-four page document. And I would write letters and answer letters for their signature and, gradually, various assignments fell to me that Mr. Langner didn't want to do or Miss Helburn didn't want to do—they were were the principal producers.

We got into new projects, such as television, and we did the first experimental, full-hour dramatic show that was done on television. It was a nonprofit experiment with NBC. It's hard to think of that because that was done in 1947, which seems like ages ago! The question at that time really was whether or not television *was* an entertainment medium. There was a lot of debate as to whether television should just be a reporting medium or possibly an entertainment medium.

Anyway, gradually I built up the job by trying to make myself indispensable, because this is a tough business and there aren't many jobs that exist—aside from the regular categories of producer, general manager, company manager, press agent, box office treasurer and so forth. They're all well-defined jobs and if you're not qualified for them and don't belong to those unions, you don't get the regular jobs. My position eventually expanded from assistant to the producers of The Theatre Guild to developing a number of productions, financing them, supervising a number of shows, and being the active producer on certain shows. We also developed a national subscription series around the country for plays put on by The Theatre Guild and by other producers. So that's my background. There are no clear cut ways to become whatever you aspire to in the theatre, as you can see from my experience.

My present position with The Shubert Organization came about simply from a kind offer by the then-president of the Organization. As Director of Theatre Operations (a fancy title!) I work on booking the shows and supervising the shows that are brought into our theatres.

I'm speaking, of course, about the Broadway theatre, and I think it would be valuable for us to have some sort of orientation. Obviously, there are other forms of theatre throughout the country—the institutional theatre, the regional theatre, the nonprofit operations, the cultural centers and so forth. But my experience has all been in the Broadway theatre.

We had a theatre congress [The First American Congress of Theatre (FACT)] last summer, for which Alex Cohen was the principal organizer. We had the same need then to define what we meant by different forms of theatre. I was on the steering committee that drew up a precis for the congress and perhaps part of that can tell you how we see the theatre that we're going to talk about here:

> The Broadway and Off-Broadway professional theatre is commonly referred to as the "commercial" theatre. Actually, this is misleading. In reality it is an art conducted as a business in a free enterprise society—and, as such, it is heir to all the vicissitudes as well as the advantages of free enterprise. More exactly, Broadway and Off-Broadway theatre might better be described as the "self-supporting" theatre. Inescapably, it must pay its own way: it has, for the most part, no subsidy, no help from any source other than private investors and its own box office. Its losses, annually, far exceed it profits.

I won't burden you with a lot of statistics, but that is a fact. Actually, a *few* shows make money but the overall picture is one of loss, and has been for the last several years.

> In essence, the self-supporting theatre is a paradox: its production activities are centered in the most expensive city in the world; it is ridden by the towering costs of production and real estate, and riven by internal feuds; it is burdened by excessive charges of labor and materials; and operates under superimposed restrictions both from within and without—a vast labyrinth of union requirements of endless and needless complexity, together with onerous laws, arbitrary rules and capricious regulations (Federal, State and municipal)—that have proliferated over a long period and exist today without any systematic design relevent to contemporary conditions.

A lot of words to say that we *are* hampered by regulations that were passed many years ago, sometimes on an emotional basis, and that don't really make any sense in today's economy.

> And yet, from all of these pressures and from the mad scrimmage known as "show business," there emerge every season works of art—challenging and thought-provoking dramas, bright comedies, and new forms of lyric theatre in which libretto and music, dance and decor are blended in arresting new productions. Somehow or other, the self-supporting theatre of Broadway and Off-Broadway which constantly struggles for its existence, does manage to bring forth year after year at least one or two pearls of great price—productions, plays, or performances which really have the incandescence of great theatre.
>
> Compared to its gargantuan sister arts, television and motion pictures, the self-supporting theatre—no longer the mass medium of entertainment—is a small, intimate profession, one of the last strongholds of individualism in this country. There are only about a hundred Broadway producers presenting plays in some thirty-four Broadway legitimate theatres. The annual volume of business in New York on Broadway alone is roughly around forty-five million dollars, and on the road approximately fifty-five million, a total of one hundred million dollars, as compared with other industries which run into the billions.
>
> Yet the self-supporting, professional theatre has unique significance, not simply as an economic stimulant for the City of New York, but as a crucible of creativity, a fountainhead maintaining high standards of excellence and a vital

artistic resource—providing properties to be performed throughout the United States and the world, as well as supplying subject matter from which films and television productions are constantly derived.

Now the other side of that coin is that, obviously, there have been changes in the past ten years, during which the resident theatres are *beginning* to make some sort of contribution to the total scene. We've seen shows like *The Great White Hope*, a marvelous show that came from the Arena Stage in Washington. *Candide*, which is now in one of our theatres here, the Broadway Theatre, was a co-production with Harold Prince and the Chelsea Theatre Center done, originally, at the Brooklyn Academy of Music. *Much Ado About Nothing*, which had a very successful Broadway run, was Joe Papp's production, developed by him in Central Park, as was *Two Gentlemen of Verona*. So there is a stronger contribution being made now in terms of original material or plays, which I'm very happy about—because if there's one thing we don't need in this business, it's a lot of needless division between the various facets of theatre. I think it's *all* theatre. It doesn't matter where it originates or comes from, it's not good to have one side of it denouncing the other side.

It used to make me very angry when I would lecture at some university or community group and they would say, "Well, the Broadway theatre is only interested in commercial things—the fast dollar—and the real art is done here in Pittsburgh or Cincinnati or wherever."

I would usually ask them to read the list of plays that they were going to do that season, and nearly every single play turned out to be a play that had been done on Broadway and developed on Broadway. So I'd say, "If you have a playwright who's able to produce a marvelous piece of work, great! That's what we want! We're not trying to monopolize theatre. But in the meantime, don't denounce us and then produce *The Odd Couple* and *Death of a Salesman* and *Liliom* and everything that *we* put on and created!"

Now I'll tell you briefly what our work is here—it's much too complex for any one session. I had the fun one summer of teaching a course in theatre production at the University of Hawaii. That went on for six weeks and that's just about how long it takes thoroughly to go into the production of a play from the time it's first acquired by a producer to the time the curtain goes up on the opening night—a tremendous amount of complexity. But let me tell you what the arrangements are with our theatres.

The Shubert Organization is the owner of seventeen theatres on Broadway, which is about half of the total scene. I mentioned before there are thirty-four theatres. In one case we only own half a theatre, the other half is owned by Irving Berlin. That's the Music Box Theatre, where *Absurd Person Singular* is now playing. As the owner of these buildings, it's our job to keep them filled and to keep them occupied with attractions.

I don't know how many of you know what the arrangement is between the theatre (ourselves) and the producer. Many people think the producer comes in, since he has the show, leases our theatre and just pays rent, like you would lease a building or a store, something of the sort. Well, it's not quite like that. It's more like a partnership or a joint venture in the sense that we usually share with the producer parts of his costs and, in turn, we share the gross receipts of the theatre with him.

Let's say the box office of a theatre with a big musical like *Gypsy* (which we now have at the Winter Garden Theatre) takes in $100,000 a week, which these days is not a large amount. The grosses for musicals actually are much larger, but we'll take that as a figure. Those gross receipts of $100,000 would then be divided between the producer of the play and the owner of the theatre in a ratio of seventy-five percent to the producer and twenty-five percent to the theatre. This is by no means a fixed amount, these terms are all negotiable, but it's an example. We're saying that out of every dollar, the producer gets seventy-five cents and we, the theatre, get twenty-five cents. Then each side pays its respective costs. The show has to pay all the costs of everything that's on the stage—the actors, the musicians in part (we usually share the musicians costs with the producers and we share the stage hands), but everyone on the producer's payroll is paid by him. He has many miscellaneous charges: accounting fees, legal fees, publicity charges. And the difference between his share at capacity—$75,000—and his *costs* represents his profit. Let's say it costs him $65,000 to run the show for the week, and he got $75,000. Then he would obviously have a profit of $10,000. And on our side, if we got $25,000 from a musical of that size, our costs would be in the neighborhood of $20,000 for the week, and we would make a profit of $5,000. This is, of course, assuming that the play does that kind of business. That's basically the arrangement, so we are in effect a partner with the producer and from the time that the show opens, consequently, we're involved with the producer in everything he does with that show.

Another example is *Pippin,* which we have in the Imperial Theatre. *Pippin* had a rather curious experience. It started off in a rather uncertain way, then came to be highly successful for a period, and then took a big drop. We thought that was going to be the end of it. But the producer came to us, saying that he thought the way this show should be conveyed to the public was through television advertising, not through the usual, stale newspaper advertising. So we created a marvelous television commercial which increased sales spectacularly and really had the effect of turning that show around from a downgrade run to the most successful musical on Broadway.

The point that I want to make is that when the producer thought that television was the way to sell this production, he came to us and asked us to share the expense of it on the theory that every ticket represents seventy-five cents for him and twenty-five cents for us. So if he could sell more tickets by this method, obviously it's fair for him to ask us to share the cost of it in some way, which we did. And we help in many other ways, wherever we can. So in effect we are partners. We're not just a landlord and tenant relationship.

I won't bore you with all the details that are involved in running the theatres—we have a manager in each of the theatres who settles things for us, and the show also has a general manager who handles its financial affairs.

Incidently, let me explain something so that you won't be disturbed by it. In the next half hour or so you'll see tracking up here a·uniformed porter from each of our theatres. Each theatre has its ticket box locked after the audience is in for each and every performance. Then the box is brought up here to be checked independently. We have a Count-Up Room in the back of this office—a very old tradition—in which the receipts are checked nightly and every matinee against what the box office has supplied. So we keep very close supervision over each box office. The Central Count-Up Room is a unique creation of The Shubert Organization, and serves the all-important function of assuring that the producer and the theatre receives a completely accurate accounting of box office sales—first through the box office itself, then through a wholly independent auditing unit responsible for certifying the accuracy of the box office figures as they come in each day.

Maybe at this point we should invite a few questions.

Questions to *Warren Caro*

QUESTION   How is it decided when to close a show, especially one that has been running for a long time?

MR. CARO   Well there are, as I've said, no subsidies and no foundations—we have to pay our own way. And in order to pay our own way we have to take in money at the box office. It's just like running a store. If it costs you $10,000 a week to run that store and you're only taking in $5,000 and you have to pay the people who work behind the counters, the delivery boys and so forth, then you will find yourself paying $5,000 week after week out of your own pocket, out of your own wallet. How long anybody can do that is a great question. There are very few producers with such resources and, besides, it just doesn't make sense to do it. So that when you think about closing is the point when your income, that is admissions at the box office, are less than your outgo, your expenses.

Now, we try in every way to pre-sell a show, to pre-sell it by theatre parties, by benefits which are purchased by organizations; we try to do it by mail order sales, by group sales. We've introduced Ticketron as a method of selling to outlying places, and credit cards are now honored by the theatres. We're constantly trying lots of ways to bring money into the box office *before* a show opens, so that there is a cushion we can ride on if the show isn't well received. Some shows overcome poor reviews, but rarely shows where there is no great advance in the box office. It's like the play which Mr. Cohen opened last night and which got unanimously poor notices. He wasn't surprised by it, because he had hoped for certain changes to be made before opening but one way or another they couldn't be worked out, and it got tepid reviews—respectful, but poor. So he knew today that there were no people coming to the box office buying tickets. Therefore, added to let's say a zero advance sale, it was still zero after he opened. That meant that for each week he ran he would be going into his own pocket to cover thé losses. So the decision is made on the basis of the break-even figure. The moment that you take in less money than you have to shell out, then you can't run any more, unless you're J. Paul Getty or somebody who just for the kick of it wants to pour money into the show and keep his ego happy.

Now *Mack and Mabel* was a show that did have an advance and up to this past week it has theatre parties and box office sales, not huge, but enough that might enable it to run. Let's say that show has to take in $80,000 a week in order to pay its expenses (which is not too far off) and it has $55,000 a week in theatre parties. The balance will have to be sold at the box office. If it *isn't* selling, you can see—you can look in the box office. You know where you are at all times, because you look at the racks and you see that those tickets have not been sold. So it's prudent to terminate.

Well, here's the expert on this: here is Mr. Alexander H. Cohen. He needs no introduction.

MR. COHEN   He needs plenty!

MR. CARO   The question, Alex, is how do you decide when to close a play?

MR. COHEN   Perfect timing!

It's really a very simple decision—the box office tells you. Sometimes you get great notices and do no business. Sometimes you get lousy notices and do big business. It's very unpredictable. But with the kind of notices we got today, it *was* predictable!

MR. CARO   And they also want to know, Alex, when you have a very successful run, as you did, let's say, with *Beyond the Fringe,* which ran four years, how do you decide when you should quit?

MR. COHEN   When it stops making money, that's all.

The one thing that I would like to say, one thing that I thought was very interesting, was that Mr. Langley sent me a transcript of the comments I made at a seminar like this one over a year ago, and I thought, "Oh, my God, I'm not going to read a transcript." But I was on a flight to Boston and I did, and was fascinated to find that I would say today *precisely* what I did then. I would be just as discouraging to people who want to go into the business aspect of the theatre today for any profit motivation as I was then.

And I'm fascinated, also, to find that you have the good taste and the great intelligence to call upon my friend Warren Caro for this session, because I believe that on an administrative level there isn't anybody who is functioning in the American theatre today who knows as much about it as Mr. Caro does. Thanks and good night.

MR. CARO   Thanks for dropping in, Alex.

Well, it really *is* that simple, because we're not subsidized. See, if you're running a theatre that is part of that community, let's say the Minneapolis theatre, founded by Tyrone Guthrie, which is very well directed, that theatre *knows* that it's going to have a deficit at the end of the year and plans accordingly and goes out to raise money from the foundations and corporations to pick up the deficit. They have tremendous losses. If they sell every seat, they will *still* come out with a deficit. So they have an annual fund-raising problem.

But here on Broadway we're still in the old-fashioned business of trying to pay our own way which, as I said, is why it angers all of us, who work pretty hard, to be criticized for supporting ourselves. I mean, what is so sinful about paying your own way?

QUESTION   Does The Shubert Organization usually help the producers find backers for their shows?

MR. CARO   No, because we are not the producers of the plays. It's the producer's job, you see, to raise the money for producing the play. However, we do help out in many other ways.

When the producer has extreme difficulty and we have some confidence in his production, we try to assist him if he cannot raise the final money for the show. Very recently, there was a show done right downstairs in this theatre, *A*

Little Night Music, and that reached the point in its financing where it simply could not raise the last $200,000 in the time available. So it was either a question of our helping in some way or of not getting the show on. We took a calculated estimate of what we thought the show was really worth in terms of its quality, and we did make that investment and fortunately we were lucky. I'm not saying that we're geniuses in this business. Whenever somebody thinks he knows it all in this business is when he should get out! But we did get our money back and made a profit besides, and we enabled the show to get on. But, normally, the theatre owner does not get involved in the financing. Our job is to maintain these buildings, which is a big enough job in itself, in terms of the maintenance, mortgages, insurance, taxes, the whole business of the real estate.

But remember there are two parties to every agreement. So when you see a show downstairs, you're seeing the show, the performance, created by a producer, and you're seeing it in the theatre owned by the theatre owner.

QUESTION How involved do you become, artistically, in the shows that come into your theatres; and does The Shubert Organization ever invest in shows?

MR. CARO Yes, indeed. We're trying to encourage productions. We know that raising money is very, very difficult. While we're not an unlimited resource, and we're very selective, we have invested in order to get certain shows on. I'll give you another recent example—*The Magic Show,* now very successful at the Cort Theatre. That show was very questionable. I was asked to go to Toronto to see a remarkable illusionist, a magician named Doug Henning. He was playing up there in a tiny little theatre and they had a pallid show surrounding him. He alone, however, was terrific. You could tell at once that he was a great magician and illusionist. So they said, "What do you think about it?"

Fortunately, the producers of the show, Lansbury and Beruh, who also produced *Godspell,* were able to convince Stephen Schwartz, who wrote the scores for *Godspell* and *Pippin,* to do the music and lyrics and Bob Randall to do the book for this show. And then it became a question of money. They were short a certain amount of money—I think it was $40,000. And, again, we invested in the show. But, having gotten it on, we sold off our investments to others, because basically it's not our business to deal with investments, but rather with the running of the theatres. But the important point is that we got that show on.

So that has been a new policy with The Shubert Organization in the past two or three years, because there has been a vast change in the administration of the Organization, which is far too complicated to go into. But the people now in control, the principal executive directors, and especially Bernard B. Jacobs who is the chief of theatre operations, are far-reaching in their vision and in their policies, and are bringing in some enlightened and innovative ideas to give energy to the theatre and to help rejuvenate the whole scene.

QUESTION   When a producer comes to you with a show, do you make a decision as to whether or not it's suitable for a Shubert theatre?

MR. CARO   Yes, we make choices. If we have theatres that are vacant and there is nothing else available other than that one show, then we'd probably book it. We'd book anything sponsored by a bona fide producer and properly financed, because we feel that everything should have an opportunity to be presented. But if there is just one theatre available and *three* people want it, then obviously a choice has to be made—an artistic and a business choice. We have a very close relationship with the producers. I mean, take a man like Alexander Cohen—I talk with him practically every day, and with other producers. He will sound you out, because he knows that eventually he's going to have to work with you. So he'll say, "What would you think of so-and-so to play such-and-such a part?" And he's talking both artistically and commercially. So we are involved in that because we're not purely a landlord sitting back renting a piece of property. And from our point of view that is significant, because it gives us a great interest in just about everything that goes on.

Very frequently the producer asks us for an opinion. I

remember when a play by Arthur Laurents, called *The Enclave,* was playing in Washington and David Merrick had the rights to bring it to New York and asked if I would come down and take a look at it. It's *tough* to take a position, because you can be quite wrong. I've been wrong many times. I mean, I'm famous for not having seen the values in *Hair!* I never knew what it was about. When they came for a theatre, I didn't see the urgency of it. Nobody else saw it either. They finally got the Biltmore Theatre, which took them almost as a favor, because everybody was saying, "What is it?" You know, *Hair* was totally new. Its success is *still* a mystery to a lot of people. So you can miss on these things. You can't be right all the time.

But, to answer your question, we are indeed involved on an artistic level. We read all the scripts, we see all the plays in London, we go out of town wherever a likely property is being presented. I've just been told this week that a new musical based on the music and lyrics of Gilbert Becaud has just opened in Buffalo, it's called *Gabrielle* and it stars Tammy Grimes and is written and directed by José Quintero. They think it's outstanding—it's gotten three or four great reviews in Buffalo, so I will fly up there on Saturday, see the show, talk with the people about how much it will cost to bring in, what kind of a theatre we have available for it, and what kind of theatre it *needs.* It's very helpful to know what you're dealing with, because the theatre itself is a very important factor. Sometimes a small show is done in an overpowering theatre where it doesn't belong. Mr. Cohen's *Ulysses in Nighttown* suffered because of that, only because there was no other theatre that we could offer him. That show did not belong in the Winter Garden, which is a big theatre. So that's, to some extent, the nature of our involvement.

QUESTION We hear so much about the pending death of Broadway and how inflation and high costs are making it impossible to produce in the traditional ways. What do you think about the future of Broadway?

MR. CARO Well, from a sane point of view, a logical point of view, we would probably be better off selling all these properties and building office buildings or just collecting the revenues. However, there is a great tradition here. The Shubert Organization is now celebrating its seventy-fifth year! Of course, the original Shubert brothers were quite some fellows! They could be pretty tough—they were often described as rough bastards—but in reality they did a great many things for the well-being of the theatre. They kept the theatres running through the Depression, they encouraged production and they produced themselves. But we're interested in the survival of theatre, because the plays that are created here eventually reach the entire world. And I'm not exaggerating. When *My Fair Lady* was originally done, or *The Sound of Music*, nobody knew whether they were going to do exactly as Mr. Cohen's show did—close on Saturday night—or if they were going to run for several years. Yet, *My Fair Lady* has been presented in every country in the world, as has *Fiddler on the Roof*, and has been made into a marvelous motion picutre, so has *Sound of Music*, which has been entertaining the peoples of the world from here to South Africa—and even in England! So we want to keep that art, if you want to call it that, or that business, going—even though it might be to our financial advantage to sell these buildings.

The building that we are now in, for example, is ridiculous economically. We haven't got any height. If you look out the window from the third story—the *top* story—of this building, next door to us you will see the Minskoff Building, which includes a theatre, but which goes up thirty-nine storys, I think, and is obviously set up to produce far more revenue.

We're in a fortunate position, however. When these properties were acquired, they were not worth nearly as much as they are today. The Shuberts had the foresight—when the theatre was centered at 14th Street, then at 23rd Street, then 34th—to realize that eventually the whole complex had to move uptown. So they bought these properties very reasonably and now they're owned outright with practically no mortgages. So The Shurbert Organization is in a sound financial position and feels that it has a duty—indeed, a mission—to keep the theatres going.

QUESTION   Have any attempts been made to utilize Broadway theatres for nontheatrical, revenue-producing purposes during the daytime hours when there are no performances going on? Wouldn't that help the economy of the theatre?

MR. CARO   Well, the way they're situated the unions can run you into a great many extra costs which you really don't need. The moment you connect the power, you've got to have electricians around. That's why some shows, like *Sergeant Pepper*, can't face all those costs, so they seek out a theatre like the Beacon, which is not unionized. I've tried myself many times to get children's theatre on during daytime hours, and it's the most difficult thing in the world! It makes perfect sense to use the theatre at hours when you wouldn't otherwise be using it. But when you start figuring out how many people you have to employ at the prevailing scales, it becomes unworkable. It is really a damned shame that these buildings are used in effect only three hours a day.

We do, occasionally, use them for other, related purposes. Last night we had a reception for Elia Kazan at the Lyceum Theatre, because he has a new book coming out and he wanted to have the reception on a stage. So we made arrangements to use the theatre for that purpose, which is related. And we use the theatres also for benefits, for ceremonies, for non-profit activities.

QUESTION   Do you think more television advertising for Broadway shows will help keep more of them open for longer periods of time?

MR. CARO   Well, I don't think that you can sell anything that's mediocre for very long. People find out about it through word of mouth. But a good production can be vastly aided by television.

The experience with *Pippin* was quite interesting, however, because when you sat in the theatre and you reached the point where they do that same scene that they show on the TV commercial, the whole damned audience got wildly enthusiastic, because they identified what they saw on television.

QUESTION I know that The Shubert Foundation gives money to help develop new playwrights. Have you ever considered setting aside one of your Broadway theatres to present new plays and playwrights, to help develop them?

MR. CARO There are already several places that do something similar to that—St. Clements has such a theatre, Joe Papp does it at his theatre downtown, there is La Mama and others. But, so far, it has just not been feasible on Broadway. We need all of the theatres to service Broadway productions and to generate enough income at least to cover expenses. But it's not a bad idea, if some foundation or private source could support it.

In fact, we *have* done something similar. We effectually *gave* the theatre to the APA-Phoenix organization—they operated in the Lyceum Theatre, had their own workshop for several years until they, themselves, couldn't make ends meet. But we didn't charge them for that theatre. It's a good idea.

But the fact is that we have to earn much more money now, because of the economy. You see, some of the theatres are just too small. The Booth Theatre that we have here (except for small productions, one man shows and the like) doesn't generate enough revenue to make ends meet for the producer or for the theatre. These costs are not of our making. Oh, in some cases they are, if you say that you don't have to pay a star $5,000 a week. But if you want that star and feel he or she is that important, you pay it—I have no idea of what they are paying Mr. Rex Harrison, who is opening in a new play right this very minute across the street at the Morosco, but they're paying him a good sum of money, I should think. Most of the costs are beyond our control. Our union costs have gone up about forty percent in the last few years, such as the musicians and the stagehands. Just like anything else, anything else you care to talk about. So we have to scale the smaller houses at much higher prices, and we're very sorry to do it. You can look at the statistics in *Variety,* we lose every year—that is, on the total—we lose more than we make.

The Cultural Centers

Norman Singer
Sir Rudolf Bing
Harvey Lichtenstein

Commentary by *Norman Singer*

Executive Director, City Center of
Music and Dance, Inc.*, New York
City

I can be described as having had a varied background, or a
lot of incomplete careers, and none of them, I would say, really led to the position I have now as Director of the City
Center of Music and Dance. I started out training to be a
lawyer and was saved from that by the war. I left law school
and began studying Russian. In the 1940's Russian was a
very exotic language and various centers had been set up
around the United States for exotic languages—Japanese,
Siamese, all the things that were not normally needed before the war. At Cornell they set up a Russian institute, so I
became a Russian fellow at the Council of Learned Societies and spent a great deal of time (actually five months) doing nothing but studying Russian. Naturally, when I got
into the army I was in the German division!

When I came back from the Army, I spent a week at law
school and became a disturbed veteran and quit. My family
has never discussed that week thirty years ago—they had all
the manuals about returned veterans. I decided I didn't
want to go to law school and so I studied sociology with a
psychology minor at Columbia University and got my M.A.
and then got all the course credits for a Ph.D. which, of

---

*Mr. Singer resigned as Executive Director on September 1, 1974, but remained as
a consultant to the organization.

course, I did not finish. I had begun by that time teaching at the Juilliard School of Music in the academic division. I suppose that's the part that pulled me over into the arts world. I had planned all along to resist my father's business in Rockaway Beach, which was right across the water from us, and to become an intellectual, no matter what happened. I struggled hard, but somehow it wasn't ever going to be possible.

At the Juilliard School of Music, teaching sociology and psychology to music students (they had a regular degree program and they needed sociology and psychology) I got involved with a group of people who were teaching in the summer at the Aspen School of Music in Aspen, Colorado. I used to complain a great deal about the fact that at the school they had no counseling service at all for students and I found, since I was teaching psychology, that questions would inevitably lead to personal problems and then to me. I felt very reluctant to get caught up in that since I hadn't had any kind of training. Coincidentally, at that time I started out to be analyzed, psychoanalyzed, and then later decided that it would be rather interesting to actually take some courses. (Unlike Daniel Ellsberg, my files are open—they're so uninteresting!) At that point I decided that I would in the most altruistic manner possible keep on with psychoanalysis and take analytic courses so I could become a better teacher. I know that sounds inane, but that was my attitude at the time. Then I was asked to go out to Aspen, Colorado. Actually, I think what they wanted was somebody who would be a dean of students, since I was organizing student activities by that time at Juilliard. They had no academic dean and in a very short time, in fact overnight, I was asked to prepare a catalogue and I became the dean of the music school, without formal training as a musician, although I had taken piano, flute and recorder lessons.

The person who was running the festival had not done a very good job and at the end of my first year running the music school I had done a comparatively good job—at least by all of the psychological principles of contrast, it *looked* as if I had done a very good job. I was asked to become the administrator of the Aspen Music Festival, as well as dean of the music school. So I gave up my psychoanalysis, I hadn't finished law school, I hadn't studied to become a Russian scholar, I hadn't finished my Ph.D. But I consider all of this very helpful because it's made me a very useful ear for a lot of hysterical artists, though in none of this was there any plan of becoming an arts administrator. Very briefly, I was at Aspen for eight years, the only one to leave of his own volition in that whole eight-year period—perhaps just in time. Then the Hunter College Concert Bureau was the next place I was for six years and then I became the director of City Center of Music and Drama.

City Center is in a sense a conglomerate. It's made up of what we might call prime constituents and affiliated constituents. The New York City Opera and the New York City Ballet are organizations for which we maintain complete responsibility and complete support. The City Center Young Peoples' Theatre, which we just began a year or so ago, is another full-fledged constituent. We have a fourth division which operates under the name of Special Productions and Foreign Attractions, a series of *ad hoc* activities which do not involve a full company or an on-going season. For example, we had several seasons of modern dance, an American dance marathon that's handled by the *ad hoc* group, we have street programs, we have senior citizen programs, we go into schools, we have students on school-time programs in the theatres themselves, we will bring foreign attractions that the Hurok or Columbia managements may not feel are going to be commercial enough, but which we think should be seen. Jean Louis Barrault came over in a production of *Rabelais*, for example. And then we allow the house at 55th Street to be booked for regular commercial showings by the Hurok and other agencies. The opera and the ballet are at the State Theatre. We also have several constituents for whom we do not assume complete responsibility, and in this case these constituents have their own boards and we either subsidize their New York season or act as a kind of foundation by ourselves and give them a subsidy.

The City Center Joffrey Ballet, which appears at the 55th Street theatre, the Alvin Ailey City Center Dance Theatre, currently at City Center (I didn't realize I was going to be able to make a plug for business!), the City Center Acting Company, John Houseman's group which came out of Juilliard and only began last year, mainly tours, but we are involved in their New York season. We are in the development stage now for the City Center Cinematheque, which is going to, it hopes, raise ten million dollars to build a cinematheque underneath the 59th Street Bridge where it will be the first and the largest cinema museum in the country (if its the first it has to be the largest, so that's an easy statement to make). They will have not only a great exhibition space but three film centers going practically all day long with the archives available to us from the French Cinematheque.

I think I've listed everybody: there are four affiliated constituents: the Ailey Company, the Joffrey Company, the Acting Company of John Houseman's and the Cinematheque. And then we have our three prime constituents: the opera, the ballet and the children's theatre. And, of course, the Center constituent, which does all the other activities and productions.

Now I'm asked to indicate or to define the difference between a producer and a manager. This was brought very clearly to mind just before I left my office today. A young Israeli choreographer, who I brought in touch with the ballet theatre and the Joffrey Theatre, because he hoped to be able to do something for them, came to see me. He had actually choreographed something for the ballet theatre and he's now working on something for the Joffrey and they're all very excited. He's been here a very short time and he's leaving tomorrow night. In their meeting they discussed decor, they discussed costumes, they are caught up with the theme which is based on *The Dybbuk*. Now they need a composer—actually what they need is not the composer, but $12,000 with which to pay the composer, the copyrighting of the music, and the preparation of the parts. This fellow came to me and asked what I could do to help him get $12,000. In other words, everybody else is having the fun, is having a creative opportunity, and the job now for the manager is to find the money so they can go on having the fun and the pleasure. I think that's a good distinction between the manager and the producer. The producer will, of course, have headaches, but he will be putting things together, he will be involved to a very large extent in the creative process, even if it's only choosing further down the line the other creative people—the composers, the choreographers, the costumers. But the manager is somebody who's going to have to assume fiscal responsibility for the operation and all of the business details. Now we have a very clear point in the City Center by-laws, which say that the board of directors, and hence the director who is responsible to the board, will not be involved in any of the artistic concerns at any point. When Balanchine or Rudel or heads of other companies feel that there *is* such interference, they have the right to appear before the board and are actually given a vote at that board meeting to present their case against such interference, presumably by the executive director or the members of the board.

Of course, assuming the fiscal responsibility and setting up the budget makes whoever's in my position, the manager's position, the one who's going to be the most resented person around, because he is going to say, "You can only have "X" thousand dollars for this production and therefore your artistic aspirations are going to have to be limited." So you have an involvement, but one only of a restraining kind.

On the other hand (Harvey [Lichtenstein] will be interested in knowing this!), there was one person I could call and did call at six o'clock tonight to get the $12,000 to organize this ballet. We have all been through this a lot and there are lots of "no's" before there is a "yes." This is the way in which you can help that creative process. You can find the money for them. It's very tedious and very boring and very rewarding only if somebody appreciates it. So the manager has a kind of restrictive job and I think one has to work very hard to feel pleased and satisfied. When I go to the Balanchine ballet, I know I really had nothing to do with it and I'm quite far removed. If somebody says "Congratulations!", I don't know which is more pretentious—to turn them away or to accept them. It is somewhere very deep down that one gets job satisfaction in this particular field.

Finally, I'm expected to give you advice but I think I'll let that pass, because I'm having a very hard life at the moment at City Center. Last year we had a four million dollar operating loss. We raised some two million, seven-hundred thousand dollars, which left a continuing deficit of one million, three-hundred thousand. This year we'll have an additional deficit of seven-hundred thousand, so that as of July 1st we'll have a deficit of two million dollars. Now "deficit" has to be distinguished from "operating loss." The operating loss each year, as I said, is about four million dollars. We hope next year (and we have five union contracts coming up for negotiation this summer) to be able to have a year where we cover our operating loss and then the year after to start paying off on the deficit. So we are working very hard to turn our situation around and we feel rather hopeful. Having gone through these couple of years, my advice of course is *don't!* But that's not what you're supposed to say to young hopefuls, so I think we'll leave it at that.

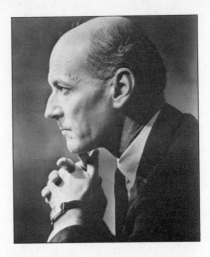

Commentary by *Sir Rudolf Bing*

Former General Manager, New
York Metropolitan Opera, Author
of *5000 Nights at the Opera*,
Distinguished Visiting Professor,
Brooklyn College of the City
University of New York.

It will be more difficult for me to tell my story, because Norman is so much younger! I span a much longer period.

I started when I was very young and studied painting and singing which, strangely enough, turned out to be quite useful later on. I knew *something* about singing—not enough, but something. Then I gave up singing and painting and wanted to be a publisher. In order to become a publisher, I was told, you must first be a bookseller and learn the public's reaction to books. So I joined a bookstore. It was in Vienna some one hundred years ago, and I loved bookselling, in fact I'm considering going back to it now. Very attractive occupation! Anyway, this bookstore had attached to it a concert agency, not unlike the Hurok operation here in New York, though it was on a little smaller scale. Nevertheless, it was the leading concert agency in Vienna. I moved from the bookstore to this concert agency, which was my first contact with performers, singers, pianists, whatever. From those days, and I'm going back now half a century, I developed personal relationships with people-like Lotte Lehmann, Fritz Busch and some others. The concert agency did pretty well and grew to include a theatrical agency—the sort where you travel to a theatre, hear the vacancies and then try to match the vacancies with available talent. I did that for a while in Vienna and eventually I was offered the job of leading a theatrical-operatic agency in Berlin. So I moved to Berlin.

I was young then and it was a dreadful disappointment because this was an official agency, it was not a private agency. It was an agency that was run simultaneously by the unions and by the heads of all the opera houses in Germany. No decent singer would come near this agency, they would all go to their private agencies. I was asked by wretched little theatres to provide Isoldes or Lohengrins for three hundred marks a month. I couldn't find anybody good enough to do that and I hated every minute of it.

Then I had my first union problem. Little did I know how it would multiply! Anyway, in Europe it is the custom if you go to an office to shake hands. You come in, "Any news for me?" meaning, is there a job for me? And I would say, "Sorry, there is nothing yet." And you shake hands again and say, "Goodbye."

So in the summer months I put a little sign on my door saying, "It would be appreciated if you would refrain from handshaking." It got rather unpleasant to shake a hundred sweaty hands during a day. The union took offense and I was instructed to take the sign down.

Then my great break came—it was in 1928. A new general manager (in those days he was called "general intendant") of the State Theatre in Hessen came to my office. He didn't know how bad an agency I was running, because he was new. He was the leading actor in Berlin and was appointed for this job. He came to me and told me about his vacancies in his theatre—a lovely, little, rather avante garde provincial theatre. Then he said, "But the most important thing is I need an assistant, because I want to direct. I need somebody with really great experience to run the theatre for me." So I said, "I have just the man for you. Why don't you take me?"

"What's your theatre experience?"

I said, "None!" and I got the job.

That took me to Darmstadt, where I was for the first time

really *in* the theatre and I enjoyed every moment. I can remember the thrill I had with my first pass key. I could go into the theatre during a performance and this sort of thing. There I was two years. Then I went to Berlin in the sort of job I could best describe as manager of an artistic department. I went to Berlin to the City Opera, which was the first time I was in the big league, and I had to deal with international artists (all long dead, none of whom you've ever heard of). But this was the first time I was in touch with people who suddenly had an engagement with the Metropolitan Opera in New York . . . where?

I was in Berlin for two or three years and really learning to run a big opera house with all its problems—nothing like what they eventually became at the Met, but nevertheless, a big league opera house. And then our friend Hitler arrived and my general intendant, Carl Ebert, and our first conductor, Fritz Busch, and I, we all left Germany and went to various places. Ebert and Busch went to Turkey, and I went back to Vienna.

In Vienna there suddenly came a strange letter from Fritz Busch, who said he had met an eccentric Englishman by the name of John Christie, who had built a little opera house sixty miles outside London in Sussex Downs and wanted to start a Mozart festival and would I be ready to engage an ensemble for it? They wanted to do *Cosi fan tutte* and *Figaro* for the first season.

I had never heard of the place—Glyndebourne—I couldn't find it on any map. But I said of course I would get the ensemble and I started to engage an ensemble, which was very difficult because I couldn't tell the people where the damn place was! As no contract existed, I had to devise some form of contract and somehow we brought them to Glyndebourne. Eventually I said to myself, "Well, having done this I want to see the place," and went to Glyndebourne on my own to look at this absolutely lovely and fascinating place where Busch and Ebert created really one of the great Mozart festivals of the day. But there was absolute chaos there because there was nobody to run the place. Mr. Christie, totally ignorant of what operatic theatres are like, had hired a manager who happened to be the manager of the Liverpool Opera House. The only trouble was that the thing was *called* "opera house," but it was a commercial theatre that booked plays and this unfortunate manager, Mr. Nightingale (long since dead), had never heard of *Figaro*, had *no* idea what *Figaro* was, no idea what *any* opera was. It was utter chaos in the rehearsals and I was asked, "Could you help out?" And I stepped in and helped out and tried to organize the first festival and was appointed general manager of the second festival.

After the second year, Mr. Christie rebuilt the house, doubled it, and from two weeks we ran to four and six and seven weeks, and it was a very, very happy time. I had an office in London and it became a full-time occupation and we ran until the war which, of course, interrupted these happy events at Glyndebourne. During the war I had met at Glyndebourne a Mr. Spedan Lewis, who was the chairman of a great chain of department stores all over the country. Obviously, anybody who had two legs was in the war. But I was still then an "enemy alien" because I was Austrian originally, and Mr. Lewis asked me whether I had anything to do. I said there was *nothing* to do, so he said, "Would you like to join in this partnership?" which I did.

I started off in a lovely department store in Sloane Square, Peter Jones, where I had a tiny desk. Rationing had just started in England and I had to provide information to the customers. A lady would come in and I would say, "No, I'm sorry, madam. Slips are four points, stockings are two, underwear is three," and so forth. And then I devised a little booklet, which became a sort of classic for all the shops. After another six or eight months I was manager of the department store, which was dreadful. I hated it. The only thing I enjoyed was ladies' hairdressing, because it reminded me a little bit of the hysterical atmosphere in the theatre. When there was trouble, I was called in and I had to put my finger to a lady's curls and say, "But, madam, it springs back beautifully!" I still don't know what it meant, but it always did the trick!

So I did rather well there and Mr. Lewis offered me a long-term contract. I said, "Yes, under one condition—if

Glyndebourne restarts after the war, whenever that may be, I will be released to go back to Glyndebourne."

Soon the war did come to an end and I suggested to Glyndebourne certain ways of restarting. Mr. Christie wasn't in a position to pour money in as he did before the war, so I thought of a market for Glyndebourne and hit upon the idea of an international festival with the music and the arts in Edinburgh. Now why Edinburgh? I first thought of Oxford, lovely city much closer to London, but somehow I couldn't get 'town' and 'gown' together, which was then absolutely necessary. You cannot have a festival just anywhere—I mean no money on *earth* could turn Cleveland into a festival! (I hope you don't come from Cleveland, it's a lovely place but it's just *not* a festival atmosphere.) Edinburgh, however, had a lovely atmosphere—an old city with an old tradition, great beauty, a castle on a hill, a little bit like Salzburg. So I went up to Edinburgh and I was very lucky with the contacts I made and eventually a little committee formed and they introduced me to the Lord Provost, which is what they call the mayor. Well he was a very nice, charming old gentleman who had never heard of Bruno Walter and never heard of Mozart, but he got the idea that at the end of the war it might be a great thing to have an international festival in Edinburgh. Britain had been starved for international artists all during the war. Yehudi Menuhin was the only artist of international standing who came to England, who braved the bombs and played there during the war. So the Festival Society was formed and I was appointed the first artistic director— wonderful, but very hard work. The festival was really built up from scratch.

The great thing was getting Bruno Walter together with the Vienna Philharmonic. I introduced to him a wonderful singer (long since dead), Kathleen Ferrier, whom he adored and whom we engaged to do Mahler songs. The Queen came to the first festival and it was a world success. I ran it for three years—'47, '48, '49. In '49 there were some plans for getting Glyndebourne to America, so I came to the United States and visited Mr. Edward Johnson, who was the

238/*Producers on Producing*

general manager of the Metropolitan, and who had visited me in London before the war. So I returned his visit. It was at the old house on 39th Street and Mr. Johnson very charmingly said, "By the way, I would like to retire and would you care to be my successor?" So I said, "fine," and here I was in 1949. I came back to the United States, was appointed general manager, started in 1950, and tried to run the place for twenty-two years until 1972 when I retired.

One of the chief reasons why I retired was, as Mr. Singer pointed out, we had fourteen unions at the Met and I had great trouble with the unions. When I retired in '72 it was the time when another round of union negotiations were to start and I couldn't face it. So I got out to give the Met a new chance. Every new manager has a honeymoon with the unions, although my successor tragically died practically before he took over.

Now to the question of my present position. Well, some months ago, the first time since I came to the United States, I had to go to the post office to buy stamps, which I had never done before. I always had secretaries, so I found it a very humiliating experience. That was part of my position! Then I had the great fortune to be introduced to the Chancellor of the City University, who introduced me to the president of Brooklyn College, who introduced me to the appointments committee, and they asked me, "What is your academic background?" and I said, "I passed only one test in my life, a driving test," and again I got the job!

Commentary by *Harvey Lichtenstein*

Director, Brooklyn Academy of
Music, Brooklyn, New York

My involvement, I guess, began when I was at Brooklyn
College as a student in the late 1940's. I was invited to a
dance performance by Martha Graham. I guess it was during that two week season, seeing about five or six performances, that I decided that I was terribly interested in
dance. So I got involved in studying dance at the College—I majored in history at the time—and during the last
two or three years of my stay, I became more involved in
dance and studied it at the Graham Studio and so on. Following that, I spent a summer at Black Mountain College in
North Carolina studying with Merce Cunningham. Then I
spent a year at Bennington College, an extraordinary year.
There were about five or six male students at the time in
theatre, dance and music and I guess there were about three
hundred and fifty females.

I left Bennington and started to dance professionally
and did that for three or four years. I danced in the corps of
the New York City Opera Ballet and toured with a number
of companies and then stopped dancing in 1957 or '58. Certain things had happened in my life. Also, it was rather
difficult to earn a living by dancing. I was traveling a great
deal all over the country and it was what is known in the
trade as a gypsy life. I decided to stop and get another job
and I got a job doing fund-raising for a college near Boston
by the name of Brandeis University. I don't know how that

followed, I'm sure there is no logical reason for that happening, but somehow it did. I worked there for about three or four years. I must say, it was one of the most important and valid experiences I ever had because, as Norman has indicated, trying to raise money for the activities that take place under your roof is an absolutely crucial activity in the arts or in any non-profit organization. So what I was doing up at Brandeis was learning the various aspects of raising money—with corporations, with foundations and with old ladies. I was still active in studying and working with a dance company in Boston.

During my third year there, I found out about a program that the Ford Foundation sponsored which was an internship program with performing arts institutions. It involved getting people who worked outside of the performing arts but had had some prior relationship with them, also somewhat mature people, at least over the age of twenty-five—and placing them with a company as salaried apprentices for a year. I took that fellowship, which was rather difficult because I was married and had a child and the money involved was not much. It was a great deal less than I was making at Brandeis University. Nevertheless, I wanted very much to do it and I was placed with the New York City Ballet, which had just moved into the State Theatre at Lincoln Center from the old City Center. I spent a year with the New York City Ballet—checking program copy and being assistant manager on a tour and reading through the files (I understand the whole business of breaking into files! It's fascinating and I used to spend hours and hours reading correspondence between artists and mangement. I'd never reveal the contents).

At the end of that year the New York City Ballet was interested in starting a subscription, which they had never had for ballet. Ballet was a problem for subscription because it wasn't like theatre or opera where each evening was taken up with one particular work. There were usually three or four works on each program. The New York City Ballet does not do *Swan Lake*, they only do one act of it. And so there was some feeling that there would be a resistance, that the subscription process would not work. In any case, they needed to jack up attendance and so this was one thing they thought they would do.

We started a subscription for the New York City Ballet and I was asked to do it. It was enormously successful, I don't think it was anything particular that I did, I think it was really just the right time at the right place for it. Then we did it for the New York City Opera, which had just moved into the State Theatre. I was there for about two years.

Subscription is a very interesting process and one that anybody involved in managing a company or a theatre really should know about, but after you do it a couple of times it gets fairly dull, it gets routine. There isn't much more you can do to it, particularly when it is successful as it seemed to be here. It was at that time that I was asked if I was interested in a position with the Brooklyn Academy of Music. I must say, Norman, your predecessor, Morton Baum, said, "You're crazy!"

Did *you* say that to me as well? Lots of people did—said it's impossible to come over and try to make the Brooklyn Academy of Music run. I remember Morton Baum saying, "I've been trying to think for ten years what to do with that place!"

Nevertheless, it is an absolutely beautiful opera house and I thought we'd give it a try and see what could be done. I've been at the Brooklyn Academy of Music now for over seven years and we're still not sure what it is that can work there and it's still a place where we're experimenting a lot. But I think a number of things which have happened have been interesting. We have, in a sense, a mini-center, because we have three theatres at the Academy and we're building a fourth one (in an old ballroom) which will be an experimental theatre, an open space theatre, so that there will be four spaces where performances can take place. We've also had some companies in residence, one of which has made a particular name for itself, the Chelsea Theatre Center. It has become one of the important theatre companies in New York City in terms of trying new and different things, doing playwrights who have not been performed, and putting on huge plays like Genet's *The Screens*, which haven't been done before in this country.

What we have tried to do at the Brooklyn Academy of Music is to build a performing arts center, but outside the core of the city. In some instances we've failed and in some instances we've succeeded. I think we've succeeded where we've been the most daring and tried to do things which other people don't do. I think we have been less successful when we've done the ordinary things that people can see in other places in New York City.

I do think that there is an important ingredient here for us in the Borough of Brooklyn—a lot of people. It consists of many people who are not served by or who don't find their way into the performing arts theatres. There are so many parts of this borough which don't respond to any performing arts center in New York City, and it is interesting to investigate and find out about these communities, to try to reach them one way or another. But this takes lots of work and lots of thought.

Questions to *Norman Singer*
Sir Rudolf Bing
Harvey Lichtenstein

QUESTION Do you think that big cultural centers are really a good thing or not?

SIR RUDOLF Well, my quarrel with cultural centers—and I don't know too much about them really except for Lincoln Center—is that many of them seem to be built from the outside rather than from the inside. They begin by building a house for millions of dollars and then, when it is ready, they start thinking of what to put in it. To wit, the Kennedy Center has been built for many millions and it turns out that the large opera house cannot house the Metropolitan Opera, cannot house the Bolshoi Ballet, cannot house the Royal Ballet, because it's simply too small and economically not viable. The Metropolitan Opera is a four thousand seat house and there's a deficit now, I think, of six million dollars. So you can imagine what would happen to the Metropolitan Opera if it goes to the Washington Kennedy Center and plays in a house that seats *two* thousand. They would have to charge fifty dollars a ticket, which is unreasonable, or they would have to be wildly subsidized, which is not always possible.

Why has nobody thought *first* "What do we build this house for?" There are great national and international institutions, like La Scala in Milan, that can come and visit here, but haven't because they would have to be so enormously subsidized.

The Lincoln Center complex, I think, really arose from the need for new buildings. The Philharmonic was then under threat of Carnegie Hall being destroyed, and the Metropolitan simply needed a new building because their old house was totally inadequate—lovely as it was inside—there was no stage equipment, no lighting equipment. I'm not even talking of fire laws. We violated fire laws every day of the year! It simply was impossible to continue contemporary production on this stage that had no side space, no back space, no nothing! Practically from the day I came I fought for a new house and it took me eighteen years until we got the new hall, which I think is very lovely. Then as Lincoln Center grew—and I cannot give you the exact details because I was not privy to all of those discussions—there was the Philharmonic and the Metropolitan first, and the State Theatre, which was originally, if I am correct, meant for the ballet. Then, subsequently, the decision was made for getting the opera in there as well. Juilliard was an afterthought, although I think a very important and useful one. And then there was the Vivian Beaumont.

The only discussion I remember was the great argument about the name, I don't know if you remember that. It was an old lady, Mrs. Vivian Beaumont, who gave three million dollars toward the building and the question was how they were going to name it. I suggested to Mr. Rockefeller, with no sense of humor, I said, "Why don't you call it 'The Old Viv?'" But eventually it was called "The Vivian Beaumont Theatre," as you know.

But where is "the cultural center?" They're totally independent, autonomous organizations. There is, I am happy to say, a very friendly relationship between the Metropolitan Opera and the City Opera. There is no real cooperation as far as the repertory is concerned. Both organizations do *La Boheme* and *La Traviata*. The City Center for a long time was very much more courageous than the Metropolitan Opera in doing avant garde things or contemporary works, which in all fairness were a little easier on an economic level for City Center to handle than for the Met with its enormous number of sets, costumes and so forth. In the mean time, I think that City Center has also come to realize that an opera company simply cannot live without *Traviata* and *Boheme,* so the repertory is largely duplicated. But even that didn't seem to harm anybody, because City Center has done extremely well as far as box office is concerned and so has the Met for many, many years. The Met has now, and this is no criticism of the new management (I don't know about the City Opera), gone down a little bit in sales, which I think has to do with theatre conditions in the city. People are frightened to go out at night. The Met has a largely aging audience and not everybody has a chauffeur-driven Cadillac. Many people are just frightened to go home at night in the subway and then walk three blocks over to the bus and then walk three blocks home and be mugged or raped or God knows what! It's a problem, not to mention the economic situation. The Met now charges $17.50 for its top price. Very few people go alone, so that is $35.00 plus taxi or a car or a dinner or a babysitter. It's quite an amount and not everybody can afford it. It costs you $50.00 or $60.00 before you really start. City Center, of course, is lower in price. But I hear the Met is doing better again now.

MR. SINGER   The Met is doing eighty-nine percent of capacity and I think we're just under eighty-eight at the moment.

SIR RUDOLF   Well that would seem very good. We used to do ninety-seven percent!

MR. SINGER   Yes, we've done better as well.

SIR RUDOLF   But there it is. For instance, our matinee is now, I hear, doing much better than we used to do, which indicates, as I said, that people are frightened to go out at night. They go out in the afternoon now.

Where the arts center comes in at Lincoln Center, I don't quite know because, as I said, there is very little cooperation—except we're all very friendly when we meet on the street—"Hi!" But there's no common policy at all that I know of. There was a time when Bill Schumann was president of Lincoln Center. He sought, indeed he wanted to make Lincoln Center another constituent, practically, which I fought. I remember a conversation with Schumann at the Lincoln Center Council when he had to admit that he made a mistake and I said, "Don't worry, Bill, to err is schumann!"

So I don't really know, it just happens to be a center geographically. They're in the same square, but that is all the center I see.

QUESTION   At the Brooklyn Academy, where you are a cultural conglomerate as it were, what are your responsibilities to the Chelsea Theatre, for instance? What's in it for them to be a constituent of the Academy?

MR. LICHTENSTEIN   Well, we have various constituents, some still there, some not. Chelsea, the Brooklyn Philharmonia Orchestra, Merce Cunningham and so on. I would say what we would *like* to do is not quite what we *do*. The reason is simply because of financial restrictions, and I know that Norman has the same problem in regard to some of his constituents. Chelsea pretty much operates on its own. We give them a theatre, they even pay a nominal rental for it. We give them office space, a costume shop, they use rehearsal space in the building. We're responsible for maintenance, cleaning, security and so forth, but they pretty much raise their own money to support their activities, they're separately incorporated, they make their own artistic decisions. That's beginning to change some now and, I hope, we're getting to the point where we can give them more help than we have in the past. We're paying for some of the services now, some of their stagehand services, and we hope to do that more and more because their activity in the building is crucial. I mean they are identified with the Brooklyn Academy of Music, they're an important aspect of what goes on, and I couldn't be more proud of their activity. So in every way, as Norman said, you support them. I would hope to get more involved with their activity, with their decisions. There was a director who just came in from England last week, whom I brought over to Bob Kalfin, who's the artistic director of the Chelsea company. We talked about directing a play, we talked about a thing I'd seen him do in London. As we get more involved with our constituents, I think we should get more involved artistically as well. It's a valid thing because we bring another point of view. That's what's happening also with the Brooklyn Philharmonia and Lukas Foss in developing programming there. Basically, they operate on their own. But we hope to get more involved with them both financially and artistically.

MR. SINGER Well, City Center is a curious situation because we are an independent entity made up of the different parts I outlined earlier. And also we are part of Lincoln Center. One of our problems is that of identity—not to be swallowed up by Lincoln Center. Lincoln Center in itself wants to do things, perfectly understandable that they do. We started out originally with just the opera company and some borrowed sets from St. Louis, doing *Martha*. I don't know what that was like, that was the opening step and then the ballet came and they did two nights, or something of that sort. Morton Baum said, "Would you like to come and be in the theatre," and *they* became a constituent. In this process over the years there's been a season of light opera, which was called the City Center Light Opera Company, but which wasn't (it was mainly revivals and used sets that somebody else had made and costumes) and it was a season, but not in the same way that the opera and ballet season is created, right from the beginning.

We have fairly close relationships, because they have this financial problem. We have a kind of love-hate relationship. I suppose the question of artistic involvement is not only a philosophical one. More important is the fact that we do have a Julius Rudel, a Lincoln Kirstein, and a George Balanchine, and nobody is about to tell them what to do. I must admit that when somebody comes and says, "Can I have an audition at the opera?" I try to make sure that they call somebody in the opera company, so it doesn't come from me and seem as if there were some special influence that I think would be counterproductive to the person involved. They jealously guard their freedom and I accept this, *faute de mieux*.

I might say that there are certain things that administrators have that are their own successes. We have certain compulsions about meeting deadlines. I would say the one thing that is never valued enough about Mr. Bing is the fact that he's known throughout the arts administration world as a superb organizer. If his bulletin board said that four years hence on a Tuesday morning there would be a rehearsal of such and such, that rehearsal took place! That doesn't happen around the world in very many places. But the problems of administration are very important and the artistic things in our situation, artistic questions, are separate. Sir Rudolf had a different involvement and a different kind of enterprise because he was not a center.

What I started to say, what I think *I'm* good at is I have a good nose for choosing what's going to be successful. I don't mean to be very humble (you know Mr. Hurok's wonderful statement, "Don't be so humble, you're not that great!") Well, the point here is that I realize I have certain strengths. One of the best things is I've been receptive to people, and people know I'm receptive, so a lot of good ideas have been brought to me. In any case, someone came to me with the idea of this children's theatre. It's a participatory theatre and I am involved in that we do discuss the program and we discuss, not the content of that day's show, or that season's show, but whether it's a good idea to go to the schools, whether it's a good idea to have certain age limits—those are artistic questions to a certain extent, but our companies are united by an umbrella that is actually a much more cohesive and friendly one, without invidious comparisons, than the Lincoln Center one. At Lincoln Center, people came together because they wanted those buildings. *Our* people are together because they share a certain kind of concept which has become a slogan for fundraising and which is: "the best possible cultural productions at the lowest possible prices." There is a certain kind of commitment, whether it's children's theatre or whatever it is to try and keep our prices low. We're now $8.95. Not very low—$9.00, $18.00, you go through the same thing all the time; babysitters, Schraff's, whatever it is, before you know it you've spent $35.00. And, you know, it's much easier to stay home for $35.00 a lot of times. So we do have a social purpose—let's say we are always trying to keep art ahead of sociology, because that's our commitment.

QUESTION   Sir Rudolf, could you tell us if there is any relationship between the deficits of the Met and Lincoln Center itself—I mean, could the Center bale out the Met if worse came to worse?

SIR RUDOLF The Metropolitan, to begin with, is no kind of conglomerate. It's the Metropolitan—period! It is itself responsible for its own deficit, which is substantial, and it pays, as City Opera does, according to some kind of fee system as a constituent of Lincoln Center, it pays something toward the general expenses—the upkeep of the plaza, the upkeep of the fountain, the security, the cleaning and so forth. That is paid "X" percent by the Metropolitan (which is the largest of the group), "X" percent by City Center, "X" percent by Juilliard and so forth. But otherwise, the Metropolitan is totally responsible for its own deficit, which is hopefully covered by fund-raising, just as all the others are. There is now a new scheme, not actually new as it started just as I left, whereby Lincoln Center does the fund-raising and the funds so raised are shared among the constituents.

We, of course, also raise very substantial funds from individuals. I occasionally had tea with an old lady. That was mainly for new productions. I, as general manager of the opera, was not involved in fund-raising for the organization at all. That was up to the board. They had their own committee for fund-raising and, indeed, did a phenomenal job. I only raised funds for individual new productions I wanted to put on, but which I could not pay out of the general funds for the Met. So if I wanted to do Verdi's *Otello* in a new production by Franco Zeffirelli, I went to Mrs. Rockefeller (who is dead, unfortunately). She was one of my greatest angels and paid, I forget, for ten or twelve productions over the years, and she never asked a question. I told her one year that I would like to do *Otello* with Zeffirelli designing and directing, etcetera, etcetera. She would say, "I think it's a wonderful idea, how much do you need?"

"Well, maybe four, five hundred thousand," and she would give me a check, and there it was!

But there ain't around too many Mrs. Rockefellers anymore!

As far as responsibility is concerned, you gentlemen

have other constituents—the Met hasn't got them, the Met is totally self-supporting, so to speak, it has nothing else but its own organization, for which it is totally responsible. It makes its own artistic decisions and its own fiscal decisions.

QUESTION   What about cooperative programming of some kind—is that ever considered?

MR. SINGER   There is an effort every so often to try to get a joint project going. For example, to try to get at minimum a Stravinsky festival whereby they'll have concert works played at the Philharmonic and the Met will do *Wozzeck* and City Opera will do *Lulu* and even the Beaumont will perhaps put on a stage version of *Wozzeck*. That never seems to come off, although it would be the minimal amount of cooperation that one could expect. But that involves a new kind of creativity and all of us are so strapped by keeping our own creativity supported that we just can't face a new kind. So there is an attempt at that, but it doesn't come off.

SIR RUDOLF   I'm sure you know as well as I do that the mere attempt to get the curtain up everyday and to schedule the various artists a year ahead, or in the case of the Met sometimes two and three years ahead, the sheer bulk of this and scheduling complications is enormous.

The other day I happened to take a small nonsinging role in *The Young Lord* at the City Opera. It was the first time that I ever worked with City Opera, and I suppose the last time! I was incredibly impressed by the precision, the sheer hard training of these people to get through a difficult, contemporary, unknown opera with a minimum of rehearsals and with a much smaller roster than we had, which meant that the man who rehearsed this morning as the Young Lord was singing Don Giovanni that night. It was just impossible to achieve that sort of thing at the Met because our singers just wouldn't do it. I'm not saying that they are that much better, but they *are* that much vainer!

The director of *The Young Lord*, a lady by the name of Sara Caldwell, is enormously talented but not exactly what

I would call disciplined in her actions and not organized. How this company withstood this and helped her and got it together I'll never understand. Mind you, I have great regard for her work. But it's a totally different operation than the Met and both of them have value on their respective levels.

MR. SINGER Getting back to cultural centers, there's one more thing I'd like to say. I hated the concept of Lincoln Center! I was teaching at Juilliard and I was scornful of all the cant that went on about "the great arts" and all the rest. We were tormented at Juilliard because, God knows, for almost eleven years nothing happened because of the attitude "well, there's no sense in doing anything because in two years we're going down to Lincoln Center." Then there was this whole terrible public relations thing about Lincoln Center. I remember those first ads about it. They hit a great many people the wrong way and one became cynical, scornful about it. But I think we have to recognize now that it has had a tremendously beneficial effect. It's a nice place to go and see all those people going in and out. There's an atmosphere there, people are always comparing it to St. Marks Place in Venice. The effect of those buildings *did* in the early years actually increase attendance. We estimated that about twenty percent of the early years' attendance was there because there was something to see. People liked going there and, after that, Harvey's subscription season was sold out. I think there is something that happens with these centers, just by being there. It's not enough to be as scornful or as cynical as we are about them—sometimes rightfully—because they sometimes get lost and come in ass backwards, not knowing what should be their first priority. I find myself every so often defending the Met, defending Lincoln Center. It's a curious position and I think it's probably, as you grow older, you stop being the young Bolshevik and you recognize some of the positive things that seem to be so anti-artistic as these big cultural centers tend to seem.

QUESTION I think I'm still confused about the difference between an "operating loss" and a "deficit."

MR. SINGER   You have a certain amount of expense to carry out your activities and you have income from the box office. The difference between these, unfortunately, is always a loss—and that's an operating loss. Just income versus expenses. That meant we spent four million dollars for all of our activities. We had to put in the amount of money we raised through contributions: National Endowment grants, New York State grants, funds from the Mrs. Rockefellers, and what we hope is to raise four million dollars. If we do that, we start the new year with a clean slate. If we don't raise that much money, then we have what we call a "carry-over deficit." Actually, the words get to be interchangeable, but unless you use them carefully you find the situation gets confused. We at City Center had a small surplus when I arrived. I'm afraid it's been eaten up in three years, so last year we had the so-called carry-over deficit. We'll have the same thing again this year because it's just very hard to raise four million dollars a year. Somebody from another center said to me the other day that they couldn't afford something. I said, "Well, you know how *we* can't afford it, we've got a four million dollar deficit."

So they said, "Well, we can't afford a four million dollar deficit!"

You don't know sometimes if you're very rich or very poor when you have a four million dollar operating loss. Then you carry on thereafter with a deficit that you haven't met.

SIR RUDOLF   I read this morning of Mr. Chapin talking about a one million dollar deficit at the Met. What it really means is the deficit is six million dollars, because the operating deficit was five million dollars. They erased five million dollars, but they are still one million dollars short!

QUESTION   Mr. Lichtenstein, do I sense that you don't consider the Brooklyn Academy of Music a true cultural center, or that you are jealous that it is not located in Manhattan or even in Lincoln Center?

MR. LICHTENSTEIN   Let me make a distinction first. I was thinking that the difference between Lincoln Center and

City Center and the Brooklyn Academy of Music is basically that those centers, both those organizations, are what I would define as national centers. That is, they not only have appeal to people in New York City but they are producing the best of what goes on in the country in the arts. They attract not only people from the city, but international visitors and tourists. The Academy, on the other hand, is more a local center. It could be in Milwaukee, or in Boston and function very well there. The one drawback that the Academy has is that it's *not* in Milwaukee or Boston, it's Brooklyn—which is fine, but Brooklyn's right across the river from what is the national center for the performing arts in this country, Manhattan. So we have to define our constituency. Who are the people we think we can attract? Obviously, we are not really thinking of attracting the tourists that come and stay at the Plaza or the Regency. Over the past few years we have come to define our basic constituency in terms of various groupings. First of all, we think one of our most important constituencies is young people. We find from studies and surveys that we have a higher percentage of young people in our general audience than almost any other cultural center or theatre or organization in the country. That's true for a number of reasons, but I think, primarily, because given the disadvantages of where we are, people almost have to be more adventurous to come to the Brooklyn Academy of Music and people who *are* more adventurous are younger people, they're not as afraid to go in subways.

Another constituency is based specifically on what we do. We've done a lot of dance, especially modern dance, and we have a dance constituency which is not necessarily limited to Brooklyn. It's a fairly small constituency, because it's the modern dance constituency as opposed to the ballet. You won't see the Sol Hurok organization putting on Merce Cunningham at the Metropolitan Opera as they do the Stuttgart Ballet or the Royal Ballet. That is simply because Merce Cunningham wouldn't be able to fill the house; so it's a small constituency in terms of the dance world.

A third constituency which we are now beginning to at-

tract more and more is the local one. We are trying to develop roots here in Brooklyn with what we do and to make
what we do more appealing to people in Brooklyn. For instance, Brooklyn has a large middle-class population and it
also has large ethnic groups. It has many different communities which are independent and which don't relate to
one another. We've decided to do things which may work
with one community, but not work with others. For example, we had a Jamaican dance company perform about a
month ago. We knew there was a large West Indian population in Brooklyn and they turned out in droves. This is not
always true when there is a population, they don't always
come, but this time they did. So our next step next year is to
do a whole Caribbean festival, working with many of the is-
lands in the Caribbean.

In terms of the middle class we also find that things that
work elsewhere work here. For instance, things of great
prestige and value, like Peter Brook's *Midsummer Night's
Dream* with the Royal Shakespeare Company, sold out in
Manhattan and they sold out in Brooklyn. So we're also
looking to do more things that are on that high level of quality. We feel more and more that our roots lie in these various constituencies. As opposed to Lincoln Center and City
Center, we think of ourselves as local—that's how we really
want to develop. That doesn't mean what we do is provincial, because it isn't. We don't do so-called "community
theatre."

QUESTION   Do non-profit arts organizations have a different relationship with the unions than the commercial organizations?

MR. SINGER   That's a very interesting thing about the union situation and a non-profit organization, because the
assumption is that if you're non-profit, you're doing good
works and so there should be some sympathy on the part of
the union. When you go down to the union and you say,
"Look at my books, we have "X" million dollars deficit,"
they're not interested in the way they would have to be if
they went to General Motors and General Motors gave them
a sheet showing that they didn't have any profits. They can

recognize this and understand this and say, "Well, there's no profit in the business, we understand that, we'll take this." But in our business, we're always involved in raising money to cover the cost between operating deficit and all the rest. So we say, "We can't raise enough money," or "We were only able to raise "X" amount of dollars."

Their response is, "Go out and raise more!" And we actually *do* go out and raise more. So it's one of those self-defeating cycles. We always have to live up to the demand, because we want to continue. But there are points beyond which you literally cannot continue. We may be able to live with a two-million dollar deficit, but we're not going to be able to live with a three-million dollar deficit. That means we owe people millions of dollars that have to be paid sometime. They may not like to have a set of *La Boheme* as their security for very long!

The problem with the unions, I think, has to be put in a different kind of concept. Let's say a musician makes $300 a week. If he makes that fifty-two weeks, that's $16,000 or $17,000 a year. That's a decent enough salary, but it's not an especially important salary for somebody who's had a long history of training at the Juilliard School. And, actually, he doesn't get fifty-two weeks of work, in any case not from City Center. He did get that from the Met, finally, but the problem for us is that $16,000 or $17,000 for him is terribly expensive for us, so we have our problem. Not that he doesn't deserve that amount of money, but we can't afford that amount of money and we're not sure that we can go out and raise it.

Now the stagehand, I think, is a different situation. Our stagehands are making a tremendous amount of money and they always tell you they work for it, as distinguished from the rest of us who just come into the theatre in the morning and stay until midnight! Their salaries are high because of certain contracts and featherbedding. This is an especially serious problem in the arts. In a business or industry if you have three men doing a job at, let's say, $300 each, it's $900 to pay those three men. Then they come and ask you for a raise. Perhaps you eliminate one of them and give the other two a raise of $150, making it $450 each, so they're still only costing $900. Meanwhile, you've introduced a labor-saving device that allows you to revolutionize the industry more. In the arts, if you have a quartet, you need four people and no matter what you do, you have to pay them the increased inflationary costs because they have to buy bread and butter for their families. So you're trapped by certain kinds of situations. A manager gets to be an ogre lots of times, but our first job is to keep our organizations alive. Of course what we should be doing at City Center is charging a fair price at the box office. Actually, our box office income is really a contribution, it's not a ticket price, because the ticket price should be much higher. Ours should be about $14 to $15, instead of $9. So what we do is let people give us a contribution of $9 tops in order to help us. We just don't have the kind of money to go on meeting inflationary costs that we can't do anything about, because we still need a hero and a heroine and a chorus and all those people.

MR. LICHTENSTEIN   I read the other day that Shaeffer Beer just had an operating loss of about a half-million for their first quarter. That was made public in the midst of their negotiations with truck drivers. So it was announced that, because Shaeffer was really in trouble, the truck drivers signed a new three-year contract without any increase. It's hard to believe that that could happen with us.

MR. SINGER   They saw the operating sheets.

MR. LICHTENSTEIN   Right. But what I'm trying to say is that there is a psychological difference. People understand that if businesses run at a loss long enough, they're going to close and the people are going to lose their jobs.

QUESTION   What do you think about government subsidy for the arts and the way it's being handed out?

MR. SINGER   I think City Center would be absolutely desperate if it weren't for government money at this particular moment. We have money from the state and federal government and a comparatively smaller amount from the city. It adds up to over a million dollars that we've been able to get, and I think they've been very good to us—without the least bit of interference in terms of what we want to do. In Russia you had government subsidy where they had to write music that Stalin could whistle! In England they give the money that Covent Garden or Glyndebourne companies need and allow them to go on doing their own thing without any restrictions, except perhaps they require a certain amount of touring, as they do influence us by requiring a touring program for dance companies. You can't get the money unless you tour.

I think that state subsidy, government subsidy, can come about in any number of ways depending on the social structure of the country in which it takes place. I don't like to be frightened by the fact that the government could take over. The government can take over if you let it take over, so you don't let it.

QUESTION Do you think government subsidy will be increased?

MR. SINGER Yes. It's becoming politically glamorous. For example, in the midst of all the cuts in every important social welfare area, Nixon increased the arts appropriation by a very large amount. Similarly, Governor Rockefeller did the same thing. It's almost embarrassing, but not so much that I would make a protest! It's politically glamorous now. We finally made it and they realize that the arts give them a certain status.

SIR RUDOLF Well I'm delighted and amazed to hear that you get that much. I don't think that the Metropolitan gets a fraction of that.

MR. SINGER Well, you see, we get it for many different things. Our opera will get two hundred thousand, and I think the Met certainly gets more than that from the state grants and current emergency grants. But it adds up because we get it for street programs, we get it for children's programs, the more we do the more we get.

SIR RUDOLF You mentioned the unions. A few years ago here is the Metropolitan Opera building a new house for forty million dollars. It's very hard for the unions to feel that such an organization is poor. These boys do work hard. They have to pay their rent, they have to educate their children, and it's pretty hard for them to understand why they cannot get a reasonable raise. The question is, what is reasonable? And also the unions have seen in the course of the years that, so far, we've always given them a raise.

When I came to this country twenty-four years ago, my then chairman (long since deceased, no doubt hastened by my activities) told me the deficit was a half-million dollars for an eighteen-week season and was absolutely impossible. It couldn't be raised and my first priority was to work on their deficit—which I did, and it was soon five million dollars! But we raised it. So it's really very tough to tell the unions you can't give that five-dollar increase.

QUESTION   Mr. Lichtenstein, how does one go about setting up a successful subscription campaign?

MR. LICHTENSTEIN   The best advice I can give you is to work in a subscription office sometime and see what goes on. When I was offered the job of running the subscription for the New York City Ballet, I'd never done it before. I did it with the advice of someone who is a traveling professional adviser on subscriptions, a fellow called Danny Newman, who is a press agent out of Chicago and whom the Ford Foundation sends around to every theatre, opera house, ballet company and orchestra to advise on their subscription. I did it with his advice and counseling.

I would say that the first rule would be scarcity. I don't think that subscription works very well unless people are forced into it by the fact that they may not be able to get tickets any other way. If you know that the house is going to be empty, or only fifty percent, then it's very difficult. What the magic number is, I don't know. Maybe seventy percent, or sixty-five, to make subscriptions really work right. Then there are all kinds of offers that were developed—offering one performance free, or other cut prices for buying a series. You're dealing with brochures, direct mail, advertising and juggling those ways of selling subscriptions. I think strong subscription is crucial in the performing arts, just as fund-raising is.

SIR RUDOLF   The Metropolitan was extremely lucky and fortunate with their subscription. We were, for many years, close to seventy percent subscribed. Now the beauty of that subscription was that it was advertised either for ten Mondays, or whatever it was. The dates were given but the performances were not mentioned and the casts were not mentioned. But the people know, "My God, this house is full! I better get my subscription."

Now last season when the box office fell off a little, the new management got into a panic and advertised what they call "trios." They announced that on the 19th of December you can have Sutherland in *Lucia,* on the 7th of January Correlli in *Romeo and Juliette,* and on the 12th of February Scotto in I don't know what. It did very well—and the subscriptions fell ten percent, because people said, "I know I can buy three performances on these days with these stars, why should I buy ten and not know what I get?"

So I thought that was a great mistake.

QUESTION   What do you think should be the relationship of a manager to a producer or a producing organization?

MR. SINGER   I would say he's completely responsible to me in anything to do with meeting his budget. If, for example, with a dance series he wants a company very badly and I have questions about it, I would be inclined to give in to him because it is his operation. But on any of the other areas of how much to spend for advertising, things of that sort, once that's established he has to maintain that.

MR. LICHTENSTEIN   I think it all depends on having, picking your own manager. I think that if you pick someone to do something whom you think is eminently capable, you trust their judgment. I think you give them some leeway, some latitude, particularly if you work in an area with which you are not as familiar as they. But basically you're responsible. I think there's no question that the director, the executive director or managing-director is the responsible party, failure or success ultimately comes back to him. But I think it's also a give-and-take situation, here maybe more flexibility, there maybe less. The important thing is choosing a manager who can work within the guidelines you set and whom you trust and whom you feel is capable of doing the job.

MR. SINGER   The hardest thing is to let go, because you know you can do everything better from selling tickets to promoting it to designing the brochure . . .

MR. LICHTENSTEIN   . . . to cleaning the toilets.

MR. SINGER   At times you can do better, you know, but it's very, very important to try and give people the opportunity to make their own mistakes. That can be very painful and I know I don't do it. But that's what you *try* to do and I think Harvey is very right about choosing someone whom you can really relax with and say, "Well, it's going to be carried out the right way." It's like choosing a director for an opera, and then going into dress rehearsal and seeing it's ghastly. You know you can't do anything about it by that time.

SIR RUDOLF   I was my own producer and my own manager. I picked the people I wanted—the director, the conductor, and the cast, and then up to a point I supervised them. But again, as you said, naturally if I have a man like Zeffirelli or Karajan—I won't tell Karajan, "This is too slow!"

QUESTION   What advice do you have about negotiating contracts with big-name performers?

SIR RUDOLF   It's changed very much over the years. Now, of course, lately, the really great stars—the Correllis, the Nilssons—don't make their own contracts. They have corporations. I have left a time bomb for my successor, because one of these days the Internal Revenue Service will wake up to this. I had a contract with Mr. Correlli's corporation in London whereby his wife is his secretary and his poodle is his manager and these were all because of tax problems. Eventually, he had to sing, but we never paid him, the money went straight to his company. *They* paid him. What they paid him is none of my business and I didn't know. It was very complicated because the company didn't get hoarse, Correlli got hoarse!

Basically, the problems are just those of demand and

supply. There are very few Correllis or Nilssons around and therefore, to a large extent, they can dictate their terms up to a point. It's just the skill of the management to try and keep these in line with what we think we can afford, to get them for the period you want, to make them sing what you want. The same applies to almost any kind of human relationship—it's a question of human relationships and the skill of negotiating and achieving what you want to achieve.

Government, Business and the Foundations as Producers

Alvin H. Reiss
G. A. McLellan
Stephen Benedict

Commentary by *Alvin H. Reiss*

Author of *Culture & Company,*
The Arts Management Handbook;
editor of "Arts Management
Newsletter"

I am most affirmatively not a representative of government!
I've written about government involvement in the arts and,
in fact, at one time did a column on government and the arts
for a magazine called *Cultural Affairs,* but let me say first
that I'm independent, I'm not organization-bound. I think
this may be interesting, since in coming years I believe
there will be a growing number of opportunities for independent activities in various aspects of the arts.

I guess I consider myself a writer, primarily, although I
am also involved in programming, broadcasting, lecturing,
etcetera. How did I begin in this field? That becomes anec-
dotal and delightful for me to tell—I haven't told this story
for a long time!

My very first job after college and the Army was as an associate to a Broadway producer—wow! This was an opportunity! Here I was ready to begin my career, and I am on
Broadway already! I worked with a man, who shall be
nameless, because of the tragic circumstances of the story. I
worked on two Broadway productions. I met prospective
backers for shows and I went on a lot of wild, hairy,
hundred-mile-an-hour trips to New Haven for try-outs. One
production we did was *Red Roses for Me,* which was beautifully done, which received good reviews and which died

in about two weeks. I had my suspicions at the time about what happens in producing. The other was an ill-fated thing called *The Innkeepers*, which didn't run very long either. In any event, after eight weeks the producer's plane crashed in Lake Erie and he was never found. I was left holding the bag for my eight week's salary of fifty dollars a week, so I was four hundred dollars in the hole.

I was engaged to be married and my father-in-law to be, a lawyer, didn't know how to respond when someone would ask what his son-in-law did. He indicated that I was somehow involved with producing, but it was clear that I had to find a job. So I wound up in the first writing job I could find. When I walked into this new job, also for fifty dollars a week, the owner of the firm said, "Write a hundred jokes!" And he left. I had never written a gag in my life. It was a publicity firm and I was writing for Broadway columns. So I stared at this blank page for an hour or so and then I started thinking, "What is a joke?" I began picking up the other jokes available around the office, sheets and columns of them, and then after about three or four hours it hit me that there were basic formulas. Anyone can write a joke if they have a basic sense of humor. Of course, I only reached number seventy-two that day when my boss came back.

I was still very deeply in love with the theatre and arts activities and wanted to get back. Somehow I drifted into PR and joined a firm. In my spare time I was an Off-Broadway press agent for the Greenwich Mews Theatre, which had a most successful production at that time called *Me, Candido*, which ran for about a year and a half. My fee was fifteen dollars, split with the nephew of the director—another lesson that I learned! Along about 1960, when I was involved in doing PR for the Museum of Primitive Art and a number of other activities, I met up with a guy named Alvin Toffler, whom you may know as the author of *Future Shock*. We became good friends as a result of our public relations involvement—me on the client end and he as a writer—and we wound up writing a show together. At least we did the prologue and the beginning of the first act, and then we started talking about other things. Al had just done a piece for *Fortune* magazine called "A Quantity of Culture," looking out around the country at developments in this field from the economic viewpoint. We became fascinated with the prospects for development in this area and the fact that there was an emerging profession—arts management— and new careerists, professional administrators.

At this point, this is 1961, there were no graduate arts management training courses as we know them now. In fact there were no courses at all linking together all the arts. There were theatre management courses and programs, symphony orchestra programs, but there weren't even national associations in some areas of the arts. So we talked about this and out of our talking came this publication, *Arts Management*, which saw the light of day in February, 1962, and which makes me a veteran in this field.

What I presently do is mostly writing. I've written about education in the arts, which is a subject that fascinates me. I have an article coming out in *Art News* next month, a rather lengthy one on that subject. I did a cover story for the *American Way* magazine on business and the arts. I am doing another story for them about a month from now. I have an *Arts Management Handbook*, which I've revised. I have written satire on the arts, believe it or not, and continue producing "Arts Management" issues and promoting my new book, *Culture & Company*. On the consulting end there are some exciting new activities. I am involved with the State University of New York now as a visiting consultant, and what I do is go around to various campuses (there are seventy-two units, so the job may be endless), working with the people who are producing arts activities on the campus and with some of the departments that are involved. Also, and I think this is a new kind of development, I work with non-arts departments—I may go into a business class and discuss the economics of the arts, or got into a sociology class and try to relate the social aspects of the arts to what they're learning. I am also involved with "town and gown" programs—bringing local arts councils together with the college. And I am a consultant with an organization called ACAE—the American Council for the Arts in Education— which begins its annual meeting tomorrow in Philadelphia.

Last year, they hosted a session in Los Angeles. It was on community arts and community survival, which was a very exciting subject.

Neighborhood arts is a field that I have been deeply involved in and loved for a great many years. I taught a course on it at the New School [for Social Research] and have written about it for a number of publications.

In the business-arts field, which is Mr. McLellan's specialty (I call him "Mac") I am running a technical assistance program which is funded by the State Arts Council. I try to provide technical assistance to corporations and business groups that want to get involved in the arts. This is strictly for New York State. In addition I become very excited at the kind of activity in which I go into a community and work with that community on a very quiet, informal, unpublicized kind of program to bring business and the arts into the same orbit. It's a very pragmatic kind of meeting, relating to business needs, the growth of the community and why business should get involved—sketching out some of the myths about the arts for businessmen. I don't lisp, but I call that particular approach "myth America."

I also do a radio show on the arts called "Monthly Arts Forum." Another activity that I am very deeply involved with is the Performing Arts Management Institute. It's an annual, three-day training workshop in arts administration given every fall. It doesn't turn out arts administrators, since it only lasts three days, but it does bring people together, it does expose a number of viewpoints and it does make participants think. Judging by the reactions we've had, it is an important program.

I am concerned with development and the social and economic context in which the arts operate. There have been a number of radical changes in the framework in which the arts have found themselves over the years, and I view any two or three recent years as several lifetimes in this field. Since 1965, a turning point for the arts, four or five things happened that helped set a new developmental framework. That year we had the first visible example of the arts as a matter of national concern—the publication of the Rockefeller Brothers Fund *Panel Report* on the state of the performing arts. Regardless of what that report said or its recommendations, I think that its primary importance was as a promotional vehicle, giving front page impetus to the arts. That was one.

Number two: we had the official entry of national government onto the scene with the Act creating the National Endowment for the Arts and Humanities. Obviously, there had been government involvement before under the Kennedy administration, both symbolically and with the appointment of August Hecksher. But this was a formal recognition of the arts, and through the creation of the Endowment we had the emergence of state arts councils with resources provided to enable states to create their own official agencies on the arts. Thirdly, a very important Act was passed, the Elementary and Secondary Education Act of 1965, which involved arts groups in the education system. There is a lot we can say about that, some of it negative. But through Title One and Title Three of that Act, arts groups were able to relate to the mainstream and bring programs into schools and this involved another kind of recognition.

Number four, if you're keeping track of the score, we were then in the midst of what I called in an *Esquire* article "the Lincoln Center Syndrome," the cultural center boom. Through the emergence and development of cultural centers and facilities, business was becoming involved more than ever before in the arts. Now there were a lot of false starts here. Sometimes that involvement only meant that business was contributing to the *symbol* of culture, rather than to culture itself. In other words, a lot of arts groups were performing within those facilities, and yet they didn't have the funds to perform. The *facilities* were being built and supported but the arts groups weren't!

All of these things, I think, have set the stage for the arts scene of today. In the late '60's, following these developments, we had another kind of force operating on the arts, which, although not affirmative at first, exerted a positive influence on the field. There were a lot of people who were in the arts but outside the action, who were criticizing the arts establishment for certain activities. You found arts groups being accused of racism, sexism and every kind of 'ism, and their most startled retort was, "But we're *for* the arts, why are we being attacked?" They were forced to find out why.

The emergence of government funds demanded a service aspect by the arts, since government was obviously concerned with the kind of service that could be rendered by an arts group, not with the arts product itself. We also had the development of neighborhood arts, the emergence of arts from the grassroots up. We had informality brought to the arts, which was very important and, I think, the youth culture played a major role in this. Some of the intimidating walls around culture were being stripped away. People could go to concerts without wearing a tie and jacket if they didn't want to.

Now, what advice can I give to someone entering the arts management field? I note five points. The first: understand the field in which you are involved, be literate. Basically, I find we are involved in an illiterate field; people don't read the material that is available to them, people become very self-centered because they are living in a very demanding situation where they must be very self-centered and concerned with what they're doing. But the material that's available, the kind of thought that can be given to this field is mind-boggling.

Two: be interested in all aspects of community life, since one of the keys to arts development in recent years has been the arts' relationship to other areas—arts and recreation, arts and education and so forth. The relationships that are emerging are important ones. Every day we learn about a new kind of relationship between the arts and another aspect of society. The arts are not at the center of things, but they're part of something that's happening, so I think you have to be concerned with everything that is happening in the city.

Number three: always question. Don't accept what seems to be there merely because it's been there. There are an awful lot of programs that exist only because they *have* existed. I think one of the worst things, especially in a creative area, is to perpetuate mediocrity. So question when you can.

Fourth, an important point: seek out artistic excellence where you can. I personally favor—and this may be very controversial—I favor artistic dictatorship. I believe that if someone has a strong artistic point of view, and knows why he is doing things, and does them well, I believe that's someone you can relate to. The best arts producers I have seen have been those who are artistic dictators and don't compromise excellence for the available dollar. Seek that out and relate to it.

I guess the last thing and the most important, is to care about people, because essentially this is a "people" area. Involvement in the arts is concerned with *people* in the arts!

Commentary by *G. A. McLellan*

President, Business Committee for
the Arts, New York City

As Mr. Benedict and I arrived here, I said I couldn't imagine anything less interesting than for you to hear about my background. But, briefly: I was raised and educated in the Midwest, attended the universities of Wisconsin and Minnesota, was drafted into the service during World War II and ended up as a major in charge of personnel work in the Air Force. That led to my going to American Airlines after the war as a personnel executive.

I stayed with American Airlines for about five years then went to the Mathieson Chemical Corporation as director of personnel. When Mathieson later merged with Olin and became Olin-Mathieson (now the Olin Corporation), I became assistant director of personnel for the joint corporations. We had forty thousand employees throughout the United States. Near the end of my time with Olin I was asked to join the White House staff with President Kennedy and later stayed on with President Johnson to develop a program to convince businessmen across the nation that they should employ, train and promote non-whites. The program was called Plans for Progress. Now it's called the National Alliance of Businessmen. The idea was to bring businessmen together at the White House and explain the advantages of hiring and training and promoting non-whites, convince them that this was something they should do, and then work with them in terms of their internal procedures, to bring about positive action.

I returned to Olin as director of public affairs and had been back a couple of years when David Rockefeller made a speech based on the Rockefeller *Panel Report* that Skip [Alvin Reiss] mentioned earlier. The speech was made at the National Industrial Conference Board, now called the Conference Board. In this speech (I think it was written by Stephen Benedict, as a matter of fact) Mr. Rockefeller said that he was convinced that the best source of the type of funds the arts needed was the business community. Essentially, he said, "If you agree with me that something should be done to interest the business community in the future of the arts, I'd like to hear from you." The response he got convinced him that he *should* do something about it.

It was about that time that I was brought together with Stephen Benedict to consider the possibility of working with a group of top businessmen to promote support of the arts by the business sector. An organization was set up and called the Business Committee for the Arts. The mission of the Business Committee is to convince all business people that the arts are important to them, that they should be concerned with the state of the arts and get involved with them and support them. It's a small group of top business people representing most communities, most states and almost all types of industry and business in the United States and Canada. The founding group, organized in September 1967, was composed of David Rockefeller, Douglas Dillon, Devereaux Josephs, who was then chairman of the New York Life Insurance Company; Gavin MacBain, who is Chairman of Bristol-Myers; Bruce Palmer, who was President of the Conference Board; Katherine Graham, Chairman of the *Washington Post* and *Newsweek* magazine; and Roger Blough, who was Chairman of U.S. Steel. We decided to invite a small group of executives to work with this founding group to implement the basic principles and rationale we thought were important for all business to accept. The invitation went out to ninety business people and we got eighty-six affirmative responses. Then we went to a group of major foundations and asked them for seed money to get the concept going, with the understanding that if it was successful in the first three years, we would ask the business community for underwriting to make it possible to continue this program. The Business Committee for the Arts has an authorized strength of one hundred and twenty-five top business heads—practically every large company that you can imagine is represented on the roll of this group which works as a national organization. We are concerned with the health of the arts in Utah, Montana and California as well as in New York, Connecticut and New Jersey. The men and women who are invited to participate as members are carefully selected for their interest in the arts, the interest of their corporation and/or their record of support of the arts.

We try to convince businessmen that they should support the arts by several approaches. First, we have a communications program geared to the business sector including a quarterly newsletter called *BCA News*. This is distributed to fifteen thousand heads of corporations across the country in an effort to convince them that they should follow the lead of those who support the arts and do the same sort of thing in their own communities or within their own industries. The newsletter is provided free of cost to the recipient, so that we don't have the problem of convincing them first that they should subscribe. We also communicate with arts organizations with a simple newsletter called *Arts-Business;* this monthly publication is sent to twelve thousand arts leaders throughout the nation, also at no cost to the recipients, and provides examples of the sort of cooperative efforts that are developing between arts and business to their mutual advantage. These ideas can be applied to their own situations. Let me give you some examples.

One of the things we wrote about in an early issue concerned an arts program of the National Shawmut Bank of Boston, one of the largest banks in the nation. Instead of giving an electric can opener or pots and pans for new accounts, they decided to give a membership in any museum in the Boston area for a new account of one hundred dollars, or an addition to an old account of one hundred dollars. They ended up financing almost six thousand new museum memberships in the Boston area!

We reasoned that this idea could be picked up by any arts organization and utilized in its own community for its own support. The program did many things. It convinced the community that the Shawmut Bank was interested in what was happening in the arts in Boston. It created a new audience and source of income for the museums by providing them with new memberships, and it acquainted a lot of people with the programs of these museums. This one article alone brought hundreds of telephone calls to our office and many to the bank in Boston. The concept has been picked up by corporations all over the country at the urging of local arts organizations.

We try to show both business and arts leaders that there are ways that the arts can be supported by other than grants of money, even though cash is always welcome.

Another article we wrote that attracted a lot of attention on a national basis concerned the creation of Heinz Hall in Pittsburgh. If any of you have visited Heinz Hall, you know it is one of the finest concert halls in the nation. It was created from an old movie theatre which was about to be torn down. A group of businessmen in Pittsburgh decided the theatre was too good to be destroyed and that the downtown area and the community needed a concert hall. This led to the decision to band together and renovate the hall. The work was financed by H.J. Heinz, Alcoa, Pittsburgh Plate Glass, U.S. Steel and other corporations in the area. This again has accomplished many things. It has provided a superb concert hall and home for the Pittsburgh Symphony, the Pittsburgh Ballet and the Pittsburgh Civic Opera. It also brings a lot of people to the downtown area of Pittsburgh who in recent years had no reason to be there after dark, because it became a no-man's land as soon as business offices closed. Shops and restaurants which were closing in early evening for lack of business now stay open to accommodate new business.

BCA also publishes hardcover books. Our newest one is *The New Patrons of the Arts.* It was published by Harry

Abrams at no cost to us and written by BCA staff. It reviews recent developments in the business-arts relationship and is the fourth in our book series.

We also communicate through an advertising campaign that some of you may have seen on television, heard on radio or read in *Newsweek, Time, Fortune, Cue, The New Yorker, Business Week*. Practically every magazine you can imagine, including the nudist magazine, has carried our ads as a public service. Our first ad used Rodin's "The Kiss" (now you know why the nudist magazine was interested). This advertising program, which is now four years old, cost us about $100,000 but has brought over twenty million dollars in free, commercial media space on television, radio and in magazines. It is aimed at the entire public, not only the business sector, and stresses the importance of the arts to each one of us. It tries to convince the viewer or reader that, although they may not be able to play in the symphony orchestra, or paint a landscape or act in the repertory theatre, they may be able to help prepare scenery or sell tickets or do many of the other things volunteers can do for the arts.

We prepare statistics on what is happening in the business-arts nexus. We are convinced that business support for the arts has increased from twenty-two million a year in 1965 to a level of one hundred and forty-four million a year in 1973. This type of support comes from two sources— from funds set aside for philanthropic giving, including funds from corporate foundations, and funds set aside for business expense purposes. Into this second area would fall money spent on arts programs that involve advertising, public relations and public affairs. The public television Masterpiece Theatre series is financed by one of our companies from business expense funds. The millions of dollars programs of this type cost has some advertising value for the sponsor because the program starts and ends with a credit statement.

We conduct conferences across the nation with groups of business people, aimed at reaching the local business executive who has never considered support of the arts. These conferences are often done on a state basis. We ask our member, if we have one in the state, or another leading executive, to act as chairman and invite a group of business leaders in his state to come to a central location and discuss the health of the arts in their state and what can be done to bring about greater involvement of the business community. We have held these conferences in Wisconsin, Indiana, California, Louisiana, Arkansas, Oklahoma, Nebraska, West Virginia, North Carolina, Iowa, Michigan and Utah. This program will continue until we have visited most major population centers and all states in the nation. We take to these conferences executives from companies that have supported the arts. They tell what they've done and, in effect, establish a pattern for the local people to follow.

BCA gives awards to businessmen for what they do in support of the arts. Jointly, with *Esquire* magazine, we gave an award to one company for the fifth time, the Schlitz Beer Company, well-known for its support of the arts. We gave them a piece of sculpture for this award. About twenty *Esquire*/BCA Awards are given each year in this program, which was initiated by *Esquire* in 1966.

We advise businessmen on involvement in the arts. If they're interested, we'll act as the catalyst between arts organizations and business. Many of the business support programs you know of have resulted from the type of marriage we have been able to establish between these two separate sectors. We try to advise arts organizations on their approach to business, because we know one of the problems they have is that they *don't* know how to approach business and therefore lose possible support or waste a lot of time.

With that I will close, except to say my advice to aspiring arts managers is that arts managers could well consider the type of person they are going to visit before they ask for support. Make certain that your own house is in order before going to business for the support you need. Most arts managers have not considered these two factors. They come to our office to talk about their plans to contact the business community and, as far as we're concerned, they're planning to see all the wrong people. A repertory theatre from Madison, Wisconsin, might plan to visit IBM and U.S. Steel and Alcoa. When we ask them, "Why?" they say, "Because they're big companies with lots of money."

The fact is that none of those companies have any interest in Madison, Wisconsin, and therefore would be hard pressed to rationalize support for the theatre in Madison—which hasn't been considered. This is why you ought to analyze the prospects whom you plan to see. If you plan to go to a company that has operations in Madison, it would make sense for that company to consider supporting a theatre in that city.

If there is anything we can do as an organization to help any of you, we would be very happy to spend as much time as we can with you. We won't give you names of people to approach, but we will tell you the type of companies to go to, the type of material to have before you go and we will give you our best judgment on your plan of action. In fact, we have a little handbook to help you do all this. If we feel that you've got a program that business might be interested in, we'll talk to businessmen and try to convince them to consider your program.

Commentary by *Stephen Benedict*

Associate, Rockefeller Brothers
Fund, New York City

I looked at the title of this seminar, "Producers on Producing," and tried to imagine what it was that I've produced
the most of. The best answer I can find is anguish, frustration and hostility on the part of most of the people who
come to see me! As you know, at a foundation we have to
say "no" to ninety-nine out of a hundred people. So that is
my principal production; but today I'll try to be a little bit
more positive.

In telling you first about myself, I preface it by saying
that there was no straight and narrow path to a career in the
arts.

After graduating from St. John's College, Annapolis, I
went right to work for a somewhat off-beat group at the
University of Chicago, called The Committee to Frame a
World Constitution. (I had been much involved in the
world federalist movements in high school and in college.)
There I was associate editor of the group's magazine, *Common Cause.* I stayed there for a year until a series of events
led me to New York following the creation by some of my
colleagues of a rather unique little charity called The Foundation for World Government, set up by Anita McCormick
Blaine, the granddaughter of the late Cyrus McCormick,
who decided to give one million dollars to set the world
aright. It didn't work, but it provided me a very interesting
job for a year as assistant to Stringfellow Barr, its president.

This led me to Europe for some conferences, and while there I quit after a while to study music, until my money ran out. After about a' year and a half, I came skulking back to the States, needing a job. While waiting for one that looked all set, I started working in the volunteer movement for Eisenhower for President. Senator Taft was about to be nominated and I thought that would be a disaster. I worked for the organization's research director and soon found myself on the White House staff. I stayed for two and a half years, in a wide variety of low-echelon administrative positions. Then I pulled myself up by the bootstraps and switched over the the U.S. Information Agency, which had interested me for a long time. There I found myself, perhaps because of my world federalist background, as a policy officer for disarmament and the United Nations, which involved attending disarmament conferences in London and in Geneva during the years 1956 through 1959. I was a press officer for the U.S. Delegation and had a variety of other duties. After four years, I started shopping around, having decided I wanted out of government and into the foundation field. I realize now, after having seen about three thousand, four hundred and eighty-six people who are sent to me and want to work at a foundation, that it was sheer dumb luck that caused me to be where I am now. I was a generalist, if ever there was one! At the Rockefeller Brothers Fund, arts projects and applications began to flow to me and that is what I have been doing now for nearly fifteen years.

Most foundations, with the exception of the three or four largest ones, such as Ford, the Rockefeller Foundation and the Carnegie Foundation, tend not to have highly specialized staffs because there really isn't that much activity in any one area. Be that as it may, there is plenty to do in the arts field where we have quite an active program in three or four separate areas which I helped develop over the years. One is an area that Skip Reiss referred to and which has been of particularly great interest to me. It's far outgrown the capacity of private or public funding sources to treat it adequately, but better *in*adequately than not at all. This is the whole so-called community or neighborhood arts movement. We have gotten quite heavily into that in New York City, that being our chosen turf because we don't have the staff or the resources to cover the country. We have gotten very heavily into black and Hispanic theatre, music, dance and related artistic activities, and into encouragingly new links between neighborhood museums and the public schools.

The second area, to which Skip Reiss also alluded, is the whole array of service organizations in the arts, which grew out of the Fund's 1965 panel report, *The Performing Arts: Problems and Prospects,* in which it was strongly recommended that existing service organizations in the arts be strengthened and that new ones be created where there seems to be a demonstrable need for them. As a result, we have been fairly instrumental in getting some of these started and helping others to sustain themselves. I am referring to such groups as a Black Theatre Alliance, the Off-Off-Broadway Alliance, Associated Councils of the Arts, Volunteer Lawyers for the Arts, Opportunity Resources for the Performing Arts, The Theatre Development Fund and The International Theatre Institute.

Perhaps the best—though obvious—piece of advice I have for anybody who is interested in arts management is to get involved as early as possible. Get involved in any way you can on a volunteer basis, get to know artists and the groups that surround them. That is, after all, what you are about in this field. You are a facilitator. That can be a fairly high calling if you do it well, but get involved. I think everybody who *is* interested in this field does that anyway, but get involved—and not just as a professional responsibility. At the Brothers Fund we are all, in our separate fields, encouraged by our trustees to spend substantial amounts of time in ways that have no direct bearing on our grant-making functions. There is an indirect bearing, clearly, because this helps enormously to give each of us a sense of what the problems are on the other side of the table when somebody comes to us with a project or a problem. In my particular field I have been President of a professional chamber orchestra and of an amateur chorus. I am now President of the Theatre Development Fund, I am on the

Committee of the Toscanini Memorial Archives, which is concerned with original manuscripts and first editions of the great composers. I have served three years on the Expansion Arts Panel of the National Endowment for the Arts and soon will switch to the Public Media Panel. All of this for me is absolutely invaluable for keeping in close touch with the prevailing needs and currents in the artistic community. Without it I think it would be extremely difficult to sit back in my perch on the fifty-fourth floor of the RCA Building and have á practical sense of what the needs are, what the trends are and what the problems in the arts are that we should be anticipating. A professional foundation has got the staff and the time to look into things which the private or corporate donor generally doesn't have. Nor do we have all the constraints which the administrators of public money at the city, state or federal level must observe.

What I am saying seems awfully elementary, but I'm afraid it's not. For someone going into the arts, it's terribly important to get a sense as soon as possible and on a continuing basis of the total spectrum with which one will be dealing. Don't go just to the opera because you like opera, or just to something else because you like it. Artists themselves, paradoxically, very seldom experience anything that isn't in their own art form. As Skip points out, it's extraordinary how illiterate the average artist is about what's going on in the rest of the artistic community. For example, the dancer going to opera or the musician going to the theatre, museum people going to any of the performing things—the crossover is not nearly as great as I think it should be, particularly as the arts become more and more and more interrelated in so many ways.

Questions to *Alvin H. Reiss*
G. A. McLellan
Stephen Benedict

QUESTION   What can you actually say to busy executives and tired businessmen to make them support the arts?

MR. MCLELLAN   Well, the first thing we point out to business people is that they can't operate their business without the arts. The presentation of their product to the public, whether it be automobiles or chemicals, depends on the way the artist packages it, paints it, colors it or shapes it. Often, businessmen don't recognize that these functions involve artists at every turn in the road. They don't realize that moving their product from the sales floor to the customer's home depends on artists. The presentation of the product on television, in magazines, on radio, all depend on artists of one type or another. We point out that, in many instances, they have made the decision to locate a new office or a new plant in a certain area due to the existence of the arts in that area. When they stop to analyze their past decisions, they realize that this is true.

I had a very interesting experience in Little Rock, Arkansas, where the sponsors of our conference were a group of men called "Fifty For The Future." They were fifty leading businessmen in the State of Arkansas who, prior to agreeing to sponsor a conference, had done little or nothing in the arts. When we finished our conference one of these fifty leading businessmen said, "Well, you know, when a company visited the Chamber of Commerce last week and talked about moving to Arkansas, they asked us first about the cultural activities in this community. They asked to see the Arkansas Cultural Center, wanted to walk through it and see what kind of collection we had there."

They realized most business today depends on the type of person who demands cultural activities for himself and for his family.

Those are some of the points we make—and many, many more.

MR. BENEDICT I would approach the answer from a very different direction, which is not to say that I'm contradicting you, Mac.

I suppose I see the arts as being the best consolidators and interpreters of experience. After all, that's what the arts are doing. They're compressing, refining, reinterpreting and putting a new impress on different kinds of experience, whether it be experience in sound or in movement or in any of the other senses. I think that many, many answers can be given about the surge of interest in the arts (I won't say *re-surgence*, because there hasn't been a comparable one before in this country). I think it relates to the deepening series of questions that America, as the leading so-called post-industrial society, is beginning to ask itself: Why are we here? What's technology all about? What's industrial society all about? What is it for the sake of which we are doing all these things, whether it be getting a formal education or an informal education or working on an assembly line or whatever else?

The arts have traditionally demonstrated and continue to demonstrate all kinds of extraordinary and provocative and annoying and illuminating things. The arts offer a whole different way of discovering purpose. By this I don't mean necessarily to describe the arts as a "means" in the sense that Mac describes the arts as a means in the context of the business community. Art, rather, has both an end and a means because a successful artistic product or a successful artist—successful in communicating, not in making money—is, after all, constantly causing questions to be asked that lead to other questions. These questions may be verbal, they may be visual, or they may be oral. They may be stated in a whole variety of different ways. In this sense I do see the arts at the center and not at the periphery or as an adjunct to the rest of experience. I think I can see them fitting just about anywhere into a well-ordered society, both as an end and a means, as a facilitator, as a communicator, as a rationale for what we do.

MR. REISS   I guess I have been asked this question a number of times and every time I come up with a different answer. But, basically, they are all the same. To me, there is an emotional feeling about the arts. The arts engage a whole person more than anything I know. They arouse feelings which are very important. I guess I could best illustrate this with several stories involving kids.

One of the key movements in the arts now is to make them part of the core curriculum in elementary and secondary schools. We're still a long way from it, but there have been some noteworthy experiments and I have been involved with some of them. I've seen what has happened and how the arts *do* engage the kids and arouse their emotions. In one instance, in a Project Impact school where there was a dancer in residence, the kids had a program every year in which they had to write a theme about the meaning of spring. This kind of annoyed the teacher, because every year the kids would come out with "spring is warm," and "spring is green," and "I like spring very much," and that was about it. Well, the English teacher turned to the dance specialist and said, "We are doing the spring thing again and let's see what we can get out of the kids."

So the dance teacher said to the kids, "Well, what is spring?"

One kid started yelling, "Spring is warm, and there is a wind!"

"But what does the wind look like?"

"Well, the wind moves."

"How does it move?"

The kid arose and started moving the way the wind moves, and another kid got up and said, "Well, if that's the wind, I want to be the kite in the wind," and that kid started moving and another kid became the tail of the kite, and so on. Soon the whole class was up and involved in the action.

Following that, they did their themes again and the themes that came out of this were so wonderful, wild and imaginative! One kid's kite was in a cave and he kept getting deeper into the cave, and suddenly it opened up into a giant building and he was at the top of it. The kids had been aroused and had learned something important about themselves.

There is a school here in New York City which you ought to visit—P.S. 51, which is in what's called the Hell's Kitchen area in the '40's and between 10th and 11th Avenues, a low income, ethnic melting pot area. In doing a story recently, I went over there as they had also been part of a program involving the arts and the curriculum. When I went out into the school yard, there was this huge mural on the wall done after the Mayan style of art. Obviously, it had been done by kids, so I said to the principal, "How did this result?" Well the kids had been studying Mayan culture and they wanted to do something themselves. So they spent weeks doing the mural.

As I was leaving, I turned around and on the very opposite wall there was another huge mural, although it wasn't quite as well done. I said to the teacher, "How did that mural happen?"

"Oh, the kids had been telling their parents about their mural for weeks. Then we had open school week and when the parents came and saw what the kids had done, they wanted to do this themselves!"

Now to me this is the best example of what the arts can do. We can also talk about the artist and what he can do. The artist is the mirror and the prognosticator at the same time. We learn not only about ourselves and our own vulnerabilities, but we also learn through the artist something about society. We learn things that enable us perhaps to think about the future kind of world we want to live in. To me, this is very important today. It's very important that we have a humanistic concern for our cities, for the problems that we have.

QUESTION What do you think about the relationship between the arts manager and the producer or artistic director of an organization? Should it be one person or several?

MR. REISS Let me say that some of the best arts administrators I've seen have been people with a firm artistic viewpoint. Let's take Joe Papp, for example. Joe Papp learned how to relate to people, learned how to plug into various resources, learned something about developing the people around him and getting them to do things. There is another administrator, a guy in Seattle, Washington, named Glynn Ross, who took an opera company a number of years ago and through managerial acumen learned how to relate, learned how to isolate publics, not one public, and learned how to relate to each of those publics and to develop his organization.

Someone like Joe Papp isn't going to take a back seat to anyone. I don't want to speak for him on what he does or, let's say, how expert he is in handing a budget. He may not have to do this, but still he has to have a feel and a pulse on everything that happens there. He's a very strong personality. There are other organizations where the artistic point of view is not as strong. Here, there may be a split—there's a need for an artist, or an artistic director, plus an arts administrator. I don't think there's one answer to this. I think it depends on the organization and the situation. Let me say I've seen it work beautifully with the single guy doing it and with a division of responsibilities also.

MR. BENEDICT An addendum to that, though only indirectly related to it: It's generally true that the skills of a particular artistic administrator or manager in one art are not transferable to another. This is curious but usually true.

MR. REISS We have an opposite view, then. I have been involved in bringing people together from many of the art forms, indicating that there *are* commonalities. I think I have seen some darn good examples of people who have moved from one field to another. I think the problem exists, if it's a problem, with artistic thrust. If there is someone so deeply motivated by an art form, then he may find it very difficult to cross that bridge. Sometimes you get a theatre man who is so deep into theatre that he couldn't go into dance. But I think I'm finding more people who can do that, and I know quite a few who are making the transition every year. The schism has always been there, but the increasing involvement on an artistic level between various disciplines has brought many of the arts closer together, certainly from a programatic point of view. If we look at the last five or six years, we see many examples of dance, theatre, opera, light shows, symphonic-rock, all kinds of things. It has been a greater mix than before and it's brought people together who have never before been concerned with another art form. If there is a split, it's between the performing and visual arts.

QUESTION Do you really believe in the necessity of artistic dictatorship?

MR. REISS I believe in an artistic viewpoint. There are an awful lot of con men around today and society encourages con men. In the arts there are a lot of people who are developing programs of various kinds because it's very easy to get support—not necessarily because they are good programs or follow a viewpoint. Programming follows available funds. You can get funds for a lot of things. This happened especially during the Title Three days when a lot of arts groups were doing things they shouldn't have done, merely because funds were available.

If I am to be a manager or administrator, I would want to become involved with someone who knows what he is doing in an artistic sense, and knows why he is doing it. This is what I call artistic dictatorship. Let's take a theatre group in Teaneck, New Jersey, or Brighton Beach, OK? Let's say the guy there doesn't have artistic thrust, doesn't know why he is doing things, and in the middle of his program he decides to stick in this or that kind of production. OK? "The audience wasn't good for the last one, so we'll do a Neil Simon now and maybe we'll get an audience." He may be right, he may get out part of the audience, but in the long run this guy is not going to succeed in a true sense. He doesn't know *why* he's doing things.

I think what I mean by artistic viewpoint in dictatorship is that someone knows *why* he's doing something. When he sticks to his artistic viewpoint, in the long run something develops and something happens. I'm looking at people like Zelda Fichandler in Washington, D.C. with the Arena Stage, Nina Vance in Texas, Joe Papp in New York, people who have a concept and have developed along with it. Those people generally attract support because people want to help those who are doing something that they believe in.

QUESTION   Briefly, Mr. McLellan, what do you think is the best way to approach a corporation for money?

MR. McLELLAN   You first expect, when a person comes in, that he knows what your corporation is, at least to the point that he thinks you might be interested in a particular community or area. Secondly, you expect he knows enough about his own organization to be able to answer questions concerning it. You'd be surprised how many people go to corporations for support and don't really know about their own organization! Next, that you have your story prepared in two forms—first a very brief presentation, one page will usually do it, supported by as much information as you want to give in addition. But make it possible for someone you're going to talk to to consider what you're talking about by reading the very brief presentation. Try to adjust to the person to whom you're talking. Try to adjust your presentation to what you think the man wants to hear. You could spend two hours saying what can be said well in fifteen minutes, if properly prepared. Few business people have two hours to spend with you.

After I got this job, a man with whom I had once worked and who was vice president of personnel for one of the largest corporations on the West Coast called me and said, "Mac, I'm very happy that you're in that job and I've convinced my board of directors that we should do something to get ourselves involved in the arts. We have never done anything, but we have ten thousand employees in this state and we really should get involved in the arts. How do you suggest we begin? I've been given the mandate by our board to do something."

I said, "Well, I would suggest without knowing more about your community that you call your local arts council and ask them to come and talk to you to give you some ideas on what you might do. At the same time we will do some research for you."

So he did. He called the head of the arts council—this is an absolutely true story—and introduced himself on the telephone and said, "I wonder if you can come and talk to me about some things that my corporation might do to help the arts?"

The director of this arts council said, "Well, I would like to talk to you, but I'm not going to be able to come for about two weeks!"

I can't imagine an arts council head being so busy he couldn't see the largest corporation in the community for two weeks. Anyway, he said, "But I'll send someone else to see you."

So the fellow came and the secretary buzzed my friend and said, "Your guest is here." She had a funny tone in her voice, so he knew that something was wrong. He went out to meet the guy, who was barefooted, had practically no clothes on and didn't have anything with him to show what the arts council was doing. Obviously, the businessman couldn't relate to this guy.

"How could I talk to him about what our corporation could do for the arts, when this guy didn't make any effort to relate to *me?*"

Well, the end of the story is that this company is doing a lot for the arts, because we helped him research what existed in his own community, got the state arts council to visit him and make a professional approach to his corporation, including suggestions as to what might be done to help the arts in the community.

MR. REISS   I'd just like to add something. What I find most important is the *quid pro quo* aspect of any business-arts alliance. I feel that if business becomes involved with the arts, it has to get something out of it. From the arts viewpoint I've been trying to fight the "non-respect syndrome," where the arts take something from someone but there's very little respect for them. Respect must be part of the *quid pro quo* for the arts.

I have three rules from an arts point of view that I try to observe in business relationships. One is that the resulting program is in good taste, in other words that business doesn't bastardize it to their own commercial needs. Two, that it be consistent with what you are doing. If it's so far afield that you can't relate to it, then it's no good. And three, is it "do-able"? So many of the kinds of projects that come about are completely non-do-able from the beginning.

Mac referred to the Shawmut Bank. There is a bank right here, the East New York Bank for Savings, that was opening a new branch on 42nd Street. They were confronted with the possibility of giving away dishes and all that kind of stuff. One of their first questions was, "We're moving here, what are the amenities we could identify with which will make us identified with this area, which will help meet our market needs?" Right across the street was one of the great cultural-educational institutions of New York, the main branch of the New York Public Library, which at that point was engaged in a giant fund-raising campaign to match a grant from the National Humanities Foundation.

Well, these big ads came out: "Choose one of these gifts below, but we'd *rather* that you donate the cost of this gift to the New York Public Library and we'll match your contribution!"

What happened was interesting. Sure, the campaign helped the library, but what was most interesting is what it did for that bank. Number one, they encouraged more new accounts and more dollar contributions than any branch that had ever opened in their history. This is a plain fact. Number two, they established an image and identity with the area. People knew them, people were writing in, the bank president was getting letters from people saying, "Gee, what a great thing you did. I love New York City, here's a dollar!" Rival bank presidents were sending him money for the library and asking why they didn't think of this first. It's true!

QUESTION   What is the best way to approach the Rockefeller Brothers Fund with a request for financial assistance?

MR. BENEDICT   The first thing you ought to do, which a lot of people don't, is to read our last Annual Report—or the report of whatever foundation you may be going to, and try to get some sense of whether what you're talking about is even in the ball park. As I mentioned, every foundation has to exclude ninety-nine percent of what comes in, because it can only focus effectively on a very small number of areas. I mentioned three or four that happen to be our focus in the arts. There are similar ones in other fields, such as population and conservation and urban affairs and housing and economic development and race relations. Find out first whether you're aiming at the right target. If you are, there really isn't any magic formula. People tend to think that fancy design and presentation and elaborate proposals encased in glassine folders make some kind of special impression. They don't. Simply present the organization or the idea or the project as clearly as possible, and along with that an indication, in fairly specific terms, of budget, and an indication of what the overall scope and operation of the organization is. Generally, every foundation of any size will want something on paper first, and they'll want it sent in, unless you already have an ongoing relationship with the group. This will generally be enough to elicit some kind of response.

I also think that anybody going into arts administration or management had better spend some time learning how to write clearly, if this should happen to be a weak spot.

While we are always looking for that wonderful, innovative idea that will justify our existence even to the most obtuse observer, the fact is that practically never happens. Almost everything that happens at the Fund grows organically out of what it has been doing.

QUESTION   What percentage of the nation's corporations do you estimate are now supporting the arts?

MR. McLELLAN   Our last statistical study indicated that eighty percent of all corporations give *something* to the arts, but that could be anywhere from a hundred dollars for a symphony to a million dollars to the Metropolitan Opera. I would say that very few give substantial amounts. If I didn't think this was true, we wouldn't exist as an organization. When the need for our work no longer exists, we'll go out of business. I don't know whether that will ever happen. But we don't want to be like the fund-raiser of a home for unwed mothers who came to a company for her annual contribution. The businessman said, "Well, ma'm, I've been reading about the effectiveness of the pill and all the other things that are happening in this area. I can't imagine that you will have need for a home for unwed mothers." And she responded, "As a matter of fact, we don't. There's no one in the home at the moment. But we're trying to think of some other use for the home and in the meantime we'd like your support!"

QUESTION   Are there any groups other than BCA that are trying to get the business and arts communities together?

MR. REISS   On the local level there's an Arts and Business Council in New York City. It grew out of a program at the New York Board of Trade, which went back to 1965. Their program basically was a business-oriented program for the arts. What has happened in the last few years, however, and hopefully it will work in the right way, is that artists and businessmen are relating together, are sitting down on a common level and meeting with each other and discussing ways to help the arts. This is what has happened with the Arts and Business Council.

To me, one of the most important factors for the arts now is respect, not only from more business people, but from more educators, from more foundation executives— everyone isn't as enlightened as Steve Benedict's foundation. There are an awful lot of foundation people whose eyes are closed to the arts. What happens at ABC is that across the table you'll see a guy from the Bed-Sty Theatre, someone from a choral group, someone from American Airlines, and it's an experiment, trying to relate them to each other. Hopefully, it will work out.

QUESTION   Is there any kind of directory that lists corporations that support the arts, and shows what they are supporting?

MR. McLELLAN   The reason we don't want to make a list is because a corporation working only with museums or only with symphonies might decide next year to do something for repertory theatre, or another completely different area. We don't want to categorize them unnecessarily and incorrectly. But we have a booklet on what companies have received awards from *Esquire*-BCA. That booklet contains over three hundred examples of what corporations have done in the arts, and it gives you a pretty good picture of what you could expect a corporation to do.

MR. REISS   I think any corporation is fair game and to list them would be to exclude some of them that might be coming into the area.

QUESTION   Can you give us any other examples about how industries and corporations are helping the arts in a non-monetary manner?

MR. McLELLAN   One of our first, which I think is the third or fourth largest accounting firm in the nation, has offered to provide free accounting and budgeting service to arts organizations that don't have this type of assistance already. Through sixty offices around the nation they have offered to go into arts organizations upon request and set up their books, tell them how to keep them properly, tell them how to budget their funds, and how to plan for the future. This is one example.

There are several companies that are doing this on the local level and I could name twenty-five companies that supply public relations services to individual arts organizations. They not only do such things as print programs on company printing presses, but help design ads for newspapers, print their tickets, etcetera. There are many building product companies that haven't seen fit to give money, but are willing to give paint or plywood or things of that sort.

MR. REISS   I think it would be accurate to say that there is scarcely a law firm or accounting firm that takes on an arts organization and that doesn't in the end provide some subsidy by lowered rates.

MR. McLELLAN   We encourage this kind of thing because we know if they get involved, the money will come also. It's a natural sequence.

MR. BENEDICT   I should have mentioned it before, and I'm sure it applies just as much to Mac and his staff at the Business Committee. In the foundation field, for those of us who work in the arts, forty, maybe fifty percent of the time we spend has absolutely nothing to do with the grant-making process. I think I spend at least forty percent of my time merely talking and giving whatever best advice and steers and reactions I can to organizations that we are perhaps already supporting, or perhaps we can't support for some reason of policy, or to those that are trying to get started and are making the rounds getting advice that has really nothing whatever to do with a grant request.

The New York State Arts Council staff, the National Endowment for the Arts staff, the Parks, Recreation and Cultural Affairs staff, as well as foundations—we all do it. There's an enormous amount of time spent that is really consultantship in management, managerial and administrative and financial problems that don't relate directly to the grant-making process, whether it be public or private monies. But it *can be* fully as important as a contribution to an arts organization. They are giving us a chance to get the feel of their problems, while at the same time we hope we may be helping them in some tangible way.

MR. REISS   Before we finish here, let's get to some of the new developments—developments that we're seeing now, which I think are a microcosm of larger things that will happen tomorrow. You know, if we look back, none of us were real clairvoyants and, yet, it was very easy to see the direction in which certain things were going.

All of us here probably made predictions two years ago that the arts were heading into relationships with other areas, and invariably they followed that. Now certain things are happening which might be the pilot occurrences which will lead to larger developments in the future, *if* there's an enlightened arts field.

One is what I call the "and syndrome"—"the arts

and . . ." There are programs now relating the arts *and* recreation, the arts *and* new towns, the arts *and* sports. There's a whole series of things which would never have been considered before, but they are now part of emerging programs.

In the business area a number of very major developments have occured. One of the key ones is that Dayton-Hudson of Minneapolis, a major department store chain which does a billion dollar a year business, has the first corporate director of arts, or director of cultural programs. It's a little bit different than the traditional corporate arts director, who might have been concerned with fine arts and graphics, since this man is essentially an ombudsman to the arts. This company is in twenty-six different states and the arts director helps arts groups in the various states. So the corporation—Dayton-Hudson—has recognized that the arts are a very important part of their concern. And this might represent the beginning of other such situations in other corporations.

The last point I want to mention is education. Here, a whole revolution is underway and a very important one. The involvement of youngsters in the arts experience at a very early level is something that all of us who are in the arts are very deeply concerned with. There have been a number of pilot projects under way and this is an interesting development. Things are happening. We see the beginning stages of something that will become more important.

The Predominance of the New York Theatre: Three Viewpoints

James M. Nederlander
Robert Kalfin
Herman Krawitz

Commentary by *James M. Nederlander*

President, Nederlander
Enterprises, Inc.

*Note: This session in the series was
held in the Nederlander offices in
the Palace Theatre Building in
Manhattan more than a year after
most other sessions included in this
book.*

How did I first become interested in the theatre? I grew up
in the theatre because of my father, who was a Shubert partner. My father was the Detroit Shubert partner and when
the Shuberts were operating under what was called a "con-
sent decree," the government came in and said that they
must dispose of several theatres. We took over the Detroit
end of it and acquired some of the theatres that they dis-
posed of. Then, later, we came to New York. We now own
the Palace Theatre and the Brooks Atkinson and we lease
the Uris. We lease the Fisher in Detroit and we lease the
Studebaker. We sublease the National in Washington. Then
we have the arts centers. We book the Merriweather Post
Pavillion and we book the Garden State Arts Center and we
book Pine Knob.

My present theatre activities? That has to do with producing shows and bringing shows over. We are the producers of *Sherlock Holmes.* I brought that over from England.
The Royal Shakespeare Company put that package together
and we bought the entire package, remodeled the scenery,
and right now we're busy recasting it because most of the

actors are going back to London. We had *My Fat Friend* on Broadway and we brought over *London Assurance* with Donald Sinden. We'll do a play next year called *Habeas Corpus* with Donald Sinden—a fine actor. He'll be great in that play. And we're working on various other projects.

We've kind of followed the Shubert pattern. Frankly, I'm a theatre operator first but in order to fill our theatres, we've gotten into producing. I've been around theatre for years and have done many, many shows, so I understand this business.

What directions do I feel the theatre will take in the future? Well, I don't know. It looks like the theatre is going to be subsidized—or, at least, a great part of it. That's what's happening now, especially with regional theatres like the Guthrie in Minneapolis, the Arena Stage, the Kennedy Center—they are subsidized theatres.

The main thing you have to do is learn the business. One of the biggest problems, especially with a lot of the nonprofit theatres, is that they don't have good administrators. The problem with the commercial theatre is simple: anybody who can raise money can become a producer, although it's not that easy. This is a business that you've got to understand, you've got to know something about it. But not everybody does. Sometimes, just because they are able to raise money, people become producers, but they don't know what they're doing half the time.

Even the commercial theatre, I think, is coming to subsidization. How much, I don't know. I think there should be more subsidy for the arts. The economics of the Broadway theatre don't make sense. I mean, here we have thirty-four threatres on Broadway and maybe twenty of them are lit. And the road—well, look at *Variety* and you see that most of the activity is in the regional theatres. Years ago, we had producers like Ziegfeld and Sam Harris and George M. Cohan and Belasco and the Shuberts and many, many more. But today there are very few producers who know anything about the theatre. They're money-raisers. We have *some* very good producers, but you can name them on one or two hands. There are fellows like Hal Prince, who is a very knowledgable producer, David Merrick is a tremendous producer, Robert Whitehead is a very fine producer and there are a few others. But there used to be all *kinds* of producers. You see, today a lot of them, like Robert Fryer, can go to the Pacific coast and make a film or a television special that is very profitable. But you produce a play and two nights later it's out of business after you've spent a year putting it together. So what the future is, I don't know. I think it's coming more and more to subsidization.

What advice do I have for aspiring producers and arts managers? Basically, I think you have to learn where it's at in the theatre. If you're going into theatre you should start from the front of the house and work back. Then you will know the problems. You begin by working in the box office, or you begin as an usher. You have to learn something about exploiting a show. All these things are valuable whether you are producing or running theatres. You just can't put a man in to negotiate labor contracts with the unions, for example, unless he knows something about the theatre. It's a highly specialized business. If you have the material but you don't understand casting and you cast somebody wrong, you ruin the play. We sat around with *My Fat Friend* for over a year before we were able to cast it. It's a very slight play, but the people who were in it were great—Lynn Redgrave, George Rose. One of the reasons it was a success was because of the casting.

Take a play like *Sherlock Holmes*—it's an old play, but the people in it, like John Wood, are great. Because of the Equity rules, many of them are leaving—John Wood's going to stay—but we're putting in Clive Revel to play Moriarty and we've got people, like Tony Tanner, who are fine performers. A play like that has to have absolutely first-rate people. The ideal would be if they allowed London actors to work over here and if they allowed American actors to work over there. I can understand the union's point of view—they want their own people to work. When a union's got a lot of people out of work, naturally they want to keep their people working. We'll see what happens with *Sherlock Holmes*.

The regional theatres have become the tryout ground for Broadway. In other words you get a play and you try it out with Paul Libin or you try it out with Joe Papp and, if it's good, it moves to Broadway, like *Championship Season* or *Scapino* or whatever. We're always looking for plays. We have somebody who reads every script that's sent in here and who sees everything. Theatre is in a difficult way, especially on Broadway, because the costs are so astronomical. It's a difficult business today. If you have a hit show in a theatre it makes it viable. If you don't have a hit show, you're in trouble. It's a business of opportunity. If you can book hit shows into your theatre you can make money, if you don't, you lose money. It's like anything else. If you make an automobile that sells, you're OK, but if the car doesn't sell one year then that particular automobile company has problems.

Most of the Broadway theatres are pretty old. If somebody came along and wanted to tear one down to put up an office building with a theatre in it, I think I would say "yes," because you would then have a new theatre. But if the building could carry the theatre, that's the way to do it because the theatre is such a hazardous business. The idea that New York had of allowing builders to add stories to a building if it would include a theatre was a good one. The problem is that the man who built these buildings can't rent the space right now because of the economy. We now have our third landlord at the Uris Theatre.

It's a difficult business. But I say, if you want to do it and you're good at it, then you'll do OK. But you have to get a background.

Questions to *James M. Nederlander*

QUESTION Do you think that television film showings of theatre productions might help increase both audiences and revenue for the theatre?

MR. NEDERLANDER It's a possibility. But you've got to realize that the theatre audience is small. A lot of shows on Broadway wouldn't get any rating at all on television because they just don't have a wide enough appeal. There are many shows, for example, that I can't book in a city like Detroit, because they're not for Detroit. They won't accept them. You know, there's New York and then there's the rest of the country—and I'm not a New Yorker. This is the most cultured area there is, I think. My home town is Detroit. But you couldn't get away with *Let My People Come* in Detroit—they'd throw you in jail! They just wouldn't allow it. Not that it's wrong or it's right: I think if a person's twenty-one, he should have the right to go and do what he wants, so long as he doesn't hurt anybody else. I think some of the censorship laws that we have are ridiculous—that's my personal opinion.

QUESTION How do you decide what play to book into what theatre?

MR. NEDERLANDER After a while you have an idea of what does business in a certain city. After you book a city enough, you have an idea that there are certain plays that the people just won't like. It's a question of experience, I guess. You either have a flair for this business or you don't, that much I can tell you. You have to make a study, you have to read all the periodicals and judge plays by what they do in other parts of the country. Then you try to figure out what kind of a community it is. You talk to the local manager and see if he thinks it will do business there.

In New York you never know what's going to happen. You can book a play here that's been a success every place else and it doesn't get the notices. You have to get notices in New York. You can *survive* bad notices in New York, but it's very difficult. People read the critics. This is where the media establishes everything—in New York City. If you have a hit in New York that has any wide appeal at all, you can send it to other cities. A play like *Sherlock Holmes* could probably go out and tour, because everybody knows who Sherlock Holmes is. *Grease* was a big success everywhere it played. You have to see the play and then make an evaluation—is this play good for Chicago, is it good for Detroit. If it isn't, you don't book it. You could take a revival and put it on the road with a television star who's a big name and it would do business. But you can't do that in New York. Just to bring a television name to New York doesn't mean anything. You've got to get notices with the play. If you'd taken *A Moon for the Misbegotten* and toured it before it had established a name for itself in New York, it wouldn't have done any business. But it came here and took off, so *now* it's good for the road, at least in certain cities. But now I'm talking about *booking*. This is very different from producing.

We compile what's called a "route book." It lists the various cities and what's playing in them—Boston, Chicago, Detroit, so forth. We know where every show is and what all the grosses are. If we want to know what such-and-such a show did in Los Angeles, for example what *Grease* did in Los Angeles during a certain week in October, we just look in this book and it tells us. It's been a bad season so far, because there are very few shows traveling.

QUESTION   What do you think would be the most helpful thing to the future of the theatre?

MR. NEDERLANDER   We need two things: we need playwrights and we need producers. We need producers who can encourage playwrights and who can put a package together. A man can write a play, but if he gets somebody who doesn't understand producing he can ruin a good piece of property. In order for a play to be a hit in New York you first have to have the material and then you have to cast it right. But if you're not an experienced person, number one you don't know a good script from a bad script and then you don't know who to put in it. This requires a lot of expertise. If a Hal Prince does a play, it might not be a hit, but you know it's going to be something well done and well produced. Maybe the play doesn't work, but he'll do it with style. In New York you've got to have style. You can't do sleezy, poorly directed plays in New York and get away with it. In some cities, yes, you can put on plays that aren't too well directed and aren't too well done and do business with them. But not in New York—no way!

Let me put it another way. I won't say that the road will always take stuff that is not well done, but I would say that you have to be much more selective in New York than you do on the road.

QUESTION   What percentage of the time would you say that your theatres are dark?

MR. NEDERLANDER   Well the Fisher is filled fifty-two weeks of the year, it has been for ten years. I personally book that theatre myself. The Palace Theatre has had very few dark weeks. I would say that it's been filled eighty-five percent of the time since I've had it.

Someone once told me that there's a policy for every theatre—you just have to *find* it! Sometimes you'll take a theatre and you'll change policies several times before you find one that works.

QUESTION   What is your attitude toward the Times Square ticket booth that distributes tickets at half price?

MR. NEDERLANDER   I really haven't made up my mind about it. I think people are always looking for bargains. Whether that takes away from the full-price theatregoer, I don't really know. I'm certain it takes away a few people who say, "Why should I buy a ticket for full price when I can buy it for *half?*" It's a merchandising gimmick. It's like the two-fer gimmick—when a show is in its last six months, you send out two million two-fers. Many a show has run many a month on those discount tickets. Another merchandising gimmick is to book a play for four or five weeks and then start advertising "last four weeks" or "last three weeks." Psychologically, that says to people, "If you want to see it, it's only going to be here for a few more weeks."

There are lots of merchandise plans—there are theatre parties, there are subscriptions. If you're a producer, you've got to be a merchandiser, too. You've got to know how to merchandise your product.

QUESTION   Do you select a script to produce because of its marketability as well as its artistic merits?

MR. NEDERLANDER   I do, yes. My theory is that the subsidized theatres should do things that have a very limited appeal. Commercial theatre has to do plays that have wider bases or it can't survive. So when I look at a play like *Habeas Corpus*, I consider whether or not it has that base. I had a young fellow read this play because I wanted to hear what he had to say about it. He sums it up in writing: "A very funny play in the English-farce tradition. It should have no problem becoming a hit on Broadway if an imaginative director can be found. No adaptation of the play is necessary."

Now this is a play that in my opinion should be a hit in New York. It was a big hit in London with Alec Guinness. I think Donald Sinden will be terrific in it. Now it's a question of putting a package together with a director who has the right style for the play.

QUESTION   In selecting a play do you also consider how many actors it has and how many sets?

MR. NEDERLANDER   It's better from the economic standpoint with fewer sets and actors—naturally, the numbers add up. But I don't produce plays that way. If I think a play is workable, I don't care how many people are in it. I produce plays because I think they're going to be successful.

Let me put it a little bit differently. When you're producing plays, you have to be emotionally involved with them or you shouldn't produce them. When you're *booking* a play you look at it in a different way—you have to fill your theatre so you do the best you can. I book a lot of plays and I have no personal involvement with them. But if I'm going to *produce* a play, like *Habeas Corpus*, then I *personally* must think that this play is going to be a hit. We've had it for nine months and we've been trying to cast it. We finally convinced Donald Sinden to do it. He loves the play. We tried to get Alec Guinness, but Alec Guinness had done it for a year or so in London and he didn't want to do it any more. Unless I can cast this play with the best actors, then I don't want to produce it because I don't think it would go any where unless we have "Tiffany actors" and a fine director who can handle this type of play. It's a funny play, but I'll tell you one thing—nobody can pick 'em! You just use your best judgement.

I brought over *London Assurance*. I loved it. But that play had a hard time catching on. The reason I didn't keep it running longer was that it was so expensive. It was a terribly expensive production with all that scenery. It didn't show a profit, but I liked the play and I thought it would be a bigger hit than it was. We opened at a bad time of the year, but there was no other way that it could be worked. It was a very complicated deal and it took us quite a long time to work it out.

On the other hand, I've optioned lots of things that never came to pass. There was a musical in France that I liked, so I optioned it but I couldn't get anybody whom I thought could do the job to adapt it. I tried all kinds of people. But they didn't like the material or they didn't like the music. The eventuality was that we dropped it. That's just one of many. Sometimes you just can't put the puzzle together.

It's a very tough business. I've been active in it since 1940, mostly as a theatre operator rather than as a producer. It's a tough field, but you pick out what you want to do in life and you try to do it, although in this business you'd better like it or you won't succeed, because it's a lot of work. Right now, as with every industry, things are not good. But I'd still say that you should try to do what you *want* to do. If you can make a living, do it! If you like the theatre and you want to be in it and you realize what a tough road it is, just go ahead. It's a very interesting business. There's no other business I know where you meet the great and the near-great as you do in the theatre business. You meet every type of individual, because they all eventually come to the theatre in one way or another. And there are jobs. There are new auditoriums going up all over—they don't know what to put *in* half of them—so I'm sure many job opportunities will keep arising in the years to come.

Commentary by *Robert Kalfin*

Artistic Director, Chelsea Theatre
Center, Brooklyn, New York

*Note: This session was conducted
about a year after most other
sessions recorded in this book.*

How did I become interested in the theatre? I found out in
college that I knew how to do it, had an instinct for it, had a
talent for it, or whatever it was. I had been miserable as a
music major in high school. I went to the High School of
Music and Art in Manhattan and I was a rotten musician
and also a terrible scholar! There were all these smart kids
at the High School of Music and Art with 99 averages and
they intimidated the hell out of me. They insisted that I
learn how to play bass fiddle, because they needed bass
fiddle players. I was a *lousy* bass fiddle player as well.

Then I lucked into a very small college—Alfred University in Alfred, New York—with a small theatre program
which was very imaginative. It was a two-man theatre department headed by C. Duryea Smith III. They had been
producing Brecht, Anouilh and Giraudoux; in the '40's and
'50's they were doing such things as turning a school gym-
nasium into a Roman arena and producing *Androcles and
The Lion* in it, or doing Greek plays, using the basketball
markings on the floor. It was *very* exciting. It turned me
onto the magic, and I started working in the theatre department in college, doing everything, but mainly being an actor. My music training helped, in that I composed the mu-

sic for some of the productions and by my last term in college I ended up directing. That's how it started.

The kind of theatre that I was exposed to in college developed further in graduate school at Yale and sort of led me into what was happening when I got out of graduate school. That was the time of the "golden age of Off-Broadway," when Brecht, Genet, Ionesco, Pinter and LeRoi Jones were being produced in the Off-Broadway theatres and, through these theatres, being picked up by the regional theatres and integrated into the American consciousness of dramatic literature. So it was a continuation of what I had been exposed to in college.

After some terrible adventures, including having produced and directed two plays Off-Broadway—some good adventures, as well—and having worked as a director in the regional theatre, I decided at some point that there were certain works that *ought* to be produced that *weren't*. The only way I was going to get them on as a director was to create the conditions to work in. Of course, there were a lot of other things that happened in between. I had worked for a while as a consultant, helping other people start theatres at the same time I was starting Chelsea. But Chelsea really grew out of this wonderfully selfish impulse of wanting to do certain works that nobody would give me the opportunity to do and which I thought should be done.

About two years before starting Chelsea Theatre, I had a rather climactic, turning-point event in my life. Having worked on a play that I wanted to direct (which I had adapted myself and worked on for seven years), I ended up with a commercial producer who, after the production was in rehearsal, took me out of the production and put himself and friends in the major parts and hired other friends who had never really worked profesionally in the theatre. If anything is going to make you want to start your own theatre, that experience will! During that particular production, I hired a Pinkerton bodyguard with a gun to go with me to rehearsals, so that I could continue to direct the play! That'll do it, you know—it helped to mold my character, and my "taurean" determination became further entrenched.

So Chelsea began out of frustration. I wanted to do a certain kind of work and, as I say, I had worked as a consultant for people wanting to start theatres. I had had two experiences to prepare me. One involved a distant relative of relatives in Portland, Maine. There was a wonderful theatre in Portland that was owned by a bank, but the bank didn't know what to do with it. So this relative said, "I know somebody who would know something about that!"

So they called me up to Portland, Maine. I was hired by the bank to travel all over America, about 1964, and find out what was going on in terms of the regional theatre and the cultural centers that were being put up. I evolved a master plan for their gorgeous theatre, suggesting that they use it as a performing arts facility, because it was an amazing building. It was incredibly designed and I thought it would work very well. But, unfortunately, the bank decided that a parking lot would be more lucrative than a performing arts center. There was nothing I could do to convince them otherwise, so they tore it down!

After that, I was hired by Actors' Equity, which was then creating what later developed into a foundation to aid people who wanted to start theatres. It was really a consulting service and, again, I was helping people start theatres. During all of this and before, I had been working as a director out of New York in regional theatre and Off-Broadway and summer theatre.

There was a building at the end of my street—West 20th Street in Chelsea—which was a church parish hall. I walked in and I said, "Hey, this would make a terrific theatre!"

I found this wonderful, open-minded priest named Father Jenks who decided he'd like to have a theatre there. I started it in May of 1965 and did two one-act plays that spring and twenty-six plays, I think it was, the following fall. I had all these plays, you see, that I wanted to do. We rehearsed each play for two weeks and then presented it with actors still carrying books in hand, with lights and with a minimal physical production. The plays were presented at the stage they were at after two weeks of rehearsal—just to see them and hear them. No one got paid and it was all free for the audiences. Of course, I wasn't directing all of the plays. I'm starting to direct again much more now, because I think Chelsea finally is in the shape where I can—I don't have to worry as much about changing the paper towels!

In any case, I went into the church and they thought it would be a fine idea and the minister gave me a hundred dollars. Of course, when you've just got out of school and you've just done your first Off-Broadway production at the expense of your relatives, which so many of us did in those days, it was very easy to call a friend who had a lighting board in the basement and another friend who had some fabric, and another with some platforms, and another with some tools, and somebody else with a couple of lights left over. And you start doing it that way. We pulled a theatre together and we were there for several months. We did a lot of plays. I'm sure there were thirty or forty plays, after which we did a play by Archie Shepp, called *The Communist*, which upset the church hierarchy very much. At that point the church (and a Bishop) decided that they wanted to use that hall for basketball for the neighborhood and things like that.

Then we were invited to go to another church up the street on 28th Street and Ninth Avenue, where we did about twenty-six plays and then opened a play in Spanish, which was the first large production that Chelsea did. It was a beautiful play by a Puerto Rican poet whom I knew. Then one of our first grants came in. I think it was for salaries— for myself and one other person. At that point I decided that it would be important to move the theatre into a more important producing format. We did Archie Shepp's play again, this time it was called *Junebug Graduates Tonight* and this time I got in trouble with an Archbishop! Shortly thereafter, we had to leave *that* church. That had been our first Equity, Off-Broadway contract. The rest had been workshops.

After that, thanks to efforts by Oliver Rea, our Board Chairman, we were invited by Harvey Lichtenstein, the new Director of the Brooklyn Academy of Music, to become the resident company there. Thanks to Oliver Rea's good idea, we got a new home in more hospitable circumstances.

We were in Manhattan for three years and we've been in Brooklyn for seven years. We started as a weekend theatre and then performed for longer and longer weekends; the whole point of view being that, if you're doing something exciting, people will come anywhere to see it. There are two and a half million people in Brooklyn.

Chelsea is very, very selfish as a theatre in the sense that it does not get bogged down in producing plays for uplifting reasons or moral reasons or social reasons or political reasons. We are truly an "art" theatre and do only what turns *us* on—sometimes we decide on works because it just might be *fun* to do certain things; sometimes it is to give a sense of what *else* is going on in the world of the theatre and to show what America might be missing if certain things are not produced. If you look at what we've done, you'll see a "through line." It may be the revival of a little-known classic, or, for example, Genet's *The Screens*, a play that everybody had talked about but no one had seen: forty-five actors, seventeen scenes, six and a half hours long! Well, I think that's what the subsidized theatre should be doing, so we did it. Turning Alan Ginsberg's screenplay, *Kaddish*, into a play; doing *The Beggar's Opera* only because *Beggar's Opera* had been done heretofore as a "stand-up" opera and it was really meant to be something else when it was first written. What we are about, as producers, is putting the elements together to make something happen in a certain creative way. Putting Hal Prince together with Eugene Lee, because *Candide* never worked and was only a score and had to work in another way by putting the right elements together. That's the kind of thing that we do a great deal.

Now the theatre that we have in Manhattan is another story. It serves two purposes for us. It started out primarily as a way of keeping alive. I mean, the last straw with *The Beggar's Opera* was that it could not support its own run-

ning cost in a commercial theatre at eighty-five percent capacity business, because the rent was so high and the service package was so high. We decided this was ridiculous,
so we got a theatre of our own which duplicates our facilities in Brooklyn and the difference between that and renting a commercial theatre is something like the difference of
$1500 a week and $1500 a month! The funding sources, too,
are getting less and less. We decided somewhere along the
line that what we know how to do is produce—why not turn
that to our own advantage to help support what we really
are about in Brooklyn? So the Westside Theatre and the
cabaret theatre that we now operate are the "workhorse"
theatres to keep the theatre in Brooklyn going.

Diamond Studs, which is a piece of fluff which we developed, was a very deliberate choice on our part to use
"the system" to support such plays as *Kaspar* and *AC/DC*.
If *Diamond Studs* is a big smash, ultimately that does us
more good than a grant which is of limited duration and
may have all kinds of conditions. It's a creative solution.
We know how to produce plays and the three of us (Michael
David, Burl Hash and myself) have been working together
for a long time now—seven years. We also have two bars
there, which make as much money as the tickets at the door.
You must understand that the Brooklyn Academy of Music
has three parking lots, the income from which helps to support it. It's called "working with the system." It's a creative
way of keeping a nonprofit theatre alive. We are also creative in other ways.

The arrangement with *Candide*, which was a precedent-
making contract, is also creative. The cost of the original
Brooklyn Chelsea production is counted on the backers'
side. We not only share in the Broadway production as co-
producers with Hal Prince, but also the money that Chelsea
orginally spent on *Candide* will be reinbursed to the
theatre. Chelsea is the largest backer of *Candide*. That's
also being creative! It also could *only* have happened with a
producer like Hal Prince, who is involved with the total
theatre scene and cares about the survival of theatres such
as ours. And it is, indeed, survival time for us *all* the time.

For the last two seasons we've had to cancel our final production. We couldn't afford them because there weren't
enough funds. We're at that point again right now. Chelsea
is not getting rich from anything. We have a trail of over
$100,000 in deficit bills which will slowly get paid off—
hopefully!

Questions to *Robert Kalfin*

QUESTION   What do you think about theatre administration programs that are being offered by certain colleges now?

MR. KALFIN   I wonder who they are turning out those administrators *for*. I don't know what theatres exist for them. I think that the most likely people who come out of those programs are those who have a determination to create something of their own. If you're going to come out of that kind of program with a degree and expect, like a doctor, to hang up a shingle somewhere and practice—forget it! On the other hand, there *is* a dearth of certain kinds of administrators.

If someone is determined to do something by hook or by crook, he will do it! It really comes down to the individual. It has as much to do with persistence as it does with talent. If someone is willing to fight the battles to create something, he will find a way. No one is going to *give* it to anyone.

I'm very lucky at Chelsea in the sense that Michael David, who's Chelsea's Executive Director, is also a set designer. Both my partners, Michael David and Burl Hash, the Productions Director (who sometimes designs lighting for us), are artists themselves. That's quite different from someone coming in and getting off on "management." They are very much part of the whole process, organically part of it.

QUESTION   Have you ever considered hiring a permanent, resident company of actors at Chelsea?

MR. KALFIN   It makes no sense for us. It makes no sense for *where* we are, *who* we are, or *what* we do. In one way there *is* a company in that, over ten years, there are people

who work with us again and again and again. In every production you'll see that a third to two-thirds of the cast are
people who've worked with us before. But you cannot set
up a monastery on 42nd Street, any more than you can do
the kind of repertory we do using the same performers! I
mean, *Slaveship, Kaddish* and *The Beggar's Opera* in the
same season? Also, in New York City you have to be better
than any place else in the world or, at least, any place else in
the country. So for our theatre we want to get the very best
people we can. An actor, a director, a designer does not like
to limit. You do not want to limit people or make them do
things that they are basically not suited for. You would end
up with a middle-rate company all the time. When you have
a choice of the best, it's silly to do that. That's why, I think,
most regional theatre is "all right," but it ain't terrific!

Here in New York, you *can* cast a play almost ideally. It
doesn't mean that you don't take chances. But in working
with people again and again you get to know certain instruments and how to play them, you know their resources. Indeed, the more I work with certain actors, the more I know
what to get out of them—things *they* don't even know they
can do.

There is a point of development in an actor's life when
he knows that, out of New York, he doesn't really have to be
quite as good. He can do the most terrific job and it almost
doesn't matter—except to himself, of course. And that begins to get to an actor. A friend of mine played Hamlet on
the West Coast and he said, "You know, people came up to
me after and said, 'how do you learn all those words?'"

You *really* don't have to be as good anywhere else. But
here in New York for each actor I hire, there is a list of
fifteen others who can replace him and be just as good.
Also, an actor reaches a stage in life when he wants to live
some place and get married and have children and a home.
A home becomes more important than living out of a suit-
case. You get to be thirty or forty and in your prime as an actor, and it's no great shakes to be terrific in Des Moines!
There's also less reward when you're not working with people who are your equal. If you get really good, you are not,
in that situation, usually going to be working with people

who are going to make you get any better. In New York the Darwinian survivors only get their appetites *increased*!

QUESTION Then shouldn't it be an obligation of regional theatres to elevate both the quality of casting and the standards that the audiences set?

MR. KALFIN You can elevate those things to a certain point. There are certain kinds of things that I would go out of New York to do, because I want to stretch myself as a director. But, unfortunately, I know that I'm not going to get as good a company as I can get in New York, so how can I stretch myself when I'm having to "make do" with what is available? Already there is a compromise. Of course, there are compromises anywhere, even here—but they're a higher set of compromises!

I'm not writing off the regional theatre. As a result of it, there are more better-trained actors in America than there have ever been before. In the '40's and '50's the predominant training was naturalistic. Many actors stopped their work after absorbing basic "method." But suddenly, the regional theatres were hiring actors to do Brecht and Shaw and Moliere and Chekhov and a modern American play and a musical—all in the same season! So our actors had to learn a *variety* of styles of theatre. They had to work on speech and voice production and learn movement and fencing, they had to learn acrobatics and *t'ai chi*, and they had to learn everything else that one *has* to learn to be equipped to do his job as an employable actor. I thank the regional theatre for having performed that service. I'm not writing it off in any way at all. But their pressures are different than ours. The first role of those theatres was to be a library, a living library for the great plays. After a while they started to change because, after all, how often can you do *Charley's Aunt* and *Uncle Vanya*? The more exciting "regionals" do original work, but even then the quality is compromised by having a resident company, because you work under that contract where you hire a single group of people to perform for an entire season. You may job in one or two actors from New York who might fit a role better, but ultimately you must compromise.

I think it's important for actors to have a variety of different experiences and to come and go, to enrich themselves by working under different people in different places and in different situations. The actor's instrument has to be recharged by a variety of input or it stagnates. What starts to happen is that people get typed and/or become too easily satisfied if they stay on one place for too long. They start getting the same kind of parts and something dies a little. I think to grow as an actor you have to keep taking terrible kinds of possibly disastrous chances. You have to dare to be really rotten and terrible and make those stretches and take those risks *all the time*! Otherwise, you play it safe and, as you get safer, you get less interesting and you start repeating yourself.

QUESTION   Are the plays which you've premiered here, such as *AC/DC* and *Kaspar* being done elsewhere?

MR. KALFIN   No, they're not done very often—not in America, anyway. But some of them are published. You see, the things we do at Chelsea are very difficult. We do very, very hard things most of the time. And most of the time as a director, I'm also involved as a writer—rewriting as I go along. When I get a chance to do a play that's finished, it seems so easy! The summer before last I did an Off-Off-Broadway production of an Ibsen play. But, again, I picked something that almost nobody does. I picked *Lady From The Sea*, which is an almost impossible play. I did it because I was fascinated by it.

If you saw *Yentl, The Yeshiva Boy,* that production *looked* very easy. But there were fifteen people backstage and those scene changes were more like a film. As I say, at Chelsea we are *about* putting elements together to make something happen. *Yentl* is an example of a project that originated as a short story. It was brought to me by a student intern who worked at our theatre about three years ago. After he saw *Kaddish* (which I had turned into a play from a screenplay), he said, "Here is something I think you could do well."

So I called Isaac Bashevis Singer, who had written it, and he said "sure," he'd like to have it done. It had been turned into a screenplay for Barbra Streisand. And I finally found someone who could work with me in making a stage adaptation of the original short story. The girl who worked with me did a first draft, and then I did a draft of her draft, then she and I would rewrite separately. Then we went over it with Singer. He had some ideas and some new things that he added and then I rewrote his and he rewrote hers *etcetera, etcetera.* I couldn't tell you now what was mine and what was anyone elses!

There are other things that I'm involved with which are not plays yet, but which may become plays. One is a novel which could (and probably should) have been written as a play. Another is a biography set in a whorehouse, which will probably be one of our bicentennial projects. I'm into a lot of things. It's like being a marriage broker. You put the director together with a playwright and a designer. But we don't just *hire* people. It's like casting in a sense. For example, *Slaveship* began as a ten-page scenario by LeRoi Jones. We hired Gilbert Moses from the Free Southern Theatre and introduced him to Eugene Lee, who designed an environmental set, and we introduced them both to Archie Shepp, who wrote the score. At Chelsea we decide *conceptually* in advance what we want. Artistically, we come up with a concept of how something might be done. So it's an artistic idea, it's not just raising money and hiring a director and a designer and hoping that *they* will come up with a concept. It's hiring the director and designer to fulfill our *pre*conception. Of course an individual director can come along with a conception of his own that knocks us out—and we can do that as well. Every production will change and grow anyway. Sometimes the marriages work and sometimes they don't.

QUESTION   How much flexibility do you have in using your space at the Brooklyn Academy?

MR. KALFIN   We started as a weekend theatre and then we gave more and more performances. As we became entrenched, we learned how to work with the space. The biggest physical change in the room itself came when we did *The Screens.* We had to rip the ceiling out and we got about five feet more height in the room. By the way, we start with the play and then design the environment that will, in our concept, best fulfill the work. We are a *guest* resident company and the Brooklyn Academy picks up a large part of the tab, which we would have to pay ourselves if we were in another building—union stagehands, the electric bill, things like that.

QUESTION   How did you go about building your audience?

MR. KALFIN   We actively went out into the Brooklyn community. We didn't worry about people coming across the bridges from Manhattan. We went out into the neighborhood and got involved with them and went into their homes. The temptation would have been to look toward Manhattan for our audiences, but we said, "There are two and a half million people in Brooklyn!"

It also has to do with what we're about. We're not a "popular" theatre. We are, as I said, a very selfish theatre, artistically. We only do what turns us on and we don't decide what we're going to do by what we think audiences would like. We do what *we* would like. And sometimes we say, "We'll do a musical, because we've had enough *sturm und drang* and we've got to have some fun around here!"

Somehow I do balance out a season, as one does a dinner menu—with a dessert and a middle course and so forth, but this is not crucial either. For our own sakes—ourselves and our staff—working in the same building all year, we want a variety of experiences. *And*, the budget also helps determine what we do. Unfortunately, the most exciting projects that come to us are very large. The bigger plays seem to deal with bigger things. That keeps happening. What do you do? I have *lists* of plays I'm waiting to produce. Now I'm sending scripts to theatres all over the country, because I don't know when I'm going to get to do them. But someone ought to do them, or they'll get stale.

Our audience is very special because the Chelsea trip is a special trip. We appeal to the adventurer instinct in people. We say, "You may not like it, but you won't see it any place else. And, if you're lucky, you might see a *Candide* here for four dollars before it goes to Broadway where you'd have to pay fifteen dollars. But you might also see *Kaspar* and get bored to death after the first act and walk out!"

We also budget our plays so they will run for at least a month, even if no one comes. We don't close a play if it gets mixed reviews. We run the play for a month because we believe in it.

QUESTION   What percentage of your audiences are on subscription?

MR. KALFIN   I think about sixty-five percent. We deliberately cut if off because we don't want to become a private club. We want people to just come and see a play if they're interested. We don't even say to the subscribers what plays we're going to do any more. We don't go out of the way to announce titles. That's gotten harder to do, anyway—this year the money from the New York Arts Council was so late in coming that we had to change our plans drastically and switch things around. We also don't do such things as offer discounts—four for the price of three, and so forth.

We sell the *idea* of our theatre and its ten years of work. As a potential Chelsea audience member, you either take the chance or you don't, which is very healthy. It relieves the pressure of having to worry about box office. The insidious thing is when you have a success like *Candide* and people say, "What are you going to do next?"

My answer is, "I hope it's a big flop—so people won't think that we're only about looking for another *Candide!*"

Of course, if something else clicks, we'll take the money, but that must always remain a lucky accident rather than policy in what we decide to do.

QUESTION   How encouraging would you be to new producers coming along and wanting to start theatres?

MR. KALFIN   There is as much room as there are individuals with an idea that fulfills a need that is not being fulfilled. If you're going to create a theatre that's doing what everybody else is doing, there's no reason for it to exist, unless you do it so very much better. I think if you're doing something that ought to be done and nobody else is doing it, you'll get the money for it eventually and people will come. But it has to be organically related to what there is out there. There's no end of material! People always ask, "Where do you get all your scripts?"

I say it depends on who is reading them, because I have a list a mile long that I never can produce and I'm sending them to other theatres. And I'm sure I get the same plays that everyone else gets, so maybe it's their readers!

Do something that ought to be done. It has to do with the force of some kind of artistic vision. I don't think it has to do with managers and boards of directors.

Commentary by *Herman Krawitz*

Yale School of Drama; City
College of the City University of
New York; former Assistant
Manager, New York Metropolitan
Opera

I've been asked to explain how I got into this profession.

Well, I went to City College in New York, entering in
1942, at the time of both the Depression and the war. Prior
to that, I had already expressed an interest in the theatre at
the high school I attended, DeWitt Clinton. For some reason at the time I went to DeWitt Clinton, theatre was very
much in the minds of many people there. They had a tradition of some famous people who had attended: Richard
Rodgers, Joseph Fields and Herbert Fields, and there were
a couple of English teachers who were deeply involved in
the arts. But the influence was not only from high school, it
was from my family, too. My brother was interested, our
close friends were interested, and it was the most natural
thing in the world for me to get involved in the theatre. I
went to school with Jules Irving, who ran the Beaumont
Theatre for some time, Frank Cosaro, who's a leading director at City Center Opera, and Michael Wager, whom some
of you may know as an actor. We were all in the same high
school class.

When I got to City College, I was involved in the Dramatic Society—my brother was the president. Another very
close colleague, who is now the metropolitan editor of the

New York Times, Arthur Gelb, was then the vice president of the Society. Then the war came and I went into the Army. When I came back, I was twenty-one—I thought I was an old man—it was 1946. One thing led to another and I produced a play at City College about the war called *Home of the Brave*, with a young man in it named Donald Madden. He was a classmate and is now a rather famous Shakespearean actor. The director was a fellow named Henry Weinstein, who later became associated with Ely Landau, producer of the American Film Theatre.

In any event, it was somewhat successful (that was my sophomore year) and as a result of that, I was asked to consider opening a summer theatre. I thought that was a great idea and so a group of us got together—my brother, Weinstein, myself—and we went to open a summer theatre on Cape Cod. We put up our own money (I had saved some money in the Army—we could do that in those days). The first play I did was *The Beautiful People*. Everybody thought I was out of my mind to do it. But Sada Thompson had the first professional part she ever played (she recently won the New York Critics' Award) and Donald Madden was in it. We were a combination of students from Yale, Carnegie Tech and City College. Then we did other plays; and other actresses in the company included Nancy Wickwire and Nancy Marchand. We were all young college people and we were called the University Playhouse. We were very lucky in our first years. We were losing money, but two people came to see the play almost immediately. One was Morton Gottlieb, whose latest production was *Sleuth*. There were young people at another playhouse on the Cape, the Cape Playhouse, and their boss was a man named Richard Aldrich. (His wife was Gertrude Lawrence, a rather famous actress at the time. She died over twenty years ago, so some of you may not know who she was, but she was Noel Coward's favorite artist.) Mr. Aldrich heard about the theatre from them, came over and admired it, and then—one of the nicest things anyone has ever done in show business—he went back to the Cape Playhouse and advised his patrons to attend *our* theatre!

A couple of years went by, we still ran the theatre, and

then Aldrich decided to open another theatre called the Falmouth Playhouse. At that time I was in my senior year—it was 1949. The theatre still stands, and Mr. Langley manages it now. In any event, hearing Aldrich was going to open a theatre four miles away from us, I called him and asked if it was so. He said, "Yes," and he wanted to see me.

I was taking my finals, I think it was January, but I went down to see him at his office in New York and he offered me the job of general manager. So I designed the theatre with the architect and organized the company for him and hired about eleven people from my own theatre. Sada Thompson worked there and, as director, we had Martin Ritt, who recently directed the movie, *Sounder.*

I stayed with the Aldrich organization about four years. I built still another theatre in Hyannis, and another in Cohasset—those were the music tent days; they're now old-fashioned, but at that time they were a novelty. Shortly after that, I started to become a consultant in the profession, and Aldrich had a friend who was the chairman of the labor committee of the Metropolitan Opera. The Met had terrible difficulties with labor (I forgot to mention, I used to produce the Hasty Pudding shows for Harvard. The stagehands used to try to organize such productions, like they just tried to do with Juilliard—and I had handled them in a way that avoided loss and minimized difficulties. And that was considered very impressive in that world. So I had a reputation by that time—I was only out of school a year—of being a labor expert).

The Met called me and asked if I would help them solve their problems—they had some chronic labor problems they never did really solve, but at least I did come in and help settle the stagehands problem and they stayed peaceful all the time I was there.

Rudolf Bing eventually asked me to be in charge of production and, subsequently, to be in charge of the business of the company. Later I became secretary of the board and assistant general manager. Around 1955, I was asked to start planning the new opera house. I was the manager of all the affairs in the planning of it until it opened in 1966. I stayed with the company until Sir Rudolf decided to leave.

I was given the opportunity to stay, but for many reasons thought that this was the time to leave. At the time, City College came into a great deal of money and came to me as an alumnus—would I become a consultant? I said, "Yes."

"Would I teach?"

I said that I had a problem because of my position at the Yale School of Drama (I forgot to mention, for about seven years I had been teaching at Yale. I organized the theatre administration program for the graduate school there). Well, City kept pressing and one thing led to another and it was announced that I was director of their new performing arts center, which was nonexistent—no building, no anything. But there will be a lovely building, the Aaron Davis Center for the Performing Arts. So currently, I am still at Yale and I'm at City College, and I'm going into private consultation and television production—I'm a consultant on other projects as well. I'm involved at the moment, for example, with a project at the Brooklyn Academy and I do consultant work with the Curtis Institute of Music. I just came back from Venezuela, and I may be doing some consulting work on a new project down there. I also do consultant work for the Joffrey Ballet. That kind of thing goes together well with teaching. And so that's how I got started in the profession.

I've been involved in the theatre and, of course, in the opera a great deal, and in all areas of music, including ballet. I arranged for most of the transactions with the Royal Ballet, the Stuttgart Ballet and the Bolshoi on behalf of the Met. Sol Hurok was actually the presentor, but he couldn't do it, of course, unless we prepared the house to receive the attractions. I acted as the Met's liaison and my office did that work, so we got deeply involved. As a side issue, I helped to found a quartet called the American String Quartet, which ultimately became the Guarneri String Quartet. So I became involved with virtually every aspect of the performing arts. The weakest area for me is motion pictures— the area, naturally, I want to go into at this moment.

Now I'd like to explain what I mean by "professional." The idea at City College or at Yale is that whatever aspect you go into, you must declare yourself willing to go into the profession. People who wish to hedge the bet and say, "I'll take so many creative courses, and take a few education courses just to protect myself so I can become a teacher. . . ." forget it! They have to have the commitment, the confidence to say, "I'm going to be a performer, a director, a musician," whatever they wish in the performing arts. They don't have to be absolutely sure which area it is, but they have to be fairly certain they want to go into performing arts. And so we are trying to create a conservatory situation within an academic area. In any event, that should bring you up to date with what I'm doing.

Where do I think the future of the theatre is in America? I'm about to complete a book on the subject. I've been writing this book for a number of years but I really got down to it when I left the Opera. I'm writing with a collaborator, Howard Klein, who just recently became the arts administrator for the Rockefeller Foundation. The nature of what we're trying to describe is a "capital city solution" to the theatre—in essence, that each capital city should have a theatre equal to its museum, its baseball team, its state university, or what have you. That is the direction in which I believe theatre will go and I think that people are beginning to get ready for it.

Yesterday there was an article in *New York Times* by Henry Hewes describing the American Conservatory Theatre in San Francisco, a theatre that is just seven years old. William Ball is the artistic director, but the management is from Yale, and they have succeeded in accomplishing the "miracle." The article indicated, which I didn't know, that they are being bid for by another capital city. Another city is trying to take them away from San Francisco, which is foolishness—let them start their own! Leave San Francisco alone, there's room enough to build another theatre. But my personal feeling is that this is the direction that theatre ought to take and will take—when theatre people wake up to the idea that they have to turn their backs to Broadway.

The River Niger is an example of what I mean I hope won't happen. A play is tried out and then brought to Broadway, thereby perpetuating the Broadway system, instead of trying out plays right where they were and making the populace go to them. This is an essential difference. As long as you play the "Broadway game" of putting on plays where you must get hit reviews, only occasionally do you win. *The River Niger* won and *That Championship Season* won. But *Much Ado* did not, *Sticks and Bones* did not; the general rule has been that far more have *not* made it than have made it. You break up a company, you break up an ensemble, and you go for broke in a way that I think is very much a disadvantage to the theatre and its economy. The world of theatre is quite different from the world of music in this respect.

No musical organization would ever think of handling their hits this way. No ballet organization would either. Take, for example, the Arthur Mitchell Ballet Company in Harlem. Mr. Mitchell may outlast the Negro Ensemble for a long time because of what he's doing. If you want to see Mr. Mitchell's work, you have to go to his place, on his terms, at his time. He's not playing any "Broadway games," he's going the "music route." If he continues to build the company the way he's building it, in another five years he'll have an outstanding, leading company.

The theatre approach has always been disastrous, because there's always a pot of gold in the theatre and every so often it is reached, thereby stimulating others to try for it. And make no mistake, people *can* still become millionaires in this profession! If you get yourself a hit play or a musical and properly exploit it, you'll become a wealthy person. In the world of music people take the attitude that they'd like to have a good fee, and most people in the world of music are better paid than people in theatre because they don't have that "hit-and-flop" syndrome. Even ballet people are now getting more money, and they were always the lowest paid. You must have steadiness of purpose and, hopefully, works that are popular with your own public. You don't necessarily try to be popular for the entire public, but your *particular* public—there is a chamber music public, a ballet public, a dance public and so forth. The theatre is the one profession that's gone through the hit-and-flop syndrome because it was the only method people knew. Whether we

like it or not, most of the important things that occurred in
the American theatre, unfortunately, occurred in that system. The musical theatre as it developed in this country occurred on Broadway—George Bernard Shaw, Eugene
O'Neill, Arthur Miller were all presented in the Broadway
type of production. So everybody got the idea that theatre
must try to make money, while music and ballet and opera
could "go for the art"! When theatre people start making up
their minds that *they're* "going for the art," you'll have the
"capital city theatres" I mentioned. I think the theatre is
moving that way, and the first sign of it is the importance of
the university theatre, which is a form of protection, a form
of underpinning providing continuity. The next step is the
regional theatre—although at this moment it is a little too
inadequate, it doesn't pay a proper living, generally. But
they're beginning to get better. Minneapolis and ACT, for
example, are beginning to get better at that. You can go now
from a university situation to a junior position with some of
these companies and do relatively well.

I've discovered with the administrators I have trained at
Yale that none of them will now accept a job at less than ten
thousand dollars a year. I have about three or four jobs beg-
ging at this time. It's the nicest thing I can tell you that's
happened; it's a sign of the times, it's a sign that people are
moving in that direction, but it's just a beginning.

Essentially what will have to happen in theatre is that
the public will learn to attend locally, de-emphasizing
Broadway. When you leave college, you ought to look
around this country and pick out the city or the territory
you like. It's empty now, it's a very empty map! There's no
professional theatre in Boston, there's no theatre in Pittsburgh, only one theatre in Brooklyn—the Chelsea Theatre,
run by two of my former students. That's an example of
what can happen. You have to make up your minds what
style theatre you want to do, according to your artistic taste
and artistic judgement. There's the whole body of literature
from the past and there are many different directions at the
present time, and there's nothing wrong with handling
something popular if it's good. There are good, popular
things in the world of music. I always have trouble with my

intellectual friends about *Aida* and *Madame Butterfly*; they always turn up their noses, but these are very great operas. So in the theatre *Macbeth* and *Hamlet* are popular, great plays; you don't have to do the new if you don't understand it or don't like it just because that's the vogue or the fashion.

This country is a continent—wide open for theatre. It's not wide open for symphony, I wouldn't particularly suggest going up to Boston and starting an orchestra; I wouldn't even suggest opening up an opera company—they have an opera company, they have a ballet company—they have no local, professional theatre. To think Boston, Massachusetts, the cultural center of the New England states doesn't have a theatre company! Chicago, Illinois, hasn't got one either, and you can find many, many other areas in similar straits.

I was recently in Philadelphia. André Gregory, who's currently at N.Y.U., at one time ran a very important theatre in Philadelphia, but he left and nobody's come there to replace him. They told me of three houses, three buildings, waiting for people—the Walnut, the Erlanger, I can't remember the third. They said to me, "Do you know any theatre groups?" I said I would mention it to my students at Yale; and I'll mention it to a few people at Brooklyn. Philadelphia is looking for a company—a city that big! This situation may not exist a decade from now, but it exists today in many places. In this sense I think it's the most optimistic time I have seen in the theatre. The foundations are there to give money, the universities are thinking in terms of training and preparing people. The idea that this kind of symposium even exists is a novel one for the professional theatre.

All this is now in the air. Don't worry about money, don't even bring up the subject! That's always a way *not* to face the problem. If you create quality theatre, the money will be there, and the audience will be there, too. That doesn't mean you can just waltz into the situation, you have to train. You can take an internship or residency work in a number of theatres and learn at somebody else's expense. If you graduate from school at twenty-two, after five years when you're twenty-seven, maybe thirty, then a few of you can get together and open a theatre. I did it at twenty-one, but those were the days of summer theatres. Summer theatres have gone out of fashion—there are only a few good summer theatres nowadays. But there are still some opportunities in summer theatre to learn while you're going to school, to learn certain techniques, to get used to the idea of working night and day, to get used to pacing yourself and all that kind of thing, and then go to the theatre of your choice. The situation is genuinely wide open right now for any kind of theatre you wish. It is particularly wide open for people of black, Puerto Rican and Asian groups. Many are noticing the vacuum and taking advantage, becoming a very important aspect in this spectrum of the theatre.

Questions to *Herman Krawitz*

QUESTION You obviously believe that the non-profit theatre is the answer to the future; but can it really make enough money to support people and pay salaries?

MR. KRAWITZ Non-profit doesn't mean that you can't make a living, you know. You can make money without Broadway. You can lead a very long life in this profession without going to Broadway, and be artistic in the genuine sense—have fun, gain satisfaction, work with other artistic colleagues, and get a very appropriate renumeration. Now you won't become rich in the sense that Neil Simon became rich on Broadway, but you'll be very comfortable.

QUESTION Why are you so down on actors, as opposed to musicians and dancers?

MR. KRAWITZ Oh, it's a long tale. Essentially, it starts from a general attitude that theatre people have: "I'd give my right arm to do *Hamlet*." And, unfortunately, they mean it, which means that they don't want to be paid. They'd rather do *Hamlet* than be paid. They fail to ask for pay, you see, and theatre people in general are always willing to take too little for opportunity. The theory is, "I'll get up on that stage, I'll do Hamlet and, of course, some producer will see me." They've seen too many Ruby Keeler-Dick Powell movies! So they all think, "All I have to do is get on stage and they'll see me." And that's the theory of most organizations, too. Therefore, they just have enough money to get the curtain up. What will happen the next day, the next week, or the next month is rarely thought of.

Musicians have a different attitude altogether, and I'm sure it's occurred to you. Musicans say, "If you want to say 'hello' to me, put the money on the table!" I know them. They'll tell you to put the money right on the table, or don't discuss the matter. At Yale I see it. Somehow, when musi-

cians come over to the School of Drama, they get paid. But
drama students go over to the School of Music and do it for
the love and glory! Musicians have a very simple attitude:
"Thou shalt pay!" And musicians *are* very well paid in this
country and they are equally skilled and as artistic, if not
much more so. Musicians are often far superior in their
skills and talent, as are singers, and as are dancers, both
modern and classical. There are some outstanding actors,
but it's almost an accident that they got through the system
as it currently exists.

Now there are attempts to change this. The sign of the
times is that article I referred to about ACT in San Francisco. Here's a theatre that is now beginning to pay an average
salary of about $290 a week. It's not a great deal, though it
sounds like a lot to students, but it's really not a great deal
of money for a professional, anyway not in the league *I*
think in terms of. But it's far better than $75 a week Off-Off-
Broadway. At least it's relatively higher and at the same
time they're doing what they want to do. They're doing the
plays they want to do, and presenting them in a way that is
also a training situation. I don't know if you know what the
American Conservatory Theatre entails—it's a training
theatre. Mr. Ball had the idea that at the same time you are
performing, you should be training. It's a very good idea.
There isn't a ballet company that doesn't hold classes, there
is not a musician who doesn't practice, but there are many
actors who just smile and hope for the best. Well, Mr. Ball
is attempting to change that and he has succeeded in raising
over a million dollars a year, which is a sign of what can be
done.

I'll tell you a funny thing about the theatre. The person
who is now the general manager was a student in my class
at Yale and one of the assignments I gave was to organize a
company. He picked San Francisco in which to organize a
theatre. He graduated and went to San Francisco and now
he runs the theatre there!

If someone had talked six years ago about a theatre having a deficit of a million dollars, you would have thought
he'd lost his mind. Jules Irving talked that way, saying it
was impossible to raise that kind of money, when right next

door to him at the Met, in one year we raised *eleven* million! And the Philharmonic in it's way has done the same, as have Juilliard and the State Theatre in their ways. Does that give you an idea? It can be done. You have to have artistic standards and you have to say, "I will not work for nothing."

It keeps coming back to the Broadway attitude: "Just get me on, just let me get my play open and I'll get Clive and he'll say the right words and away we go!"

It *does* happen sometimes and away they *do* go and they live richly, happily thereafter, and so the next guy wants to try it. I'm sorry to tell you that most regional theatre companies are artistically inferior and the best theatre is still on Broadway. Quality theatre in this country is usually found on Broadway—real quality theatre in my opinion exists in very few places. Real quality dance, music and opera *do* exist across this continent. If you go to the Cleveland Symphony or to the Chicago Symphony, or to the New York Philharmonic, or to the Boston Symphony, you will be listening to one of the world's greatest orchestras. But in Chicago, Philadelphia, Boston and Los Angeles there are no really great theatres. With all due respect, the Arena Stage, the Guthrie Theatre and even ACT are really modest companies. Chelsea Theatre in Brooklyn occasionally does some very nice things, but Chelsea is not really a *company.* They put on one play at a time. It's under continuing management, but it's not a company of continuing actors.

Broadway is still where the quality technicians and craftsmen gather, I regret to tell you. When it really gets down to it, the best plays I've seen have usually been in Broadway theatres. The best American play I've ever seen was *A Streetcar Named Desire.* I was a student at the time. The highlights of my theatre-going, at least American theatre-going, have been on Broadway, under the Broadway speculative system. It's unfortunate, but it's true. And that's the whole problem—nobody has been able to establish quality outside that system. It's not a simple problem—it won't be solved overnight. Theatre people like to concentrate on Broadway because they know they can get other competent people to work with them there. At some of these other places, they get together some good actors but they don't pay them properly. They give them $198 a week and think they are going to keep these actors. Well, you'll discover fast enough that no professional can live on that basis. You work seasonally, but it's just too difficult to maintain a professional career after four or five years at those rates and so you're driven into making a commercial, or a movie, or into teaching, or a combination of teaching and acting, so you can live comfortably. The theatre drives away more talented people than any other group.

For example, the Lincoln Center chamber group is a phenomenon in this country! They're going to have a five-million dollar endowment very shortly. I don't know if you understand the limited appeal of chamber music in this country, but it is the single most unpopular of the performing arts.

There's also another theatre in Brooklyn run by a classmate of mine, the Living Theatre. Julian Beck is here and they're preparing a show which I think is going to open next fall. It takes nine months to do what they do: "their own thing," always. From the time they left school to this day Julian Beck and Judith Malina had their own special dream and no other company can do their works. Did you see *Frankenstein* when they did it? That was *their* company's play, not transferable to anybody else. The Theatre of the Deaf is that kind of individual thing, as is the Grotowski Company, and chamber musicans take that attitude—"we're just going to do this and only this." They do it of such high and superb quality that there is no fault in it.

So when you ask about theatres in America—do they do a good job—generally speaking, most theatres are pretty mediocre, if the truth be known. It doesn't mean they *have* to be. Why should the English have better quality? People there are accustomed to it; they set the standards and there it is. We influence the world in dance, in music, in opera, in the visual arts, in the contemporary arts from jazz through rock and soul music. If you go anywhere in the world you'll find the American point of view is the dominant one in almost every one of these fields. In the theatre, English theatre is dominant and we are inferior—there's no other way of putting it.

QUESTION   What do you think about unionism? Has it helped or hindered the growth of the performing arts in this country?

MR. KRAWITZ   I think unionism in this profession has helped enormously. I was the chief negotiator for the Met management *with* the union—not "against" it; I rather resented that use of the word. I think unions are essential to the performing arts and I think most of them have been helping, although most of them have been misunderstood. I think of the groups in general, the weakest has been Actors' Equity, which has taken the attitude that I described earlier. It reflects the membership attitude that to get on stage is more important than to get a proper salary. They have to make up their minds to close every marginal theatre in this country that won't pay an actor a decent salary. People must be paid properly to appear on stage. There isn't a musician in this country who will appear anywhere without being paid for it, the union musician is paid properly and most musical organizations are thriving. Equity's theory seems to be that theatres will close up all over the place if you pay the actors a proper salary. I just don't see it.

You know, I never found a non-profit organization that didn't pay the electric bill. They pay exactly what Consolidated Edison tells them to pay, not one penny off! Now if they can pay the electric bills, they can pay a living wage. So I'm very much for unions in that respect and I try very hard to bring up the lower-paid people. I can tell you how we did it at the Met, if you're interested.

You see, there's always a fight *between* unions—those who are better paid don't want the others to be paid more. Let's say some are getting $100 a week, and others are getting $150 a week, and others $200. The "A's" are getting $200, the "B's" $150 and the "C's" $100. It's increase time. What do the "A's" say? "The fairest thing to do is to give everyone a six percent increase."

Somebody else argues five and a half percent, somebody

else argues seven percent. Percentage sounds fair to everybody, but here's what happens: the "A's" go from $200 to $210, the "B's" go from $150 to $157.50 and the "C's" go from $100 to $105. Notice what happened: *before* the negotiation the "C's" had $100 less than the "A's," *after* the negotiation the "C's" have $105 less than the "A's!" Percentages always favor the higher-paid person, always. Whenever you hear a union talk about percentages, you can be sure that the high-salaried people are in control.

Now the opposite is to give dollar increases. For example, everybody gets $10.00 increase. What's the problem with that? If you give the "C's" $10.00, if you give the "B's" $10.00 and you give the "A's" $10.00, the "A's" suddenly notice that the "C's" got ten percent while they're only getting a five percent raise! That's a very serious problem in all labor negotiations—newspaper people, typographers, all of them—the top people want the percentage and the lower people want the dollar increase. The argument goes back and forth and there's no answer. There are two different ways of measuring, and they're incompatible, they cannot be resolved. So arguments go on for weeks and months. How do you solve it?

It was discovered that "fringe benefits" treat every individual as an individual. sometimes lower-paid people have larger families, so if you give them family Major Medical, you've given *them* far more. How can anybody argue against that? How can "A" dare say that his colleague in a lower level isn't entitled to his Blue Cross, Blue Shield or Major Medical? He can't. So we gave the finest fringe benefit program in the performing arts at the Met. It's the only way we could equalize it. People have to be able to buy milk and bread. You must see to it that the lowest-paid people are paid higher, or at least above the subsistence level, regardless of what happens to the higher-paid people.

The gap will get wider. But I always tried to keep this problem in the front of my mind, and of course, I worked very hard to bring up the ushers, the porters and the service personnel, because they need to live, *too*.

QUESTION   You seem to be quite optimistic about the opportunities available in professional theatre. Could you elaborate further on that subject?

MR. KRAWITZ   When I went to Yale I was aware of this problem and I made up my mind that I was going to use my professional influence to open up the doors for my own students, and I did so. For the administration students right from the start that was part and parcel of the program as I conceived it. They are now starting a program with directors that's somewhat similar, though directors are less in demand. Do you know what a director ought to do? He ought to open his own company, that's the easiest way: get a group of actors and don't worry about money, just direct them. Go back to the simplest theatre: a group of actors performing. Forget about all this paraphenalia—arts services and buildings and so forth—forget it! Just get actors acting, don't worry about money.

When you're in a university I assume you're a student or you're a member of the faculty, so you have some funds; compensation is not your main concern at this point. When you're a student you impress each other, it's like dropping pebbles into a lake, you know—just a little ripple, just you and three or four friends. That's exactly how I created my group. Who knew then what I was doing at City College? The other students, my colleagues, knew, and I knew their work. To this day that same group talks to one another, to this day the people who started together in those years know of each other's work. Those whom we respected, we still respect; and the opposite holds—those whom we didn't respect, we *still* don't respect!

So out of this group you first get your friends and classmates impressed with each other, and then their families get involved, and then their friends, and then maybe the faculty will notice you, and then it goes to the student audience at large, or your local newspaper takes notice, and suddenly you begin to be known. That's how it happens, but first you've got to impress the people you know right now, your colleagues.

There's a program starting at Williamstown that I can tell you about. They are going to take ten directors, train them for three years, and give them stipends. They're making a deal with the regional theatres in the country. One person will go to ACT, another will go to the Arena Stage, and they'll be the assistant director at these various places. It's an interesting program, but the best thing, frankly, is to develop your own project. Students have some advantages—free labor and a lot of other similarly interested people. Help each other, cooperate—it's a collaborative art, you'll learn that very quickly. You actors and directors get together and produce plays of your own choice or do original pieces. Dream up your own versions and do them morning, noon and night. Somehow you'll influence each other and something will happen, and if something doesn't happen, you'll become good audiences! Not everybody can become a professional. ·

To be a professional takes great work, great intensity. Did Sir Rudolf tell you the hours he kept? Did anybody ever ask him? He used to work ninety hours a week. This man, who is now in his early seventies—ninety hours a week! He'd be in that office at roughly 9:30 and be there frequently until midnight, straight through—six days.

In my early years we had to train him to get away from *seven* days a week! When I first came to the Opera, they used to work seven days a week many, many times. I remember one time with labor negotiations, I worked seventy days in a row without a break. That's what this profession is about—very long hours. Get used to the idea that when everybody else is going off on holiday and weekends, you're rehearsing, you're working. If you don't like it, find out now.

I see it as a very optimistic time and also as a deplorable time, with the economy and inflation very difficult to handle. But it is far better than the '30's and '40's, don't let anybody tell you that those were "the good old days." They were desperate times. People were poor then, starving. I remember fellow students at City College so poor that we had to chip in to buy milk for them, and under certain school programs milk was a penny a bottle. I knew people who couldn't afford it! Whatever has happened, that extreme poverty has been eradicated a little. Also, there's a much greater receptivity toward the arts, although as yet there is no public need for art. It's a need for those who are *in* it, but not for the majority of the public. I belive it's a need toward which the public must be educated.